ROUTLEDGE LIBRARY EDITIONS: CONTINENTAL PHILOSOPHY

Volume 10

ZARATHUSTRA *CONTRA* ZARATHUSTRA

ZARATHUSTRA *CONTRA* ZARATHUSTRA
The tragic buffoon

FRANCESCA CAUCHI

LONDON AND NEW YORK

First published in 1998 by Ashgate Publishing Ltd

This edition first published in 2018
by Routledge
4 Park Square, Milton Park, Abingdon, Oxon OX14 4RN
605 Third Avenue, New York, NY 10017

Routledge is an imprint of the Taylor & Francis Group, an informa business

© 1998 Francesca Cauchi

All rights reserved. No part of this book may be reprinted or reproduced or utilised in any form or by any electronic, mechanical, or other means, now known or hereafter invented, including photocopying and recording, or in any information storage or retrieval system, without permission in writing from the publishers.

Trademark notice: Product or corporate names may be trademarks or registered trademarks, and are used only for identification and explanation without intent to infringe.

British Library Cataloguing in Publication Data
A catalogue record for this book is available from the British Library

ISBN: 978-1-138-06315-0 (Set)
ISBN: 978-1-315-10580-2 (Set) (ebk)
ISBN: 978-1-138-08936-5 (Volume 10) (hbk)
ISBN: 978-1-138-08947-1 (Volume 10) (pbk)
ISBN: 978-1-315-10922-0 (Volume 10) (ebk)
DOI: 10.4324/9781315109220

Publisher's Note
The publisher has gone to great lengths to ensure the quality of this reprint but points out that some imperfections in the original copies may be apparent.

Disclaimer
The publisher has made every effort to trace copyright holders and would welcome correspondence from those they have been unable to trace.

Zarathustra *contra* Zarathustra
The tragic buffoon

FRANCESCA CAUCHI

Ashgate
Aldershot · Brookfield USA · Singapore · Sydney

© Francesca Cauchi 1998

All rights reserved. No part of this publication may be reproduced, stored in a retrieval system, or transmitted in any form or by any means, electronic, mechanical, photocopying, recording or otherwise without the prior permission of the publisher.

Published by
Ashgate Publishing Ltd
Gower House
Croft Road
Aldershot
Hants GU11 3HR
England

Ashgate Publishing Company
Old Post Road
Brookfield
Vermont 05036
USA

British Library Cataloguing in Publication Data

Cauchi, Francesca
    Zarathustra *contra* Zarathustra : the tragic buffoon. -
    (Avebury series in philosophy)
    1. Nietzsche, Friedrich, 1844-1900. Also sprach Zarathustra
    I. Title
    193

Library of Congress Catalog Card Number: 97-76930

ISBN 1 84014 351 7

Printed and bound by Athenaeum Press, Ltd.,
Gateshead, Tyne & Wear.

What must a man have suffered to have such a need of being such a buffoon? Is Hamlet understood? Not doubt, certainty is what drives one insane. But one must be profound, an abyss, a philosopher, to feel that way. We are all afraid of truth.
        Friedrich Nietzsche: *Ecce Homo*

The wise through excess of wisdom is made a fool.
        Ralph Waldo Emerson

Contents

Acknowledgements	ix
List of Abbreviations	x
Introduction	1

THE FALL
The Parable of the Ropedancer

1	Realism versus Idealism	13
2	Ropedancer as Buffoon	20

CONVALESCENCE
The Eagle and the Serpent

3	Cunning Reason and Proud Imagination	37
4	Physicians as Metaphysicians	51

PILGRIMAGE
The Higher Men and Zarathustra's Shadow

5	The Art of Self-Overcoming	69
6	The Decadence of Modernity	76
7	The Decadence of Christianity	112

APOTHEOSIS
The Tragic Buffoon

8	Ignoble Lies and Insolent Truths	149

Conclusion	169
Texts and Translations	171
Bibliography	172
Index	180

Acknowledgements

I would like to thank the following for their help and encouragement: Michael Tanner, Neil Gascoigne, Michael Henry, Mike Walters, Terry Llewellyn and Paul Hewett. I would also like to thank Corpus Christi College, Cambridge, for furnishing me with a handsome set of rooms under the eaves of Leckhampton House where most of the ideas contained in this book were originally conceived.

List of Abbreviations

A	The Anti-Christ
AS	Attempt at a Self-Criticism
BGE	Beyond Good and Evil
BT	The Birth of Tragedy
CW	The Case of Wagner
DD	Dionysus-Dithyrambs
D	Dawn
EH	Ecce Homo
GM	On the Genealogy of Morals
GS	The Gay Science
HH	Human, All Too Human
KSA	Kritische Studienausgabe
NCW	Nietzsche contra Wagner
TI	Twilight of the Idols
TL	On the Truth and Lies in a Nonmoral Sense
UM	Untimely Meditations
Z	Thus Spoke Zarathustra

See 'Texts and Translations' for full bibliographical information.

Introduction

Who is Nietzsche's Zarathustra?

Who is Nietzsche's Zarathustra? Broadly speaking, responses to this question vary according to whether or not the respondent (a) attends to the contextuality of Zarathustra's utterances; (b) deems the end of Part III of *Thus Spoke Zarathustra* to mark the completion of Zarathustra's *Bildung*; or (c) acknowledges the importance of Part IV as a means of gaining additional insight into the "character" of Zarathustra.

(a) Contextuality

In his essay, 'Who is Nietzsche's Zarathustra?', Heidegger insists that, in order to answer his question, 'it is not enough merely to compile sentences showing what the advocate and teacher says about himself. We must heed *how* he says it, on what occasions, and with what intention.',[1] Three excellent suggestions, to which I would add a fourth: the even greater need for meticulous attention to how (and on what occasions, and with what intention) Zarathustra speaks about *others*, especially his 'higher men'.

In response to his own question, and his own interpretative precepts, however, Heidegger completely disregards the *how* of Zarathustra's discourse by failing to interrogate its possible ironic, parodic, satiric, rhetorical, fictional, confessional function within *Zarathustra*. As for heeding the context of Zarathustra's utterances, Heidegger only per-

---

Notes

1. Martin Heidegger, in David B Allison (ed.), *The New Nietzsche* (London: The MIT Press, 1988), p. 65. In a footnote to his chapter on Heidegger's interpretation of Nietzsche, Alderman refers to a conversation that he had with Heidegger on 24th May 1973, in which Heidegger maintained that the above cited essay contains the best summary of his Nietzsche interpretation. See Harold Alderman, *Nietzsche's Gift* (Athens: Ohio University Press, 1977), p. 177.

2 Zarathustra contra Zarathustra

functorily complies with this hermeneutic injunction. Finally, when Heidegger looks for Zarathustra's intent, he looks not within the context of *Zarathustra*, nor within the larger context of Nietzsche's published works, but in Nietzsche's posthumously published notes where, according to Heidegger, the sole source of 'Nietzsche's philosophy proper'[2] is to be found.

Heidegger's reliance on Nietzsche's *Nachlaß* is unsurprising given the former's specific philosophical preoccupation, but it is a methodological prejudice that inevitably leads to a highly idiosyncratic reading of Zarathustra. Seeing Nietzsche's protagonist principally, if not solely, in terms of 'the relation of Being to the human being',[3] compels Heidegger to reformulate his question thus: 'who is this being who appears within metaphysics at its stage of completion?'[4] This reformulation effectively removes the subject of the question from his natural habitat and places him in a (Heideggerean) world that is entirely alien to him.

(b) Delimitation

Many Nietzsche commentators consider Part III of *Zarathustra* to mark the completion of Zarathustra's *Bildung* and accordingly dismiss Part IV as little more than a postscript to the "whole" which precedes it. Hollingdale's assessment is typical in this respect: 'the glowing conclusion of the third part is the book's true climax and the seal upon what was by then a complete philosophical outlook on the world'.[5] Lampert, however, while endorsing Hollingdale's judgment thus: 'Everything points to the end of Part III as The End',[6] and accordingly confining his discussion of Part IV to a (relatively) brief appendix, unwittingly defends the significance of Part IV by insisting that 'the existence of a fourth part *violates* the end of Part III' (emphasis

---

2. Heidegger, *Nietzsche* Vol I, trans. David Farrell Krell (San Francisco: Harper & Row, 1991), p. 8. See also Heidegger, *What is Called Thinking?* trans. J Glenn Gray (New York: Harper & Row, 1968), p. 73.
3. Heidegger, in Allison (ed.), p. 78.
4. Ibid., p. 77.
5. R J Hollingdale, *Nietzsche: The Man and His Philosophy* (London: Routledge & Kegan Paul, 1965), p. 190.
6. Laurence Lampert, *Nietzsche's Teaching: An Interpretation of* Thus Spoke Zarathustra (London: Yale University Press, 1986), p. 287.

added).⁷ If this violation is intentional - and this book submits that it is - then Part IV is vital to an understanding of Parts I to III.

Another involuntary defender of Part IV's integral relation to the book's preceding parts, is Ackerman, who points to its expository function: 'These additional materials seem to have been added after the first version had seemed incomprehensible to readers, in the hopes of facilitating communication, at least to Nietzsche's close friends'.⁸ Once again, if this suggestion concerning Nietzsche's possible motive for writing Part IV were to be removed from its context - in this case, from Ackerman's largely descriptive account of *Zarathustra*⁹ - and wantonly 'deconstructed'¹⁰ from the perspective of violation and disclosure, then the suggestion that Parts I to III (which deal with a predominantly affirmative protagonist) might have seemed incomprehensible (inauthentic, certainly) to Nietzsche's more discerning readers, until exposed as mere bluster and bravado by the addition of Part IV, is remarkably *apropos*.

Part IV is most frequently condemned on stylistic grounds, and Lea's judgment in this respect is representative: 'Part IV, an after thought [...] is also an anticlimax. Diffuse where the other [parts] are concise, allegorical where they are figurative, it took far longer than they to write, and the reason is all too plain: it is uninspired.'¹¹ But if the stylistic excesses of Part IV lead Lea to reject this final part as 'a baroque extension',¹² they provoke Fink to a far more damning condemnation: 'the fable now erupts violently, even insistently; it comes to an embarrassing and terrible derailment; the entire fourth part is a fall. Somehow the poetic-intellectual vision seems

---

7. Ibid.
8. Robert John Ackerman, *Nietzsche: A Frenzied Look* (Amherst: The University of Massachusetts Press, 1990), pp. 57-8.
9. Ibid., pp. 43-59.
10. One way of defining the verb 'to deconstruct' is to separate the text from its author and to place it in a 'semiotic' no-man's land that lies (to borrow Derrida's formulation) 'beyond the mythology of the signature [and] beyond the authorial theology'. See Jacques Derrida, *Spurs: Nietzsche's Styles*, trans. Barbara Harlow (London: The University of Chicago Press, 1979), p. 105.
11. F A Lea, *The Tragic Philosopher* (London: Methuen, 1957), p. 226. To cite the allegorical style of Part IV as a methodological 'defect', however, is tantamount to criticizing poetry for not being prose, since 'the absence of a sustained analysis or argument in support of [its] assertions' is simply the nature of the allegorical beast. See Irving M Zeitlin, *Nietzsche: A Re-examination* (Cambridge: Polity Press, 1994), p. 35.
12. Ibid., p. 252.

exhausted. This fourth part of the work is added like an evil, malicious satyr play that opens up a new, tragic view of the world.'[13] Fink is, I believe, correct in ascribing Zarathustra's 'fall', from the azure heights of poetic-philosophical vision to the stygian depths of tragic insight, to crude authorial intrusion. To assert, however, that 'Zarathustra as the thinker of new thoughts stands beyond Nietzsche's psychology'[14] is to impose upon the author an objectivity which the author himself categorically repudiates. Indeed, it is this thinly veiled *publication* of Nietzsche's psychology - his tragic *Weltanschauung* which in Part IV threatens to break through the exquisite fabric of Apollonian illusion and to destroy the carefully wrought Zarathustran persona of Parts I to III - that makes Part IV so worthy of detailed analysis. For, ultimately, neither the private publication of Part IV nor its allegorical form could prevent the exposure of that which Nietzsche had hoped to keep secret, namely, the profoundly tragic nature of his heroic self-projection. 'Nietzsche is tremendous', claims Fink, 'as long as he speaks, thinks and teaches, as it were, *as* Zarathustra - he becomes weak when he talks over Zarathustra. There he is not enough of a poet.'[15] But it is precisely *there*, at the point where the lying poet yields to the penitential author, that this book seeks to probe most deeply.

---

13. Eugen Fink, *Nietzsches Philosophie* (Stuttgart: W Kohlhammer, 1968), p. 114. It is a great pity that Fink did not pursue his satyr play analogy, since a more detailed comparison of Part IV with certain aspects of satyric drama - for example: its customary performance, after a set of three tragedies, for the purpose of relieving the seriousness of the tragic trilogy; its subject matter, which, like that of a tragedy, was taken from an epic or legendary story; its tragic element, which was diminished but by no means absent; and, as in tragedy, the comic function of its 'wanton, saucy, and insolent' chorus, which generally comprised twelve or fifteen persons (see Oskar Seyffert, *A Dictionary of Classical Antiquities*, rev. and ed. Henry Nettleship and J E Sandys [London: William Glaisher, 1894] p. 559) - might have persuaded Fink to re-evaluate Part IV on grounds other than stylistic.
14. Fink, p. 115. Cf. Halévy's similar indictment: 'Zarathustra the judge has only insults and lamentations upon his lips [...] This is no longer the hero whom Friedrich Nietzsche had created so superior to all humanity; it is a man in despair, it is Nietzsche, in short, too weak to express anything beyond his anger and his plaints'. See Daniel Halévy, *The Life of Friedrich Nietzsche*, trans. J M Hone (London: J Fisher Unwin, 1911), p. 263.
15. Ibid., p. 118.

(c) Rehabilitation

Standing apart from the detractors of Part IV is a handful of Nietzsche commentators struggling, by various means, to give it the critical attention which it deserves. Most prominent[16] among these critics are Higgins[17] and Shapiro,[18] whose respective approaches to Part IV are primarily informed by modes of interpretation that place far greater emphasis on external than on internal sources of explication. For example, both Higgins and Shapiro rely heavily upon Mikhail Bakhtin for theoretical support, while Higgins drawing on Nietzsche's personal correspondence and prolonged immersion in classical philology, compares the distinctive style of Part IV – a style so bafflingly dissimilar to the style of Parts I to III of *Zarathustra* – to Menippean satire.

Higgins' striking insight concerning Part IV is that it is 'a satire constructed on the model of Apuleius' Golden Ass'.[19] Certainly, the structural parallels facilitated by Bakhtin's (*The Dialogic Imagination*) analysis of *The Golden Ass,* and the formulaic parallels provided by Northrop Frye's (*The Anatomy of Criticism*) characterization of Menippean satire, are highly persuasive. So, too, are the deeper resonances discovered by Higgins in the shared folly, pretensions and asininity of Lucius and Zarathustra. For both characters, she argues. 'Error and its unfortunate consequences serve the positive function of expediting insight that makes a new level of maturity possible'[20]. Indeed. And as the following chapters will endeavour to show, it is the pained self-knowledge consequent upon such insight that generates the highly self-conscious buffoonery of Zarathustra Part IV in its studied attempt to create a form of ironic distance between the later protagonist and his naively confident, two-dimensional predecessor in Parts I and II. Returning to Higgins, it is on the

---

16. Less prominent, but more notable, is James Ogilvy, whose highly original interpretation of Part IV, to be found in his study of *Many Dimensional Man* (New York: Oxford University Press, 1977), is remarkable not least for its freedom from the type of methodological dogmatism currently under review.
17. Kathleen Marie Higgins, *Nietzsche*'s Zarathustra (Philadelphia: Temple University Press, 1987).
18. Gary Shapiro, *Nietzschean Narratives* (Bloomington: Indiana University Press, 1989).
19. Higgins, p. 206.
20. Ibid., p. 229.

basis of her comparative study of Lucius and Zarathustra - the respective "asses" whom she sees united not only in their folly but, more importantly, in their ability to see their folly 'as valuable for its instructive incitement to wisdom'[21] - Higgins concludes that 'the straightforward thematic insistence on Zarathustra's own folly and pretensions in Part IV [...] casts a new and important light on the material in the preceding parts. It brings to completion in unmistakable clarity Nietzsche's effort to modify Zarathustra's doctrinal message with reflections of its limited nature.'[22] Unwittingly expanding on what Higgins has identified as the 'self-ironical satire' of Part IV, this book will bring the Zarathustra of Part IV into direct dialogue with the Zarathustra of Parts I and II with a view to exposing the aforesaid limitations of the earlier parts. Not only does the later Zarathustra deride his earlier effusions, but in doing so, significantly undermines the robustly affirmative dimension of his earlier teachings – a dimension, moreover, that Nietzsche scholars are wont to underscore. [23]

Rigidly distinguishing between parody and burlesque, allegory and carnival, Shapiro asserts that 'a radical shift in the narrative from the mode of allegory to that of carnival and festival'[24] occurs midway through Part IV of *Zarathustra*. This division of Part IV into discrete parts results, most significantly, in the destruction of the parodic and allegorical continuity which this book argues is manifest throughout Part IV in the allegorical higher men's relentless parody of Zarathustra. Further, instead of placing the carnivalesque Zarathustra in the context of the self-ironical festivities of the Middle Ages[25] (self-irony being, perhaps, Zarathustra's most endearing and, on my reading, most prominent character trait), Shapiro turns to Bakhtin's (*Rabelais and His World*) reconstruction of the popular carnival of the late Middle Ages. This over-reliance on Bakhtin, especially concerning the nature of carnival laughter and carnival thrashing,[26] leads Shapiro to overlook the self-referential aspect of Zarathustra's (internal) carnival, and to underplay the highly ambiguous nature of Zarathustra's

---

21. Ibid., p. 232.
22. Ibid., p. xvii.
23. Ibid.
24. Shapiro, p. 107.
25. In his *Concept of Irony*, Kierkegaard notes how on certain feast days the Roman Catholic Church in the Middle Ages 'conceive[d] itself ironically, eg., in The Feast of the Ass.' See Søren Kierkegaard, *The Concept of Irony with constant reference to Socrates*, trans. Lee M Capel (London: William Collins Sons, 1966), p. 270.
26. Shapiro, pp. 110 and 105-6 respectively.

seemingly playful, triumphant, affirmative and, at times, even *übermenschliche* stance.

Shapiro's positive assessment of Zarathustra's buffoonery stems from his perception of an ironic distance separating Zarathustra from his higher men.[27] Whilst sharing this perspective, this book submits that the ironic distance is neither as great nor as sustained as Zarathustra would sometimes have us believe, and marks the point at which its reading of Part IV breaks with tradition (such as it is). With one glaring exception,[28] it is the received view that while the higher men represent the fragmentary and chaotic nature of Nietzsche/Zarathustra's many-souled self,[29] Zarathustra nevertheless stands beyond them. The most emphatic proponent of Zarathustra's self-assured superiority is Alderman, who claims that '[t]he gap between Zarathustra and the higher men consists of [*sic*] the fact that they lack Zarathustra's prudent attention to the arguments of experience which teach the craft of appropriate affirmation.'[30] But if, on the contrary, the higher men symbolize precisely those 'arguments of experience' which have taught Zarathustra the "art" of prudent affirmation' - the experience, that is, of decadent modern culture and decadent ancient culture - then the alleged gap between Zarathustra and his higher men becomes significantly more problematic. As Nietzsche observes with his characteristic acuity: 'It is not in how one soul approaches another but in how it distances itself from it that I recognize their affinity and identity' (*HH*.II 'Opinions and Maxims' 251). On this reading, Zarathustra's buffoonery in Part IV is closer to exigency than complacency, and less akin to the comedy of *A Midsummer Night's*

---

27. Ibid., p. 99.
28. 'It is a shame', laments Lampert, 'that so many have misunderstood the superior men of part IV as parodied fragments of Nietzsche himself, as if his hard joke on the best of his contemporaries were a joke on himself' (p. 289). It is an even greater shame that, as a result of his own misunderstanding of the higher men, Lampert attacks Nietzsche's portrayal of them as 'low and laughable, fit objects for Zarathustra's pity and even for ours' (p. 291). The point that Lampert misses here is that the higher men are perceived as contemptible "figures" by Zarathustra not 'because [Zarathustra] brings a new measure of what is high in man' (ibid.), but, on the contrary, because the higher men represent precisely what Zarathustra perceives to be 'low and laughable', and hence deserving of mockery, *in his own "character"*.
29. Fink, p. 118; Ogilvy, pp. 176-7; Alderman, p. 117; Shapiro, p. 104; Leslie Paul Thiele, *Friedrich Nietzsche and the Politics of the Soul: A Study of Heroic Individualism* (Oxford: Princeton University Press, 1990), p. 59 (footnote 4), *et al.*
30. Alderman, p. 135.

Dream[31] than to the tragi-comedy of Hamlet's 'antic disposition'. What Zarathustra desires from his art is not 'to delight in his own nature [... but] to get over and away from his nature for a time' (*HH*.II 'Opinions and Maxims' 371); not, as Alderman believes, 'revelation and celebration', but 'escape'.[32]

Autobiographical Perspectives

Who, then, is Nietzsche's Zarathustra? As we have seen, this question is not one that can be answered simply or definitively. The most that one can hope for is 'a *variety* of perspectives and affective interpretations' (*GM*.III.12), and it is in this joint spirit of 'perspectivism' and subjectivism that the question will here be addressed. With regard to subjectivism, one can do no better than to recall Nietzsche's observation that 'ultimately, no one can extract from things, including books, more than he already knows. What one has no access to from experience, one has no ear for' (*EH* 'Why I write such good books' 1). In respect of perspectivism, if, as Nietzsche claims, 'the poet dips *only* from his own reality' (*EH* 'Why I am so clever' 4) and, as Zarathustra claims, 'poets lie too much' (*Z*.II.17), then Zarathustra both is and is not Nietzsche.[33]

Autobiography and fiction are, therefore, the dual but not discrete perspectives from which the character of Zarathustra is here viewed, and the deployment of Nietzsche citations now in support of, now in opposition to, Zarathustra serves to highlight the skein of psychological contiguity that ensnares author and reader alike. For, more than any other, Nietzsche's work exposes and dissolves the artificial boundaries between literature and philosophy, subjectivity and objectivity, author and text; as Nietzsche observes: 'every great philosophy has hitherto been [...] the personal confession of its author and a sort of unconscious (*ungewollter*) and unintentional (*unvermerkter*) memoir' (*BGE*.6).

---

31. Ibid., p. 115.
32. Ibid., p. 135.
33. It is not, therefore, sufficient to say that *Zarathustra* is 'Nietzsche's allegorical autobiography' (Thiele, p. 153, footnote 10).

Focusing on Nietzsche's unconscious as opposed to conscious memoir, this book draws primarily on his published works[34] and, given the anachronic nature of unconscious memoir, eschews any retrospective and hence to some extent contrived periodization. By means of an intertextual mode of argumentation that juxtaposes Nietzsche's philosophy and Zarathustra's buffoonery, both Nietzsche and Zarathustra are judged on, and specifically *with(in)*, the terms of the other. This form of 'immanent critique' (to borrow a phrase from Adorno) serves, on the one hand, to demonstrate how Nietzsche's philosophy, as taught by the prophet Zarathustra in Parts I and II (and, to a lesser extent, Part III), is severely undermined by the self-parodying Zarathustra of Part IV, and on the other, to underscore the intensely ironic[35] nature of Nietzsche's relationship to this most romantic of quixotic heroes.

Literary Conceits

The specific aim of this book is to reveal, by means of a detailed analysis of the allegorical/parabolical figures dramatized in the Prologue and Part IV of *Thus Spoke Zarathustra*, the ineluctable pessimism and nihilism lurking behind the affirmative mask of the prophet of redemption. It is submitted that Zarathustra is a man of *ressentiment*: a quintessentially romantic figure who resents his time, struggles incessantly to overcome it, and fails.

Chapters 1 and 2 take a close look at the parable of the ropedancer and show how the latter's ignominious fall at the hand of the buffoon prefigures Zarathustra's ultimate mortification by the scourge of bad conscience.

Chapters 3 and 4 examine Zarathustra's emblematic eagle (proud imagination) and serpent (cunning reason), and disclose the extent to which

---

34. In view of the highly dubious status of *The Will to Power*, this book makes no reference to it at all. For an illuminating account of this non-book's chequered history, see Bernd Magnus, 'The Use and Abuse of *The Will to Power*' in Solomon and Higgins (eds.), *Reading Nietzsche* (Oxford: Oxford University Press, 1990), pp. 218-35.
35. For a provocative and incisive analysis of Nietzschean irony *vis à vis* Zarathustra, see Robert B Pippin, 'Irony and Affirmation in Nietzsche's *Thus Spoke Zarathustra*' in Michael Allen Gillespie and Tracy B Strong (eds.), *Nietzsche's New Seas* (London: The University of Chicago Press, 1991), pp. 45-71.

Zarathustra's deep-rooted *ressentiment* is reliant upon a proud and deceptive consciousness.

Chapters 5 to 7 demonstrate the way in which the seven 'higher men' personify the effects and affects of decadence which infest Zarathustra's soul. The effects of decadent modern culture are allegorized in turn by the soothsayer (pessimistic philosophy), the king on the right (sovereign abdication), the conscientious man of spirit (scholastic science), and the sorcerer (theatrical/histrionic art); and the affects of decadent Christian culture by the last pope (faith, hope, and love), the ugliest man (bad conscience, shame, and pity), and the voluntary beggar (meditation, benevolence, and philanthropy). Finally, the decadent soul turns penitent and casts its shadow across the pilgrim's path; in its grim reflection of the anarchy obtaining within Zarathustra's soul, this shady spectre is seen to foreshadow the death of hope.

Chapter 8 deals with the tension between self-loathing and masquerade. The forced gaiety of the 'Last Supper' is atoned for in the malicious self-parody of the 'Ass Festival', and this ritual cycle of release and repentance, despair and deluded hope, is employed to support the contention that Zarathustra's last confession is ultimately a confession of bad faith that *a*ffectively explodes the Zarathustran myth. Perfidy, flushed out in the penultimate section, is flaunted triumphant and transparent in the closing section, and the prophet's mask of affirmation and redemption is torn away to reveal the pathetic figure of a tragic buffoon.

THE FALL

The Parable of the Ropedancer

1 Realism versus Idealism

The Drama of the Soul[36]

> Then something happened, that silenced every mouth and fixed every eye. For meanwhile, the ropedancer (*Seiltänzer*) had begun his art: he had emerged from a little door, and was proceeding across the rope, which was stretched between two towers so that it hung over the market and the people. Just as he had reached the middle of his course the little door opened once again and a motley fellow, like a buffoon (*Possenreißer*), sprang out and followed the former with rapid steps. 'Forward, lame-foot (*Lahmfuß*)!' cried his terrible voice, 'forward sloth, smuggler, pale-face! Lest I tickle you with my heel! What are you doing here between towers? You belong in the tower, you should be locked up, you are blocking the way of a better man than you!' And with each word he came nearer and nearer to him: but when he was only one step behind him, there occurred the dreadful thing that silenced every mouth and fixed every eye: he emitted a cry like a devil and sprang over the man standing in his way. But the latter, when he saw his rival thus triumph, lost his head and the rope; he threw away his pole and, faster even than this, shot into the depth, a whirl of legs and arms. (Z.Prol.6)

In an aphorism entitled 'To move the crowd', Nietzsche writes: 'Must not anyone who wants to move the crowd be an actor who plays himself? Must he not first translate himself into grotesque obviousness and then *perform* his whole person and cause in this coarsened and simplified manner?' (*GS*.236). In the parable of the ropedancer, 'the Dionysian drama of "the Destiny of the soul" (*GM*.Pref.7), is brought centre-stage. This parable of the fall encapsulates the story, and prophesies the fate, of Zarathustra. Picking his tentative way towards the dark tower,[37] where 'the *lie* of the ideal'

---

36. An earlier version of this chapter appears in *Nietzsche-Studien*, 23 (1994), 42-64, under the title 'Figures of *funambule*: Nietzsche's Parable of the Ropedancer'.
37. '... I had so long suffered in this quest, / Heard failure prophesied so oft, been writ / So many times among 'The Band' - to wit, / The knights who to the Dark Tower's search addressed / Their steps', Robert Browning, "Childe Roland to the Dark Tower Came", ll. 37-41.

(*EH*.Pref.2) lies hidden, the ropedancer symbolizes the Zarathustra of Parts I to III; his fatal fall, precipitated by the buffoon, foreshadows the death, in Part IV, of Zarathustra's idealism, devoured by the worm of bad conscience. As for the buffoon, his raillery sets the tone for Zarathustra's 'downright wicked and malicious' (*GS*.Pref.1) self-parody of Part IV, while his triumphant leap over the ropedancer hints at the ironic distance to which Zarathustra aspires, but ultimately fails to realize, in Part IV. To support my claim of parabolic prophecy, it will be necessary to examine in detail the symbolic function served, in the first instance, by the parable's *mise-en-scène* and, in the second, by the dialectical relationship of its two principal actors.

Madman and Prophet

The market square setting is highly significant insofar as it registers a thematic link between the parable of the ropedancer and the earlier parable of the madman (*GS*.125). The market square[38] represents the parochial world of fixed values (see Z.III.12.8) and easy virtue, of provincial 'poverty, filth and wretched contentment' (Z.Prol.3). In Book III of *The Gay Science*, the madman runs into the market square screaming "I seek God! I seek God!" and generally lamenting the cataclysmic death of God; the jeers of the crowd are testimony to the prematureness of his apocalyptic message (*GS*.125). One year later,[39] the madman returns to the market square, only this time in the guise of the visionary prophet Zarathustra. Despair wears the mask of hope, and the aching need for metaphysical comfort is assuaged by the vision of a new redeemer: 'I teach you the *Übermensch*' (Z.Prol.3), says Zarathustra; once again, the jeering crowd testifies to the untimeliness of his meditation. In both these scenes, the significance of the market square would appear to be that the news of God's death and the coming of a new messiah is, to a Christian throng, simply a tale told by the village idiot.

---

38. In traditional symbolism, the square 'represents limitation and therefore form. The square is the perfect type of enclosure [...] symbolizing permanence and stability'. See J C Cooper, *An Illustrated Encyclopaedia of Traditional Symbols* (London: Thames and Hudson, 1990), pp. 157-8.
39. Books I to IV of *The Gay Science* were written in 1882 and *Zarathustra* was commenced in 1883.

Both parables share the same basic presupposition - the death of God - and the same existential legacy - the exigency of finding a surrogate god. According to Nietzsche, this almost childlike need for metaphysical comfort is one of the deleterious effects of religious indoctrination: 'Under the rule of religious concepts, one has become accustomed to the idea of "another (behind, below, above) world" - and, with the destruction of religious delusions, one feels an uneasy emptiness and deprivation, and out of this feeling grows once again "another world", but now merely a metaphysical one that is no longer religious' (*GS*.151). Despite the obvious parallels between the two parables, there is, however, a distinct shift of emphasis from pessimism to optimism, from alienation to self-creation. Whereas, in the earlier parable, a new god is desperately being sought, in the later one he has been found. The madman and the prophet constitute Zarathustra's two most vividly painted masks, and placed back-to-back, they form the Janus-face of Zarathustra's psyche. Fearful of the vacuous and meaningless present, the madman looks behind and bewails what has been lost:

> What were we doing when we unchained this earth from its sun? Whither is it now moving? Whither are we moving? Away from all suns? Are we not plunging continually? And backward, sideward, forward, in all directions? Is there still an above and a below? Are we not straying as through an infinite nothing? Do we not feel the breath of empty space? Has it not become cold? Is not night and more night constantly approaching? Do we not need to light lanterns in the morning? (*GS*.125);

while the prophet looks ahead, to the redemptive figure of the *Übermensch*, for deliverance from 'the night, the absent sun, [and] the father's murder'.[40] In other words, the madman represents the impulse towards the real in contrast to the prophet who represents the opposite tendency towards the ideal (whether imaginary or fictitious). And in the parable of the ropedancer, this reaching 'for an upper air, while describing plunges [and] prostrations',[41] typifies the romantic preoccupation with *Doppelgänger*[42] motifs.

---

40. Stefano Agosti, 'Coup upon Coup: An Introduction to *Spurs*' in Derrida's *Spurs*, p. 23.
41. Karl Miller, *Doubles* (Oxford: Oxford University Press, 1987), p. 23.
42. 'I am a *Doppelgänger*, I have a "second" face in addition to the first. And perhaps also a third' (*EH* 'Why I am so wise' 3).

Nature and Anti-Nature

'The contradictory nature at the bottom of the German soul' (*BGE*.244), or what Hamann refers to as the idealism and realism instinct in all philosophy,[43] is represented by the two towers between which the human rope is *stretched*: 'Man is a rope, tied between beast and *Übermensch* - a rope over an abyss. A dangerous crossing, a dangerous wayfaring, a dangerous looking-back, a dangerous shuddering and standing still. What is great in man is that he is a bridge and not a goal' (*Z*.Prol.4). Accordingly, he who strives towards the *Übermensch* must walk the tight-rope.[44] But if, as the two towers suggest, the human rope-bridge symbolizes an evolutionary continuum formed by 'all beings hav[ing] hitherto created something beyond themselves' (*Z*.Prol.3), then the ignoble fate of the ropedancer necessarily calls into question the value of the *Übermensch* and the merits of such a doomed pursuit.

On Nietzsche's showing, the *Übermensch*, as an image of man in his ideal state of moral (in the disciplinary sense of a 'high spirituality [that] is the spiritualization of justice' *BGE*.219) and cultural (in the sense of a cultivated, 'transfigured *physis*'[45] *UM*.III.3) perfection, represents 'a type of supreme achievement' (*EH* 'Why I write such good books' 1). He is a type of man that 'conceives reality *as it is*: he is strong enough for that - he is not estranged or removed from it, he is *reality itself*, he still has in himself all that is terrible and questionable in reality, *only thus can man possess greatness*' (*EH* 'Why I am a destiny' 5). 'To acquire power so as to aid the evolution of the *physis* and to be *for a while* the correction of its follies and clumsiness' requires 'great health' (see *GS*.382 and *GM*.II.24) and is the 'exalted and transfiguring overall goal' of man and, ultimately, humanity (*UM*.III.3). But, as the fatal fall of the foolishly idealistic and clumsy ropedancer serves to demonstrate, such striving for a ' "higher culture" [that] is based on the spiritualization of *cruelty*' (*BGE*.229) will, 'by its

---

43. Johann Georg Hamann, in Ronald Gregor Smith, *J G Hamann: A Study in Christian Existence* (London: Collins, 1960), p. 255.
44. On this reading, the ropedancer is not, as Parkes claims, an 'image for the *Übermensch*'. The *Übermensch*, by definition, is 'over man'; it is only man who needs to go under in order to go over and across *to* the *Übermensch*. See Graham Parkes, 'The Overflowing Soul: Images of Transformation in Nietzsche's *Zarathustra*', *Man and World* 16 (1983), p. 341.
45. Greek for 'nature', and as ambiguous as the English equivalent.

nature' (or, more precisely, 'anti-nature' - see *TI* 'Morality as Anti-Nature'), lead at best to defeat and at worst to death: 'for what and how much is amenable to any kind of improvement at all, in the individual or in the generality?' (*UM*.III.3).

Noble and Ignoble

The human rope is composed of many *twisted* strands, and in this chaotic 'psychic household' the meanest and noblest strands are inextricably entwined (*BGE*.244); accordingly, the distinction between what is noble and what is mean is not easily discernible. To begin with, the positioning of the tight-rope high above the hidebound herd would seem to suggest the nobility of such an *elevated* endeavour, but, then, the *suspension* of the tight-rope might also be deemed to signify the ropedancer's need for a willing suspension of disbelief so that his ideal of the *Übermensch* - Nietzsche's ignoble lie - can exert its normative influence over the personal (as opposed to universal)[46] moral sphere before the critical voice of practical reason reveals the illusory nature of all ethical ideals; or, in the words of Coleridge, 'so as to transfer from our inward nature a human interest and a semblance of truth sufficient to procure for these shadows of imagination[47] that willing suspension of disbelief for the moment, which constitutes poetic faith.'[48]

Second, the ropedancer, seen striving towards his exalted *vision* of human perfection, might at first glance appear noble, and the buffoon, as the instrument of the ropedancer's death, not only mean but also dæmonic (in

---

46. See Nietzsche's repudiation of Kant's 'categorical imperative': 'What? You admire the categorical imperative within you? This "firmness" of your so-called moral judgment? This "absoluteness" of feeling that "here everyone must judge as I do"? Rather admire your *selfishness* in this respect. And the blindness, pettiness, and simplicity of your selfishness. For it is selfish to experience one's own judgment as a universal law; and this selfishness is blind, petty, and simple because it betrays that you have not yet discovered yourself nor created for yourself your own, your very own, ideal - for that could never be somebody else's let alone that of everybody, everybody!' (*GS*.335).
47. Zarathustra confides that 'The beauty of the *Übermensch* came to me as a shadow' (Z.II.2).
48. Samuel Taylor Coleridge, *Biographia Literaria*, Ch. XIV.

the Judæo-Christian sense)[49] and even cynical (in the Nietzschean sense).[50] Upon closer inspection, however, the buffoon can be seen to represent a type of nobility: his perfect balance symbolizing the equipoise of the ironic higher man who, through the creation of 'artistic distance' (*GS*.107), transcends his dual impulse towards the real and the ideal, or, in Nietzschean terms, the contradiction of his will to honesty with his life-preserving will to artifice; and his triumphant leap over the ropedancer gesturing towards the 'noble soul [...] which rises little and falls little, but dwells *always* in a free, translucent atmosphere and height' (*HH*.II 'Opinions and Maxims' 397). Whereas the ropedancer, whose high-flown 'ideal has [...] driven him so impetuously that midway along every path he has got out of breath and had to stand still' (*HH*.II 'Opinions and Maxims' 350), and whose dithering equivocation has cost him his life, can be seen to possess those 'midway' qualities more akin to mediocrity than nobility.

Upon even closer inspection, however, the buffoon can also be seen to represent the idealism of Zarathustra's missionary intent. As a marginal figure simultaneously inside and outside society, the buffoon 'holds the social world open to values that transcend it'[51] in the same way that Zarathustra - oscillating between mountain and valley, solitude and society - offers the multitude transvalued moral values. But if the buffoon's leap over the ropedancer effectively brings him closer to the *Übermensch* and, by implication, to the cultural and moral idealism which it signifies, the

---

49. Köhler preposterously equates the buffoon with the Judæo-Christian Devil despite Nietzsche's emphatic repudiation of all such anthropomorphisms and Zarathustra's insistence that 'there is no Devil and no Hell' (Z.Prol.6). See Joachim Köhler, *Zarathustras Geheimnis: Friedrich Nietzsche und seine verschlüsselte Botschaft* (Nördlingen: Greno, 1989), pp. 424-26.
50. Lampert identifies the buffoon with 'the serviceable cynic described as a "jester" in *Beyond Good and Evil*' (p. 27): one of those 'so-called cynics [...] who simply recognize in themselves the beast, the commonplace, the "rule" and yet still have that degree of spirituality and that itch which constrains them to speak of themselves and their kind *before witnesses* [...] Cynicism is the only form in which common souls brush against honesty; and the higher man must prick up his ears at every coarse and refined cynicism and congratulate himself whenever a buffoon without shame [...] speaks out in his presence' (*BGE*.26). For a detailed critique of Lampert's and Köhler's entirely negative reading of the buffoon see Francesca Cauchi, 'Figures of *funambule*: Nietzsche's Parable of the Ropedancer', *Nietzsche-Studien*, 23 (1994), 42-64.
51. William Willeford, *The Fool and His Sceptre* (London: Edward Arnold, 1969), p. 137.

ropedancer's consequent fall dramatizes the gravitational pull of social conditioning and, by extension, the mortal danger in all idealist undertakings. Like the cripple in Browning's "Childe Rolande to the Dark Tower Came", the buffoon is 'the bizarre muse of the poetic solipsist, directing him to the site of the absolute he seeks and of absolute self-destruction.'[52] While the buffoon, by virtue of his *lofty* values, is seemingly able to distance himself from the stagnant social mores 'peddled in the thoroughfares',[53] the ropedancer, as his ignoble fall seems to suggest, is unable to free himself from the old morality. Indeed, as Nietzsche confesses in his *Nachlaß*: 'What will be the hardest [task] for Zarathustra? *To free himself from the old morality*' (*KSA*, Vol.10, p. 180).[54] Once again, the parable of the ropedancer - with the buffoon's figurative promise of radical individualism and the ropedancer's parabolic social bondage - dramatizes a further type of romantic duality: that which 'promises that bounds may be passed, bonds broken, that nature and society may be deserted, while also, on many occasions, retracting the promise.'[55]

---

52. Bernd Magnus, Stanley Stewart, & Jean-Pierre Mileur, *Nietzsche's Case: Philosophy as/and Literature* (London: Routledge, 1993), p. 142.
53. W B Yeats, *A Prayer for my Daughter*.
54. All future references to the *Kritische Studienausgabe*, eds. G Colli and M Montinari (Berlin: de Gruyter, 1980), will be by volume and page number - eg., Vol 10, p. 180 will read *KSA*.10.180.
55. Miller, p. 46.

2 Ropedancer as Buffoon

Dionysus and Apollo

If man is a rope, then the allegorical *funambulist* is a *higher* man, or, to be more precise (given that both the ropedancer and the buffoon emerge from the tower symbolizing 'beast'), a higher beast. This higher beast, referred to by Nietzsche as 'Dionysian man' (*BT*.8), is a divided man, a proud man, but above all, a broken man. His *dédoublement* is a psychological split between the will to health (and thus necessary illusion) and the will to integrity[56] - or, in the parabolic symbolism of *Zarathustra*, a psychological split between the ropedancer and the buffoon, respectively. Having glanced into the horrifying abyss of nature, Dionysian man finds himself caught between the Scylla of life-denying pessimism and the Charybdis of life-preserving optimism; the latter necessitating a debasement of the self and the former an annihilation of the self in the form of a Schopenhauerian denial of the will to live.[57] It is the 'terrifying Either/Or' situation envisaged by Nietzsche in Book V of *The Gay Science*: ' "Either abolish your reverences or - yourselves!" The latter would be nihilism; but would not the former also be - nihilism?' (*GS*.V.346). In the figure of the ropedancer, Zarathustra's equivocation between illusion and integrity is seen to be his undoing, while in the figure of the buffoon a way out of this nihilistic dilemma is suggested: an improvised stance which neither negates nor denigrates life but affirms it: redemption through dissimulation.

'[F]olly itself is the mask for an unhappy, all too certain knowledge' (*BGE*.270), and like Hamlet, whom Nietzsche compares to 'Dionysian man'

---

56. This *dédoublement* is noted by C G Jung in Lecture VII of his *Nietzsche's Zarathustra: notes of the seminar given in 1934-1939*, Part I, ed. James L Jarrett (London: Routledge, 1989), pp. 110-28.
57. For a discussion of Nietzsche's ambivalent relationship to Schopenhauer and pessimism see Francesca Cauchi, 'Nietzsche and Pessimism: The Metaphysic Hypostatised', *History of European Ideas*, 13:3, (1991), 253-67.

(*BT*.7), Zarathustra seeks to conceal the ugly face of tragic knowledge behind a mask of impudence and foolishness: 'I myself have now murdered all gods in the fourth act, for the sake of morality. Now, what is to become of the fifth act? From where am I to take the tragic solution? - Should I begin to think about a comic solution?' (*GS*.153). Just as in the fifth act of *Hamlet*, the tragic solution lies in Hamlet's Pyrrhic victory - vindication at the cost of death - so, in the ignoble fate of the ropedancer, Zarathustra's moral victory is a tragic one: intellectual integrity at the cost of moral idealism and spiritual well-being. In the victory of the buffoon, however, tragedy is recast into a tragi-comic mould, and Hamlet's 'antic disposition' (I.v.180), revived in the ambiguous figure of the buffoon, is now seen to typify the tragi-comic hero.

In the parable of the ropedancer, the tragic myth, which is 'to be understood only as an illustration of Dionysian wisdom through Apollonian artifices' (*BT*.22), is reborn. Consider the following passage from *Birth of Tragedy* and its allegorical transposition into the parable:

> In the overall effect of tragedy, the Dionysian once again achieves predominance; tragedy closes with a sound which could never have resounded from the realm of Apollonian art. And thus the Apollonian illusion shows itself as what it is: as the constant veiling during the performance of the tragedy of the real Dionysian effect; but the latter is so powerful that in the end it pushes the Apollonian drama itself into a sphere where it begins to speak with Dionysian wisdom and where it denies itself and its Apollonian visibility. Thus the difficult relation of the Apollonian and the Dionysian in tragedy may really be symbolized by a fraternal union of the two deities: Dionysus speaks the language of Apollo, but Apollo, finally, the language of Dionysus; and so the highest goal of tragedy and of art in general is attained. (*BT*.21)

The ropedancer plays the role of the tragic hero who has peered into the abyss. To a courageous, noble hero, neither the 'Buddhistic [desire] for nothingness, Nirvana - and no more!' (*GM*.I.6) nor what Goethe describes as the romantic's 'suffocation on the rumination of moral and religious absurdities' (*CW*.3) is a worthy option. Rejecting these quietist and disquietive forms of life-denial, the Dionysian hero invokes the life-affirming and joyful *Übermensch*; just as the Greeks invented the Olympian world as a 'transfiguring mirror' and a justification of human existence (*BT*.3), so the ropedancer invented the *Übermensch* as redemption through Apollonian illusion from Schopenhauerian (and Leopardian) pessimism.

As Nietzsche himself confessed in his *Nachlaß*: 'in order to bear *this* extreme pessimism (it can be heard here and there in my *The Birth of Tragedy*) and to live alone "without God and morality" I had to invent a counterpart for myself. Perhaps I know best why man alone laughs: he alone suffers so deeply that he *had* to invent laughter. The unhappiest and most melancholy animal is, as is fitting, the most cheerful' (*KSA*.11.571). This contradictory urge towards truth and falsity, towards the real and the ideal, exemplifies the decadent disposition as described by Nietzsche: 'decadents *need* the lie - it is one of the conditions of their preservation' (*EH* '*The Birth of Tragedy*' 2).[58] Is not this, ironically, the 'psychological problem in the type Zarathustra [...] how the spirit who bears the heaviest of destinies, a fatality of a task, can nevertheless be the lightest and most otherworldly (*jenseitigste*)' (*EH* '*Thus Spoke Zarathustra*' 6)?

In striving towards the *Übermensch*, therefore, the Dionysian ropedancer figuratively 'speaks the language of Apollo', but the colossal force of ineluctable Dionysian wisdom eclipses the beautiful illusion of the *Übermensch*. 'The self-overcoming of morality out of truthfulness' (*EH* 'Why I am a destiny' 3) is analagous to Zarathustra's putative self-overcoming in Part IV. As the reflexive Zarathustra of the fourth part comes to realize, an aesthetic transfiguration is less a justification than a deprecation and denial of man; in the parabolic terms presently under scrutiny, the ropedancer's will to the life-affirming *Übermensch* is ironically a life-denying will to the '*lie* of the ideal' (*EH*.Pref.2).[59] 'What justifies man is his reality - it will justify him eternally. How much more valuable an actual man is compared with any sort of merely desired, dreamed of, odious lie of a man? with any sort of ideal man?' (*TI* 'Expeditions of an Untimely Man' 32). If the mark of the ideal (*übermenschliche*) man is the ability to see and live reality '*as it is*', the mark of the actual (Zarathustran) man, who lacks the strength for '*amor fati*' (*EH* 'Why I am so clever' 10), is the

---

58. Cf: Ogilvy: 'the display of opposities so characteristic of decadence' (p. 177); and Furtwängler: 'That [Nietzsche] was at odds with himself, unable to come to terms with himself, is the surest mark of decadence'. See Wilhelm Furtwängler, 'The Case of Wagner', in Ronald Taylor (ed. and trans.), *Furtwängler on Music: Essays and Addresses*, (London: Scolar Press, 1991), p. 83.
59. Clark makes a similar point. See Maudemarie Clark, *Nietzsche on Truth and Philosophy* (Cambridge: Cambridge University Press, 1990), p. 275.

ability to see himself as he really is and 'to laugh at [himself], as a man ought to laugh' (Z.IV.13.15). Enter the buffoon.

In the guise of the buffoon, 'the whole "divine comedy" of life, including the inferno' (*BT*.1) is now to appear. With the tragic death of the ropedancer, the tragedy does indeed close with a tragi-comic image which 'could never [have come] from the realm of Apollonian art.' The 'tragedy of the real Dionysian effect' is thus the juxtaposition of the spectacular and almost farcical failure of the ropedancer to attain *übermenschliche* 'wholeness and manifoldness' (*BGE*.212), and the ropedancer's terrible and inescapable realization (represented by the mocking figure of the buffoon) that his failure is inevitable. As Nietzsche painfully observes, 'the corruption, the ruination of higher men, of more strangely constituted souls, is the rule' (*BGE*.269), a fate which might have been avoided had the so-called higher men heeded the following words of Blake, 'The Errors of a Wise Man make your Rule / Rather than the Perfections of a Fool.'[60] It is thus the dying words of the ropedancer - spoken with 'Dionysian wisdom' - which finally articulate 'the language of Dionysus': 'I am not much more than a beast that has been taught to dance by blows and meagre morsels' (Z.Prol.6). In short, Dionysian man has two masks: the real and the ideal. Through the ideal mask of the *Übermensch* (a mask utilized by the prophet Zarathustra) Dionysus speaks the language of Apollo, and through the real mask of the buffoon (a mask which the latter most likely borrowed from the madman) Apollo speaks the language of Dionysus.

Wise Fools and Foolish Wisdom

The function of the buffoon *vis à vis* the ropedancer is analogous to that of the fool's mirror in one of Holbein's illustrations to Erasmus' *Praise of Folly*, which depicts a fool looking searchingly at himself in a mirror (a motif that Holbein borrowed from the illustrations to Brant's *Narrenschiff*), and the reflection sticking out its tongue at him.[61] Traditionally, the fool's mirror - either held symbolically like the jester's bauble or represented by the jester himself - is a dramatic device employed to reveal the folly of whomsoever the mirror (real or metaphorical) is held up to.

---

60. William Blake, Epigrams, Verses, and Fragments, written about 1808-11.
61. William Willeford, p. 35.

24   *Zarathustra contra Zarathustra*

In Shakespeare's *King Lear*, the Fool acts as a mirror to Lear. Both characters wear cracked masks: through the Fool's mask of foolery, wisdom can be discerned, whereas folly is seen to reside behind Lear's mask of regal wisdom. (A similar relationship obtains between Gloucester and Edgar's 'Poor Tom'.) Just as the Fool offers Lear his coxcomb (I.iv.95), so the buffoon informs the ropedancer that he should be locked up in the tower where fools and madmen belong.

Incarcerated in his own imaginary tower, the "mad" protagonist in Pirandello's *Henry IV*[62] represents the madness of a world in which people live at the behest of dogmatists who propagate outmoded concepts and values:

> And every moment of the day, them wanting everyone to be as *they* want ... *that's* not persecution, of course ... oh, no! That's just their way of thinking, feeling, seeing ... well, to each his own! [...] You're just a flock of sheep ... paltry, ephemeral, hesitant sheep. And they take advantage of that, they make you submit and accept *their* way, so you'll feel and see like them! At least they delude themselves they do! But what do they actually succeed in imposing on you? Words! Which they all interpret and use in their own ways [...] Do you think this [*that is, his desire to live the role of Henry IV*] too, is a practical joke, that the dead go on making life? Yes, it is a joke, in here. But go outside, into the living world [...] say hello to all the old traditions for me! Say hello to all the old customs! Start talking ... use all the words that have ever been said! You think you're living? You're just chewing over the life of the dead! (Act II)

Compare this with Zarathustra's view of 'the new idol' - the state:

> Confusion of tongues of good and evil; this sign I give you as the sign of the state. Truly, this sign indicates the will to death! Truly, it beckons to the preachers of death!
>
> Far too many are born: for the superfluous the state was invented!
>
> Just look how it lures them, the far-too-many! How it devours them, and chews them, and re-chews them! ...
>
> It will give *you* everything if *you* worship it, the new idol: thus it buys for itself the splendour of your virtues and the look of your proud eyes.

---

62. Luigi Pirandello, *Three Plays*, trans. Julian Mitchell (London: Methuen, 1986).

It wants to use you as bait for the far-too-many. Yes, a hellish device has here been devised, a horse of death jingling with the trappings of divine honours!

Yes, a death for many has here been devised that extols itself as life: truly, a heart-felt service to all preachers of death!

I call it the state where everyone, good and bad, is a poison-drinker: the state where everyone, good and bad, loses himself: the state where the slow suicide of all - is called "life". (Z.I.11)[63]

In Büchner's *Leonce and Lena*,[64] Valerio mocks, in particular, the idealism of poets:

> I shall lie on the ground and allow my nose to peep out between the grass blades. When the bees and butterflies rock themselves upon it, as upon a rose, I shall receive poetical impressions [...] How I feel for nature, sir. (I.i) -

compared with Zarathustra's remarkably similar satire in 'Of Poets':

> But all poets believe this: that whoever pricks up his ears as he lies in the grass or on lonely banks, will learn about some of those things that are between heaven and earth (Z.II.17) -

and, in general, the folly of mankind: 'Who will barter his madness for my good sense?' (I.i).

Lastly, in a chaotic monologue exemplifying the loss of centre in a Godless world, the hapless Lucky in Beckett's *Waiting for Godot*[65] manages to articulate the fact that man, 'for reasons unknown' and in spite of his physical and intellectual labours, is in full decline. This decadent type of man is what Zarathustra contemptuously terms 'the last man': 'You have made your way from worm to man, and much in you is still worm. Once you were apes, and even now man is more of an ape than any ape' (Z.Prol.3).

---

63. Cf. 'New ways I go, a new speech comes to me; weary I grow, like all creators, of the old tongues. My spirit no longer wants to walk on worn soles' (Z.II.1).
64. *The Plays of Georg Büchner*, trans. Victor Price (Oxford: Oxford University Press, 1986).
65. *The Theatrical Notebooks of Samuel Beckett*, Vol. 1, *Waiting for Godot*, eds. McMillan and Knowlson (London: Faber and Faber, 1993).

26 *Zarathustra contra Zarathustra*

Masks and mirrors are the stock-in-trade of the fool, and the predicament of Dionysian man is exemplified in the figure of Till Eulenspiegel. The fool's mocking and ambiguous mirroring of the owl (a symbol of wisdom) is analogous, in the private sphere, to the 'refracted light' by which Zarathustra, in a moment of spiritual gloom and weakness, ironically *reflects*[66] upon the foolish wisdom of his inexorable will to truth: 'Here are my faults and blunders, here my delusion, my bad taste, my confusion, my tears, my vanity, my *owlish* seclusion, my contradictions. Here you can laugh' (*GS*.311, emphasis added); and, in the public sphere, analogous to the cunning masks of self-preservation which are required by the initiate of Dionysus: 'how much falsity I shall *need*, if I am to allow myself time and again the luxury of *my* truthfulness' (*HH*.I.Pref.1). Buffoonery is the studied 'art of *appearing* cheerful [... and] above all healthy and malicious', although a 'sharper eye and sympathy will nevertheless not fail to notice [...] that here a sufferer and self-denier speaks as though he were *not* a sufferer and self-denier' (*HH*.II.Pref.5). In the reflection of the jester's mirror, the transfiguring image of the *Übermensch* appears as the wilful self-deception of a melancholy fool and poet:

> "The wooer of truth? You? - so they jeered -
> No! Only a Poet!
> A beast, cunning, preying, prowling,
> That must lie,
> That knowingly, willingly must lie:
> Lusting for prey,
> Colourfully masked,
> A mask to itself,
> A prey to itself -
> *That* - the wooer of truth?
> No! Only a fool! Only a poet!
> Only speaking colourfully,
> Only screaming colourfully out of fools-masks,
> Clambering around on mendacious word-bridges,
> On colourful rainbows,
> Between false heavens
> And false earths,

---

66. It is to reflection or reflexivity that the title of this book refers; for that which *reflects on* is distinct from (*contra*) that which is *reflected upon*.

Roaming, hovering about, -
Only a fool! *Only* a poet! (Z.IV.14.3)

The buffoon symbolizes mocking self-reflection: the ropedancer's painful realization that the tight-rope, stretched between beast and *Übermensch*, is only a metaphorical rope-bridge, a mendacious word-bridge 'signifying nothing' (except, perhaps, the 'colourful rainbow' which appears after a flood of tears.) And if the buffoon mirrors the ropedancer, then both reflect Zarathustra's dual nature. It is a retrospective reflection, however, to which Zarathustra was blind when he ironically *reflected* that 'To men I am still midway between a fool and a corpse' (Z.Prol.7), and when the buffoon taunted him with the memory of the mocking crowd and the fact that Zarathustra truly spoke like a buffoon (Z.Prol.8). Indeed, it is precisely because he is neither wholly vanquished by his Dionysian wisdom (a corpse) nor so triumphant over it that he can wholly dispense with 'powerful delusions and pleasurable illusions' (*BT*.3) (a fool), that Zarathustra initially fails to recognize himself in the extreme representations of his *dédoublement*.

Gravity and Levity

In Part III of *Zarathustra*, in the section entitled 'On the Vision and the Riddle', the parable of the ropedancer is retold with figurative variations:

> Recently, I walked gloomily through a deathly-grey twilight, gloomy, dour and tight-lipped. Not only one sun had set for me.
> A path that ascended defiantly through scree; a wicked, solitary path that was no longer cheered by herb or shrub; a mountain path crunched under the defiance of my foot.
> Striding silently over the mocking clatter of pebbles, crushing the stone that made it slip: thus my foot forced its way upward.
> Upward - despite the spirit that drew it downward, drew it towards the abyss, the Spirit of Gravity (*Der Geist der Schwere*), my devil and arch-enemy.
> Upward - although he sat on me, half dwarf, half mole; crippled (*lahm*), crippling (*lähmend*); dripping lead into my ear, leaden thoughts into my brain.

> 'O Zarathustra,' he whispered mockingly, syllable by syllable, 'you philosopher's stone! You have thrown yourself high, but every stone that is thrown must - fall!
>
> 'O Zarathustra, you philosopher's stone, you catapult, you star-destroyer! You have thrown yourself so high, but every stone that is thrown - must fall!
>
> 'Condemned to yourself and to your own stoning: O Zarathustra, far indeed have you thrown the stone, but it will fall back upon *you*!' (Z.III.2.1)

Half dwarf, half mole, the spirit of gravity allegorizes the negative aspect of the buffoon; he is, as it were, the buffoon stripped of his motley-dress. And with this identification of the negative force of the buffoon with the grotesque spirit of gravity as depicted above, further characteristics of the buffoon are disclosed.

In the first place, the spirit of gravity's mocking allusion to Newton's law of gravity provides further corroboration that part of the signification of the buffoon is reflexivity. Just as the imagination soars upward into the ethereal realm of beautiful illusion, and just as 'intellectual conscience' (*GS*.335), with censorious looks and salutary reminders of man's limitations, drags it back down to reality; so is the ropedancer's tentative advance towards the *Übermensch* checked by the scoffing buffoon, and his plunge into the market square a less than salutary reminder that visionary ideals have no *business* in the market place. Here, poetic dreams, like mountebanks' elixirs, will be treated with scorn and ridicule:

> Alas, there are so many things between heaven and earth of which only the poets have let themselves dream!
>
> And especially *above* heaven: for all gods are poets' parables (*Dichter-Gleichniss*), poets' artifice (*Dichter-Erschleichniss*)!
>
> Truly, it draws us ever upward - namely, to the realm of clouds: upon these we seat our motley puppets and call them gods and *Übermenschen*.
>
> For they are just light enough for these chairs - all these gods and *Übermenschen*.
>
> Alas, how tired I am of all the inadequacies (*Unzulänglichen*), that should be definitely acknowledged (*Ereigniss*)! Alas, how tired I am of the poets! (Z.II.17)

'Who alone has grounds for *lying his* way out of reality? He who *suffers* from it' (*A*.15). And as the ropedancer's plunge into the market-square amply demonstrates, it is precisely this mendacity which serves to underscore the inescapable *reality* of suffering. It is the sick, solitary man who reifies his need for spiritual and material sustenance into palpable, living beings: as Nietzsche confesses in one of his late prefaces,

> Thus when I needed to I once also *invented* for myself the "free spirits" to whom this melancholy-valiant book with the title *Human, All-Too-Human* is dedicated: "free spirits" of this kind do not exist, did not exist - but, as I have said, I had need of their company at that time so as to remain among good things while surrounded by bad (sickness, solitude, alienation, apathy, inertia): as brave companions and phantoms with whom one can chat and laugh when one feels like chatting and laughing, and whom one can send to the devil when they become tedious - as compensation for the friends I lacked. That free spirits of this kind *could* one day exist, that our Europe will have such lively and daring fellows among its sons of tomorrow and the next day, palpable and in the flesh, and not, as in my case, merely spectres and hermit's phantasmagoria: *I* would like to have the least doubt about it. (*HH*.I.Pref.2)

But when the spirit of gravity exposes the necessary connection of the 'melancholy' with the so-called 'valiant', of the sickness of man with the robust health of the *Übermensch*; when he goads Zarathustra with incessant reminders of the nemesis that awaits all forms of hubris, then Zarathustra, despite all heart-felt wishes to the contrary, is bound to suffer the *greatest* doubt concerning the future existence of 'free spirits'. As Nietzsche writes in his *Nachlaß*: 'I am a seer, but my conscience casts an inexorable light upon my vision, and I am myself the doubter.'[67]

In the second place, the spirit of gravity is described as 'crippled' and 'crippling', which recalls the disdainful epithet with which the buffoon harangues the fated ropedancer hesitantly making his way along the tightrope. ' "Forward, Lame-foot!" ' he cries, putting the ropedancer's "heroic" endeavour into its bathetic context of inevitable failure. Pouring scorn on the ropedancer and whispering in Zarathustra's ear, the buffoon is a prefiguration of the spirit of gravity who drips lead into Zarathustra's ear and whom the latter, in a fit of pique, calls 'Lamefoot' (Z.III.2.2). It is precisely these crippling, leaden thoughts which paralyze the ropedancer - hence the (Freudian) projection and (Nietzschean) *'ressentiment'* implicit in

---

67. Cited in Daniel Halévy, *The Life of Friedrich Nietzsche*, trans. J H Hone (London: J Fisher Unwin, 1911), p. 277.

Zarathustra's infantile name-calling. Reflexivity denies the ropedancer the pre-reflexive comfort of 'the splendid dream-birth of the Olympians' (*BT*.3) and so, bereft of his beautiful illusions, he wavers and plunges into the abyss of pessimism. In this context, Newton's law of gravity is of particular relevance. Just as the planets are kept in their orbit by the force of gravity, and would drift aimlessly in the event of the sun's disappearance,[68] so the ropedancer maintains his balance by the gravitational force of the *Übermensch*, but loses it as soon as the illusion evaporates. The spirit of *gravity* can thus be seen to operate on two (psychological and linguistic) interrelated levels, namely, the *seriousness* (1) of pessimism which acts as a psychological *depressant* (2).

Lastly, in the allegorical spirit of gravity the *devilish* quality of the buffoon is illuminated. Far from being Satan, however, the spirit of gravity is a "devil" only insofar as he represents for Zarathustra the destructive powers of acute self-analysis and consequent pessimism. If Köhler insists on a devil threatening to drag the ropedancer down to hell,[69] then the devil is the voice of intellectual conscience and hell the abyss of pessimism. That Zarathustra constantly felt himself in danger of falling into the eternal night of self-doubt, self-loathing, and paralytic nihilism is, I would argue, ironically borne out by the exuberantly imaginative and emphatically affirmative Zarathustra of Part I and, to a large extent, Part II. The buffoon is not, therefore, one of Satan's cunning disguises, but rather the sinister, self-mocking mask of one who suffers from the lingering disease of pessimism. And this juxtaposition of the infernal buffoon with the ropedancer epitomizes the *Doppelgänger* in its 'psychologically realistic form [...] combining the characteristically romantic extremes of exact self-analysis and exuberant imaginativeness.'[70]

---

68. This metaphor is, of course, the one used by the madman as he struggles to express the *horror vacui* from which he suffers as a result of the earth being unchained from its sun.
69. For a discussion of Köhler's startling, Christian interpretation of the parable of the ropedancer see Cauchi, 'Figures of *funambule*'.
70. Ralph Tymms, *Doubles in Literary Psychology* (Cambridge: Bowes & Bowes, 1949), p. 120.

Integrity and Irony

In his discussion of irony, with constant reference to the buffoonery of Diderot's eponymous anti-hero, Rameau's nephew, Trilling asserts 'the intellectual value of the ironic posture' implicit in 'the doctrine of masks'.[71] He then provides etymological support for associating the idea of the mask with the concept of irony by noting that the word 'irony' derives from the Greek word for a dissembler. It is not surprising therefore that the fool or jester, with his multiple masks and revealing mirror, is often dramatically conceived as a highly ironic figure.

Leaping over the ropedancer, the *transcendent* buffoon gestures towards the ironic attitude of 'simultaneous immanence and transcendence'.[72] This lofty activity of the buffoon can be seen as a metaphorical analogue of Friedrich Schlegel's 'transcendental buffoonery' (*transzendentale Buffonerie*).[73] Schlegel uses this expression to characterize the way in which the romantic ironist[74] aesthetically transcends the paradoxical fabric of life. 'Paradox is the *conditio sine qua non* for irony, the soul, source and principle',[75] writes Schlegel; it is, as I have argued above, the irresolvable dialectic instinct in Dionysian man. Oscillating between the will to illusion and the uncompromising will to truth, between necessary error and the 'Minotaur of conscience' (*BGE*.29), between what Bourgeois[76] refers to as 'false naïveté and terrible lucidity', the ropedancer is the victim of an existential irony that simultaneously declares and disdains man's intrinsic

---

71. Lionel Trilling, *Sincerity and Authenticity* (London: Oxford University Press, 1972), p. 120.
72. D C Muecke, *The Compass of Irony* (London: Methuen, 1966), p. 337.
73. Friedrich Schlegel, *Kritische Ausgabe*, Vol II, ed. Ernst Behler, (Paderborn: Ferdinand Schöningh, 1967), p. 152, § 42. All future references to the *Kritische Ausgabe* (*KA*) will be by volume, page, and section number - eg., Vol II, p. 152, § 42 will read *KA*.II.152.42.
74. For a comprehensive overview of romantic irony in general and Nietzsche's attitude towards the early romantics in particular, see Ernst Behler's following articles: 'Nietzsches Auffassung der Ironie', *Nietzsche-Studien* 4 (1975), 1-35; 'Nietzsche und die Frühromantische Schule', *Nietzsche-Studien* 7 (1978), 59-87; 'The Theory of Irony in German Romanticism', in Frederick Garber (ed.), *Romantic Irony*, (Budapest: Akadémiai Kiadó, 1988), pp. 43-81.
75. Ibid., *KA*.XVI(1981).174.1078.
76. René Bourgeois, 'Modes of Romantic Irony in Nineteenth Century France', in Garber (ed.), p. 119.

need for a justificatory and redemptive vision of the world. (Is this also, perhaps, God's irony: that His death simply serves to reinforce man's vital need for metaphysical comfort?) As the ropedancer's fate amply demonstrates, to relinquish one's ideals is to cast away the rod of hope and to plunge into the abysmal hell of nihilism.

Painfully aware of this fundamental contradiction at the core of life, both Schlegel and Zarathustra turned to the putatively resolving figure of the buffoon. Recognizing the futility of trying to effect a reconciliation between his contradictory impulses, the Zarathustra of Part IV, in common with the romantic ironists, *assumes* an ironic attitude towards them. In doing so, he is engaged in the *art* of hovering 'poetic reflection' which Schlegel terms 'irony'. The romantic ironist can, 'on the wings of poetic reflection, hover (*schweben*) midway between the represented (*Dargestellten*) and the representing (*Darstellenden*), free from all real and ideal interests.'[77] This artistic freedom is also apotheosized by Nietzsche in *The Gay Science*:

> At times we need to take a rest from ourselves, to look upon, and look down upon, ourselves and, from an artistic distance, laugh *over* ourselves or weep *over* ourselves. We must discover the *hero* no less than the *fool* in our passion for knowledge; we have to be happy in our folly to enable us to remain happy in our wisdom. Precisely because we are, in the final analysis, grave (*schwere*) and serious human beings, and more like weights (*Gewichte*) than human beings, so nothing does us as much good as a *fool's cap*: we need it in relation to ourselves - we need all exuberant, hovering, dancing, mocking, childish, and blissful art lest we lose the *freedom above things* that our ideal demands of us [...] We should also be *able* to stand *above* morality - and not only to stand but also to hover (*schweben*) above it and play. How could we, then, possibly dispense with the anxious stiffness of a man who is afraid of slipping and falling at any moment, with art - and with the fool? - And as long as you are in any way *ashamed* before yourselves, you do not yet belong with us. (*GS*.107)

Herein lies the key to the parabolic significance of the buffoon's triumphant leap over the ropedancer. From this 'artistic distance' the elevated buffoon can mock both the heroism of the ropedancer and the integrity of the buffoon in their respective quests for truth; he can also see the spirit of gravity instinct in both hero and fool; in other words, how pessimism is the

---

77. Schlegel, *KA*.II.182-3.116.

cause of the former's idealism and the effect of the latter's resolute reflexivity. Morality dictates the gravity of their respective endeavours: a weighty earnestness which is detectable in the ropedancer's rigid fear and in the buffoon's uncompromising honesty which not only shames the ropedancer out of his idealism, but which cruelly and dangerously 'never ask[s] whether truth is useful or fatal' (*A*.Foreword). Levity is required: the hero must be able 'to stand with relaxed muscles and [an] unharnessed will' (*Z*.II.13) and the fool must beware lest his honesty lead him and others 'to nausea and suicide' (*GS*.107). Accordingly, the Zarathustra of Part IV essays the artists' art of self-dramatization, because

> Only artists, and particularly those of the theatre, have given men eyes and ears to see and to hear with some amusement what each man is himself, experiences himself, desires himself; only they have taught us the value of the hero, the hero that is hidden in every one of these ordinary men; only they have taught us the art of viewing ourselves as heroes - from a distance and, as it were, simplified and transfigured - the art of "staging" ("*in Scene zu setzen*") ourselves in front of ourselves. Only in this way can we get over some of the base details in ourselves. (*GS*.78)

According to Schlegel, the romantic ironist, from this elevated position, can purportedly 'raise this [poetic] reflection to higher and higher powers and can multiply it, as it were, in an endless array of mirrors.'[78] But if Schlegel conceived these infinite powers of reflection as the 'freest of all licences'[79] and as 'beautiful self-mirroring',[80] Zarathustra senses the nihilistic dangers implicit in such powers. Having countless mirrors and masks at his disposal, Zarathustra arguably fears that this 'endless array of mirrors', each with its own ironic reflection, will ultimately preclude any possibility of authenticity. For if every mask is seen to conceal another mask, and so on *ad infinitum*, then one is led finally to suspect that the last mask, rather like the smallest box in a set of Chinese boxes, will conceal *nothing*. As Kierkegaard incisively observes: 'the ironic individual has most often traversed a multitude of determinations in the form of possibility, [and] poetically lived through them, before he ends in nothingness.'[81] It is this

---

78. Ibid.
79. Ibid., *KA* II.160.108.
80. Ibid., *KA* II.204.238.
81. Kierkegaard, p. 298.

nothingness which Zarathustra, as early as Part II, perceives lurking behind all those ethereal gods and *Übermenschen* (Z.II.17).

Unlike Schlegel, therefore, Zarathustra did not view his 'transcendental buffoonery' as an expression of infinite poetic freedom, but rather as a masquerade born out of prosaic necessity. Nor did he believe that true objectivity was the prerogative of poets. On the contrary, even those great poets,

> for example - men like Byron, Musset, Poe, Leopardi, Kleist, Gogol - are and perhaps must be men of fleeting moments, enthusiastic, sensual, childish, frivolous and sudden in mistrust and trust; with souls in which they usually try to conceal some fracture; often taking revenge with their works for some inner contamination, often seeking with their high flights forgetfulness of an all-too-faithful memory; often lost in the mud and almost in love with it, until they become like will-o'-the-wisps around swamps and *pretend* to be stars - the people may then call them idealists - often struggling with a long nausea, with a recurring spectre of unbelief which freezes them. (*BGE*.269)

Endorsing Kierkegaard's critique in this regard, I believe that one of the principal objections to the romantic ironists is, paradoxically, their intrinsic *lack* of irony. They failed to discern that their ironic attitude, far from being the easy detachment of an impartial spectator, was merely the mask of a disillusioned actor. What distinguishes Zarathustra from the proponents of romantic irony is his will to integrity, which compelled him to reflect upon his own *assumed* ironic attitude and the cathartic need underlying the art of transfiguring self-projection. And just as an unrelenting moral imperative compelled Nietzsche to confess, not only to himself, but (most unambiguously in his 1886 prefaces) also to his readers, that his ability to overcome with courageous laughter the irony of the human condition was no more than an *attitude*, a 'tenacious *will to health* which often ventures to clothe and disguise itself as health already achieved' (*HH*.I.Prol.4); so a rigorous will to honesty compels the Zarathustra of Part IV to warn his higher men that 'a wise man is also a fool' (Z.IV.19.10). Unlike the romantic ironists, Zarathustra did not lack 'the courage of conscience' to remove his mask(s); 'the good taste' to warn a friend or foe of his dissimulation; nor 'the exuberance' necessary for self-mockery (*BGE*.5).

CONVALESCENCE

The Eagle and the Serpent

3 Cunning Reason and Proud Imagination

Prudent Imagination

> And behold! An eagle swept through the air in wide circles, and from it hung a serpent, not like a prey but like a friend - for it coiled itself around the eagle's neck.
> 'It is my animals!' said Zarathustra and rejoiced in his heart.
> 'The proudest (*stolzeste*) animal under the sun and the cleverest (*klügste*) animal under the sun...'[82] (Z.Prol.10)

Like much of the symbolism in *Zarathustra*, the eagle and the serpent are hackneyed emblems which Nietzsche makes no effort to revivify through novel employment: accordingly, we have the *proud* eagle and the *clever* serpent. Traditionally, the eagle represents the aerial and the spiritual, and the serpent the chthonic and the material,[83] but whereas the eagle straightforwardly symbolizes the solar and is thus implicitly associated with divine wisdom and intuitive knowledge, the serpent is notoriously polyvalent, symbolizing both life and death, good and evil, knowledge and blind

---

82. Both Kaufmann and Hollingdale refer to the serpent as 'the *wisest* animal under the sun' (emphasis added). This very generous rendering of '*klügste*' necessarily proceeds from a positive reading of Zarathustra's character; for if Zarathustra is deemed to be a noble figure, then *his* animals will be seen to symbolize *his* noble qualities. If, on the other hand, Zarathustra is perceived to be more base than noble, more reactive than active, more *Mensch* than *Übermensch*, then his animals will be taken to represent his ignoble qualities. On this latter reading, Zarathustra's serpent appears to have less of the genius about him than the ingenious: far from being the wisest animal under the sun, he is the cleverest animal under the sun. For a discussion on the significance of partiality in Nietzsche translation see Cauchi, 'Rationalism and Irrationalism: A Nietzschean Perspective', *History of European Ideas*, 20:4-6 (1995), 937-943.
83. For a history of these two symbols with respect to *Zarathustra*, see David Thatcher, 'Eagle and Serpent in *Zarathustra*', *Nietzsche-Studien* 6 (1977), 240-60.

passion, healing and poison, perversion and destruction.[84] This serpentine ambivalence is particularly evident in the shift from Greek to Christian mythology, from the serpent's Apollonian association symbolizing medicine, music, and light, to its Satanic association with guile, "evil", and destruction.

In *Zarathustra*, this symbolic ambivalence is retained, a circumstance which is best explained by reference to Nietzsche's repeated exposure of the intrinsic conection between seeming opposites on the grounds that 'there are no opposites, except in the customary exaggeration of popular or metaphysical interpretations, and that a mistake in reasoning lies at the bottom of this antithesis' (*HH*.I 'Of First and Last Things' 1). The root of this error, Nietzsche suggests, can be found in man's 'reas'ning pride',[85] in man's natural aversion to the idea that good might possibly be rooted in bad, or the ideal, the beautiful, and the moral in the real, the ugly and the non-moral. Pride - a Greek virtue symbolized by the eagle, and a Christian vice symbolized by the proud Lucifer - is that which unites Zarathustra's eagle and serpent. It is the clever serpent's "earthly" and earth-bound knowledge of the necessary kinship between good and bad, and the concomitant threat to man's self-esteem, that leads him to enter into conspiratorial relations with the creative genius of the air-borne eagle.

On this reading, then, the soaring eagle finds its psychical analogue in imagination, and the clever serpent in the subtle and convoluted practices of reason. Proud and prudent reason courts proud imagination, and together - the serpent coiled around the eagle's neck - they redeem man from his proud shame. Placing Zarathustra's animals within this complex psychical framework, I will argue that the proud eagle represents the pride of imagination; that the clever (*klug*) serpent represents the prudence (*Klugheit*) of reason; and that their union symbolizes the 'proud, deceptive consciousness' (*TL*.1) of the man of *ressentiment*.[86]

---

84. Cooper, op. cit., pp. 146/7.
85. Alexander Pope, *An Essay on Man*, ll. 119-122.
86. While I have chosen to retain the French word '*ressentiment*', I do not share Kaufmann's misgivings concerning its English equivalent 'resentment'. Harraps' French-English Dictionary gives 'resentment' as the *primary* translation of '*ressentiment*', and one wonders why Nietzsche necessarily had another meaning in mind, as Kaufmann seems to imply. Rather, Nietzsche's originality could be seen to lie not in giving '*ressentiment*' a new "meaning" (I do not believe that he does), but in extending its application to the moral sphere: *ressentiment* as the source of herd and

Disease: Civilization

Almost fifty years before Freud's supposedly seminal work, *Civilization and its Discontents* (1929), Nietzsche had analysed the irreparable psychological damage wrought by civilization on man. According to Nietzsche's speculative anthropology, the "taming" of animal man was a world-historical event of unparalleled cruelty: henceforth man would wage war on himself. Restrained by law from discharging his aggressive drives, the romanticized noble savage was forced to turn his combative and predatory instincts back upon himself. But just as prohibition drives that which is prohibited underground, so the primal instincts, undeterred and undiminished in their thrusting lust for power,[87] resort to subterfuge (*GM*.III.13). Instinctual aggression, formerly directed outward, must now reckon with a new (internal) opponent called consciousness, which must likewise develop subtlety and cunning if it is not to be overcome by the more formidable and resourceful powers of the unconscious:

> They were awkward in the execution of the simplest tasks; in this strange[88] new world they no longer possessed their former guides, their regulating, unconscious and commanding (*sicherführend*) drives: they were reduced to thinking, inferring, calculating, combining cause and effect, these unfortunate creatures; they were reduced to their "consciousness", to their poorest and most fallible organ! I believe that there has never been such a feeling of misery on earth, such a leaden discomfort - and at the same time the old instincts had not suddenly ceased to make their usual demands! Only it was hard and seldom possible to comply with them: as a rule they had to seek new and, as it were, subterranean gratifications. (*GM*.II.16)

'The weak in courage is strong in cunning',[89] and so it is that man's 'poorest and most fallible organ' develops into his shrewdest and most sophisticated organ. Fearfully exposed to the wanton flux of instinctual and phenomenal nature, consciousness learns the *art* of reasoning and turns casuist. Only by

---

slave morality (see *GM*.I). In choosing the French word rather than the German, Nietzsche's purpose might simply have been to draw attention to his novel application of this noun.

87. 'Every drive is tyrannical' (*BGE*.6).
88. This adjective (*unbekannt*) is absent from Kaufmann and Hollingdale's joint translation.
89. Blake, *The Marriage of Heaven and Hell*, 'Proverbs of Hell', Plate 9.

adopting and refining its opponent's strategies can the 'small reason' of the mind succeed in outwitting the 'great reason' of the body (Z.I.4).[90]

Symptom: *Ressentiment*

In the transition from wilderness to society, the prototypical man of *ressentiment* is born. *Ressentiment* is defined as an indignant sense of injury received, and the man of *ressentiment* is characterized by the *shrewd* (serpent-like) way in which he reacts[91] to this feeling. Resentful of the loss of instinctual freedom and the suffering attendant upon relentless internal warfare, the man of *ressentiment* avenges himself as only the weak can: through cunning and artifice. The man of nature becomes a man of reason, 'active forces become reactive',[92] and in the struggle for survival, subtlety and prudence usurp the former rights of brute force.[93] Just as Prince Hal/Henry V rejects Falstaff - who is 'not only witty in [him]self, but the cause that wit is in other men'[94] - so consciousness seeks to deny its unconscious determinant and thus its chaotic and subtle foundations. Asserting legitimacy by the denial of its historical contingency, the Pretender, intellect, disingenuously planks over the flux of existence (Z.III.12.8); metaphysics becomes the comfort food of vain philosophers.[95]

Daunted and dispirited by the inexorable will to power inherent in nature, reason, with the aid of imagination, devises the reassuring but false

---

90. Cf. 'Energy is the only life, and is from the Body; and Reason is the bound or outward circumference of Energy'. Blake, *The Marriage of Heaven and Hell*, 'The Voice of the Devil', Plate 4.
91. Deleuze stresses that it is the *type* of reaction (in fact, a failure to re-act) that designates the man of *ressentiment*: '*Ressentiment* designates a type in which reactive forces prevail over active forces. But they can only prevail in one way: by ceasing to be acted'. See Gilles Deleuze, *Nietzsche and Philosophy*, trans. Hugh Tomlinson (London: The Athlone Press, 1986), p. 111.
92. Deleuze. Man's active and reactive forces form the basis of Deleuze's critique of Nietzsche and inform his excellent readings of the will to power, *ressentiment* and bad conscience.
93. Freud discusses the consequences of this transference of power from the individual to the community in Chapter 1 of *Civilization and its Discontents*.
94. William Shakespeare, *2 Henry IV*, I.ii.9-10.
95. 'If such Metaphysiques [...] be not Vain Philosophy, there was never any.' Thomas Hobbes (*SOED*), p. 1315.

polarities of real and ideal (Plato); spirit and matter, immortal and mortal, good and evil (Christianity); noumenal and phenomenal (Kant). As Nietzsche avers: ' "Reason" is the cause of our falsification of the evidence of the senses' (*TI* ' "Reason" in Philosophy' 2), and with her contempt for the body and her devaluation of the sensible in favour of the suprasensible, reason imaginatively invents the "noble" lie and thereby ushers nihilism into the annals of history.

Physic: Nihilism

Within the context of Nietzsche's work as a whole (and his *Nachlaß* in particular), the term "nihilism" displays formidable versatility. This is not the place, however, for a detailed discussion of Nietzsche's idiosyncratic employment of this term;[96] suffice it to say that Nietzsche distinguishes between four basic forms of nihilism, which might be termed optimistic or idealist nihilism, pessimistic nihilism, apathetic nihilism, and affirmative nihilism. The first three types are characterized by a denial of life, and the fourth by a denial of life-denial. The optimistic nihilist denies the value of this world of becoming by weighing it against the (believed/imagined) supreme value of an ideal (believed "true") world of being; the pessimistic nihilist denies the value of this world and the existence of any other, and inveighs against both; the apathetic nihilist, or what Zarathustra contemptuously refers to as 'the last man', is a resigned pessimistic nihilist who has found contentment in stagnation; and finally, the affirmative nihilist, posessed of an *übermenschliche* love of life as it *really* is, denies himself all forms of life-preserving life-denial.

The history of optimistic or idealist nihilism is the 'history of an error' (*TI* 'How the "True World" Finally Became a Fable'), an error perpetrated by the man of *ressentiment*: first by the shrewd reason of the philosopher-king (Plato); then by 'the *diseased* reason in the priest' (*TI* 'Morality as Anti-Nature' 6) (Christianity); and finally, by the "pure practical reason" of

---

96. For a clear and concise exposition of Nietzsche's diverse treatment of the term "nihilism" see Chapter 2 of Alan White's *Within Nietzsche's Labyrinth* (London: Routledge, 1990). For a more schematic exposition see Robert C Solomon, 'Nietzsche, Nihilism, and Morality', in Robert C Solomon (ed.), *Nietzsche: A Collection of Critical Essays* (New York: University of Notre Dame Press, 1978), pp. 204-9.

the philosopher-theologian[97] (Kant). In his breathtakingly concise six-part history entitled 'How the "True World" Finally Became a Fable', Nietzsche dissects the metaphysical malaise and charts the decline and fall of the so-called "true world". Parts 1 to 3 rehearse the gradual refinement and rarefication of this bastard child of reason and imagination, and parts 4 to 6 depict the dawn of positivism, of a world-view purportedly unclouded by theology and metaphysics.

> 1. The true world, attainable to the wise, the pious, the virtuous man - he lives it, *he is it*.
> > (Oldest form of the idea, relatively clever (*klug*),[98] simple, convincing. Transcription of the proposition 'I, Plato, *am* the truth.')

Nietzsche's application of the adjective '*klug*' here is significant: it suggests that Plato's idea of the Forms is simply a clever ruse, a "noble" lie, devised by one who seeks to authenticate his truth claims. It is a *relatively* clever idea by virtue of its simplicity and in contradistinction to those ingenious ideas which lack credibility by being too-clever-by-half (see 3 below). Plato's idea of a "true world" is intelligible in both senses of the word: it is an idea that is both comprehensible (to all) and apprehensible (albeit to philosopher-kings only).

> 2. The true world, unattainable for now, but promised to the wise, the pious, the virtuous man ("to the sinner who repents").

---

97. As Heidegger argues in his excellent reading of Nietzsche's 'history', Kant's noumenal, suprasensuous world does not appear 'on the grounds of basic philosophical principles of knowledge but as a consequence of uneradicated Christian-theological presuppositions. In that regard Nietzsche on one occasion observes of Leibniz, Kant, Fichte, Schelling, Hegel, and Schopenhauer, "They are all mere Schleiermachers" ([*Grossoktavausgabe*] XV.112). The observation has two edges: it means not only that these men are at bottom camouflaged theologians but also that they are what the name suggests–*Schleier-macher*, makers of veils, men who veil things. (Heidegger, *Nietzsche*, Vol I, op. cit., p. 206). In a similar vein, Nietzsche remarks: 'Fichte, Schelling, Hegel, Schleiermacher, Feuerbach, Strauss - all theologians' (*KSA*.11.152).
98. Hollingdale here renders '*klug*' as 'sensible', which, in its given context, is extremely misleading. The "true world" of Plato's Forms is a transcendent, *supra*sensible reality, a world, therefore, which is apprehensible to the intellect and *not*, by definition, to the senses.

> (Progress of the idea: it becomes more cunning (*feiner*), more insidious (*verfänglicher*),[99] more incomprehensible - it becomes woman, it becomes Christian ...)

Once again, the adjectives '*feiner*' and '*verfänglicher*' draw the reader's attention to the increasing subtlety of reason in its desperate bid to deny and vilify the more *sensible* truth claims, as it were, of the instincts. The incomprehensibility of the idea *lies* in its cunning removal to an "afterworld", to a world from which no-one ever returns; a world, therefore, which can neither be proved nor disproved. In this, of course, lies its enticing mystery; but, for Nietzsche, the cosmetics of mystery, like those of woman, are meretricious.

> 3. The true world, unattainable, unprovable, unpromisable, but even as thought, a comfort, a duty, an imperative.
> (The old sun, basically, but seen through fog and scepticism; the idea grown sublime, pale, northern,[100] Königsbergian.)

Here is Kant's postulated noumenal world, a world which lies beyond the phenomenal, beyond the empirical, beyond the sensible, beyond the causal and the conditioned, and so, for Nietzsche, beyond the pale. Here is the same old sun: bright enough at first to cast a shadow in Plato's allegorical cave, then growing hazy as the sun becomes shrouded in mystifying mists and clouds of frankincense, and finally eclipsed by Kant's categories of the understanding. But just as the eclipsed sun shines forth in a halo of light, so the Platonic and Christian incandescence of 'pure spirit and the good in itself' (*BGE*.Pref) irradiates Kant's halo of pure practical reason and the 'categorical imperative' of its postulated moral law.

> 4. The true world - unattainable? Unattained, in any case. And if unattained also *unknown*. Consequently, also not consolatory, redemptive, obligatory: to what could something unknown obligate us?
> (Grey dawn. first yawnings of reason. Cockrow of positivism.)

---

99. By translating '*feiner*' as 'more refined', and '*verfänglicher*' as 'more enticing', Hollingdale effaces the subtlety and treachery that Nitezsche is at pains to emphasize.
100. This reference to northern climes, suggestive of fog and pallid complexions, nicely juxtaposes the literal and the metaphorical, the physical and the ethereal.

> 5. The "true world" - an idea which is no longer of any use, not even an obligation, - an idea which has become useless and superfluous, *consequently*, a refuted idea, let us abolish it!
>> (Broad daylight; breakfast; return of *bon sens* and cheerfulness; Plato blushes for shame; pandemonium of all free spirits)
>
> 6. The true world we have abolished: what world remains? the apparent world perhaps? ... But no! *with the true world we have also abolished the apparent one!*
>> (Noon; moment of the shortest shadow; end of the longest error; highpoint of humanity; INCIPIT ZARATHUSTRA)

According to the above history, then, nihilism finally an*nihil*ates itself; but does it? If one scrutinizes the whimsical asides of parts 4 to 6, an autobiographical dimension reveals itself. In the cockcrow of positivism, the cheerful pandemonium of the free spirits, and the clarion call of INCIPIT ZARATHUSTRA, one can hear the distant echo of Nietzsche's respective and retrospective efforts - in *Dawn*, *The Gay Science* and *Zarathustra* - to extricate himself from the metaphysical mire. But, as we shall see in chapter 6 below, positivism is just another, more refined form of nihilism; and with the arrival of Zarathustra and his prophecy of the coming *Übermensch*, we seem to have come full circle. For if Nietzsche can congratulate himself on having abolished the "true world", he must surely be blushing for shame at his need to invent a character who is courageous and heroic enough to be true to a world whose truth is both ungodly and unsightly. Zarathustra's *Übermensch* represents the 'highpoint of humanity': a man who not only lives truly *in* this world - he 'lives it, *he is it.*' But if this real world is truer than Plato's ideal world, Zarathustra's ideal lover of this real world is truly just another "noble" lie.

In *The Gay Science*, Nietzsche had argued that man's contempt for life and himself would begin to ebb 'as soon as he ceases to *flow out* into a god' (*GS*.285). Zarathustra's propehtic beginning, however, is a veritable flood, an outpouring of vitriol against the contemptible 'last man' and a promised redemptive sea into which the latter can 'flow out': 'In truth, man is a polluted river. One must be a sea to be able to absorb a polluted river and not be defiled. Behold, I teach you the *Übermensch*: he is this sea, in him your great contempt can drown' (Z.Prol.3). The *Übermensch* is, of course, an (perhaps *the*) affirmative nihilist who, giddy with happiness and exuberant dancing, ecstatically embraces life. It is, however, an optimistic nihilist who, in prophesying the redemptive *Übermensch*, weighs man against the (believed) supreme value of an ideal of human perfection, 'a type of supreme achievement, in *opposition* to "modern" men, to "good" men, to Christians and other nihilists' (*EH* 'Why I write such good books' 1).

On this showing, then, history repeats itself. Nihilism is self-perpetuating rather than self-defeating: no sooner is one idol obliterated (whether it be the Forms, God, or the '*Ding-an-sich*', or any of its secular manifestations such as socialism and positivism), than another blossoms in its place.

'*Incipit Zarathustra*', writes Nietzsche, and *beginning* (as we saw in Chapter 1) where his illustrious forbears left off, Zarathustra enters the market square peddling his latest (*übermenschliche*) "form" of the old ascetic ideal. The question is, of course, whether Zarathustra realizes that his *Übermensch* is but another nihilistic lie; another subtle strategy of a proud and deceptive consciousness.

Physician: Prudent Pride

> In reas'ning Pride (my friend) our error lies;
> All quit their sphere and rush into the Skies.
> Pride still is aiming at the blest abodes,
> Men would be Angels, Angels would be Gods.[101]

The philosopher, according to Nietzsche, is 'the proudest of men' (*TL*.1), and just as Eve felt that her divine origin entitled her to a share in divine knowledge, so the philosopher/metaphysician, with his ontological and epistemological pretensions, lays claim to divine wisdom. In *Beyond Good and Evil*, Nietzsche mocks the 'subtle pride' of those 'philosophical labourers [who,] after the noble model of Kant and Hegel, must establish and press into formulas [...] some great facts of high regard - that is, former *positings* of value, creations of value, which have become dominant and for a long time been called "truths" ' (*BGE*.211). But this will to conceptualize and systematize, to abstraction and simplification, is nothing compared to Kant's and Hegel's vaunted claims to absolutism. Indeed, Kant's audacious attempt to lay the groundwork to a *metaphysic* of morals on unconditional, "free" and hence groundless grounds, and Hegel's conviction that '*das*

---

101. Alexander Pope, *An Essay on Man*, ll. 119-22.

absolute Wissen' can only be consummated in philosophy, would seem to suggest, after the noble model of Plato and Pythagoras, nothing short of the divine right of philosopher-kings. The 'magnificent arrogance' of these two archetypal philosopher-kings leads to their denunciation in *The Gay Science* as 'monsters of pride and self-satisfaction' (*GS*.V.351).

It is with apparent pride and self-satisfaction that Zarathustra sings of his 'wild wisdom', which became pregnant upon lonely mountains (Z.II.1), and with impetuous desire (Z.III.12.2) now proudly wings its way across the sea (Z.II.8). But a glance at Nietzsche's anguished *Dionysus-Dithyramb*, 'Amid Birds of Prey', leads one to suspect that Zarathustra's wild wisdom is but an instance of proud reason, having fallen heavily pregnant with the gravity of its knowledge, seeking periodic relief in flighty imagination.

> Now -
> alone with yourself
> twain in self-knowledge,
> amid a hundred mirrors
> false before yourself
> amid a hundred memories
> uncertain,
> weary from every wound
> cold from every frost,
> strangled in your own ropes,
> *Self-knower*!
> *Self-executioner*!
>
> Why did you bind yourself
> with the rope of your wisdom?
> Why did you lure yourself
> into the old serpent's paradise?
> Why did you sneak into yourself
> *yourself* - yourself? ...
>
> Now an invalid
> sick with the serpent's poison; [...]
> towered over by a hundred burdens,
> overloaded by yourself,
> a *knower*!
> a *self-knower*!
> the *wise* Zarathustra! ...

> You sought the heaviest burden:
> there you found *yourself* -,
> yourself you cannot throw off ...
>
> [...] And only recently so proud!
> on all the stilts of your pride!
> Only recently the hermit without God,
> co-dweller with the Devil,
> the scarlet prince of all high spirits!

The serpent's *gift*[102] of knowledge is here seen to be received at the behest and self-bequest of pride, and the biblical link between pride and the Fall is rehearsed. Just as proud Lucifer, the angel of light, waged open war on the plains of heaven, fell into darkness, and must now rely on cunning and artifice to satisfy his pride; so a proud and godless Zarathustra, having entered into mortal combat with his battalion of inner selves and fallen from wounded pride, makes a pact with the devil and cunningly creates for himself a new god. Armed with this new amulet, Zarathustra enters the fray once more (Z.Prol.3-5), is defeated by injured pride once more (overthrown by the mocking, rope-dancing buffoon Z.Prol.6), and must once more resort to subtlety and disguise if he is to retain a modicum of human dignity.

A distinction must be made between clever (*klug*) and wise (*weise*). Just as man is 'a manifold, mendacious, false, and devious animal, uncanny to the animals less on account of his strength than on account of his cunning and cleverness' (*BGE*.291), so *klug* is a consummate and versatile actor, and a German etymologist might well raise an eyebrow or two at those Nietzsche commentators who display a tendency to mistake the role for the actor. *Klug*'s repertoire includes clever and intelligent, witty and sophisticated, wise and sound, prudent and shrewd. And in the following dialogue from Lessing's play *Nathan the Wise* (*Weise*), Nathan gives a shrewd account of the incestuous relations obtaining between clever and wise:

> *Saladin*: I have long wished to know the man whom [the people] call wise.
> *Nathan*: And what if he was mockingly so called? If wise to the people was nothing more than clever? And clever only he who knows where his advantage lies?

---

102. '*Gift*' in German means 'poison'.

48 Zarathustra contra Zarathustra

> *Saladin*: His real advantage, you mean?
> *Nathan*: In that case, of course, the most selfish would be the cleverest; in which case, of course, clever and wise would be one. (2,272)[103]

Is not Zarathustra's "wisdom" only mockingly so called, and his 'wild wisdom' merely an imaginative conceit 'And Reason in her most exalted mood'?[104] As evidenced by the following textual references, imagination is inextricably bound up with Zarathustra's so-called wisdom: his youthful wisdom - possessed at a time when he had 'wanted to dance beyond all heavens' - resided in (Wagnerian) 'visions' and (Schopenhauerian) 'consolations' (Z.II.11); his 'laughing, wakeful day-wisdom that mocks all "infinite worlds" ', finds the courage to do so - that is to say, without the aid of his metaphysical crutch, the *Übermensch* - only in a dream, a dream in which the finite world appears to him in the utopian splendour that imagination alone can supply (Z.III.10.1); his 'wild wisdom' is, 'in truth', a 'wise' and 'great desire with rushing wings' (Z.III.12.2), an exalted *feeling* and a passionate *longing*; in a chapter appositely entitled 'Of the Great Longing', Zarathustra sadly recalls how he gave his soul 'all new wines and also all immemorially old strong wines of wisdom', and how even these *heady* intoxications are insufficient to cure his soul of its heavy melancholy (Z.III.14); and finally, in a chapter entitled 'Of Human Prudence',[105] one encounters Zarathustra's imaginary '*Übermensch* joyfully bathing his nakedness in the burning sun of wisdom' (Z.II.21).

Klugheit loves to strut about in the golden[106] robes of *Weisheit* - 'At all times *arrogance* has rightly been called the "vice of the knower (*Wissende*)" ' (*HH*.II 'Opinions and Maxims' 26) - and Zarathustra himself, as his animals betoken, is no stranger to this dissembling art. He learns that amongst the nauseating and pitiful herd his 'best wisdom' (*beste Weisheit*) is to 'forget and pass by' (Z.III.9). Furthermore, it is precisely his disgust at the sight of the 'polluted river' of mankind, that prudently creates for itself

---

103. Jacob Grimm, *Deutsches Wörtebuch*, Vol. 5, 'klug', p. 1275.
104. William Wordsworth, *The Prelude: A Parallel Text*, ed., J C Maxwell (New Haven: Yale University Press, 1981), Book XIV, l. 192.
105. Hollingdale misleadingly translates '*Menschen-Klugheit*' as 'Manly Prudence', in spite of the fact that Zarathustra's prudence is cowardly, and therefore typically *human* rather than *manly*.
106. It is submitted that all references to 'gold' or 'golden' in *Zarathustra* connote a mythical world as envisaged by fools and poets.

the redemptive sea symbolized by the *Übermensch* (Z.Prol.3), and 'wings to soar away into distant futures' (Z.II.21).[107] In short, Zarathustra's all-too-human prudence consists in disguising himself so that he may 'misjudge' himself and others (Z.II.21). But to what effect? A conscious counterfeiter, as opposed to an unconscious counterfeiter (see *EH 'The Case of Wagner'* 3), cannot afford the luxury of self-deceit. Herculean effort and selective blindness may enable Zarathustra to 'pass by' suffering humanity with, at best, an air of studied indifference, but his brutally suppressed pity threatens anarchy with every passing step. And 'to soar away into distant futures' is, at the very least, a disingenuous activity for one who exhorts man to be 'true to the earth' (Z.Prol.3). Only when intellectual conscience and bitter irony are, as it were, up-staged by reason and imagination, can Zarathustra tolerate himself, humanity, and life. Life, like wisdom, is for Zarathustra in all things a woman: 'fickle and defiant', and perhaps 'wicked and false', wisdom and life share the same serpentine qualities (Z.II.10). Is it any wonder, therefore, that so many readers of *Zarathustra* confound prudence and wisdom, and fail to see the man of *ressentiment* hiding behind the mask of the prophet, and the wizened face of prudence grimacing behind the joyful mask of 'wild wisdom'?[108] Above all else, Zarathustra is a clever man, a prudent man, a resentful man; a man who, in the interests of self-preservation, would rather 'conceal and deny [a] broken, proud, incurable heart' (*BGE*.270) than choke to death on self-contempt.

'Prudence is a rich, ugly old maid courted by Incapacity',[109] and time and again in Nietzsche's work, amidst a barrage of vitriol, contumely and general polemic, one encounters this contemptible figure. One of Nietzsche's favourite *bêtes noires*, this exceptionally clever beast is almost invariably exposed as a wolf in sheep's clothing. Nietzsche has, of course, particular sheep in mind, namely, the Christian "flock". According to Nietzsche, prudence masquerades as morality, and the Christian virtues are a motley collection of cunning disguises. Just as the ugliest man in Part IV of *Zarathustra* decks himself out in a crown and purple (symbolizing sacerdotal power) sashes - 'for, like all the ugly, he loved to disguise and

---

107. Alan White makes a similar point (p. 82).
108. Cf. '[Wisdom] is a screen for philosophers, behind which he saves himself from weariness, old age, cold and hardness; as a feeling that the end is near, like those instincts of prudence which animals have before they die - they go off by themselves, become still, choose solitude, crawl into caves, and become *wise*' (*GS*.V.359).
109. Blake, *The Marriage of Heaven and Hell*, 'Proverbs of Hell', Plate 7.

beautify himself' (Z.IV.11) - so weakness cloaks itself in strength, vice in virtue. These 'protean arts' (*BGE*.230) of prudence owe their subtlety and ingenuity to the circumspect leaders of the Christian movement, those Church Fathers 'who are clever, clever to the point of holiness' (*A*.59), and whose 'Serpent Reasonings us entice / Of Good and Evil, Virtue & Vice.'[110]

Zarathustra is (apparently) no Christian prophet, but, as an ironic man of *ressentiment* struggling and failing to overcome his cultural past, he is forced to recognize his own deep implication in the priestly heritage; the ironic man of *ressentiment* acknowledges that he is a man of *ressentiment*. If consciousness developed with the aid of the intellect, then the supreme sophistication of the latter was achieved by clerical casuistry. A cunning prudence invented morality in order to instil pride, to establish *morale*,[111] and so counteract the fatal consequences of self-loathing. Out of the same materials (prudence and cunning), Zarathustra fashions for himself gaily painted masks: self-love masks self-contempt; pride, shame; and the prophet of the redemptive *Übermensch* masks the madman who fears the nihilistic consequences of the death of God (*GS*.125) and his dire need of metaphysical comfort.

The Christian God and the "anti-Christian" *Übermensch* are two sides of the same metaphysical coin in the currency of shame, hope and redemption. The old morality, invented by the priestly caste and perpetuated by the pride and prudence of rational imagination, is embodied in Zarathustra's animals. Far from symbolizing Zarathustra's noble, *anti-Christian* virtues,[112] the proud eagle and clever serpent typify the Christian "virtues" so often denounced by Nietzsche; and on Nietzsche's own admission, the hardest task for Zarathustra will be to free himself from the old morality. As early as the Prologue to *Zarathustra*, this task is seen to be impossible, an impossibility that, as we shall now see, the periodic appearances of Zarathustra's animals serve to underscore.

---

110. Blake, *For the Sexes: The Gates of Paradise*, 'Of the Gates', ll. 5-6.
111. A '*moral* condition [...] especially with regard to *confidence* and discipline' *SOED* (emphasis added).
112. 'These animals [...] symbolize the virtues of pride and cleverness, vices from a Christian standpoint' (Lampert, p. 29); 'Pride and cleverness are consciously chosen attributes, they stand in a sought after opposition to humility and that poverty of the spirit before which the wisdom of this world becomes stupidity - they are anti-Christian' (Fink, p. 70).

4 Physicians as Metaphysicians

Zarathustra's Disease: Intellectual Conscience

Following the market square fiasco, Zarathustra's animals come in search of the proud "prophet" who, looking for all the world like a mountebank hawking another placebo, has come among 'the unteachable flock'[113] to prophesy a new "anti-Christian" redeemer; but who, in an untimely moment of shamefaced self-reflection, has rashly let fall his mask upon discerning at the root of his redemptive *Übermensch* his own profoundly Christian need for hope and redemption ('The need for *redemption*, the quintessence of all Christian needs [...] is the most honest expression of decadence [...] The Christian wants to be *rid* of himself' *CW*.Epilogue). As the parable of the ropedancer serves to demonstrate, moral idealism (the ropedancer) will always be brought low by scoffing reflexivity (the buffoon). Hearkening to the voice of his 'intellectual conscience' (*GS*.2), to the rigorous demands of 'unconditional honesty' (*UM*.III.1), Zarathustra abandons his 'proud, deceptive consciousness' (his animals), and plunges ignominiously to his *dramatic* death. Thus it is that Zarathustra's forsaken animals come to ascertain whether the erstwhile "prophet" is still alive. He is not, of course, as the corpse of the ropedancer somewhat crudely demonstrates. Reminiscent of the manner in which Leonce, in Büchner's *Leonce and Lena*, lays out his love's corpse in his head (I.i), Zarathustra lays the corpse of the ropedancer 'in a hollow tree at his head' (Z.Prol.8); the so-called prophet has laid to rest his ideal of the *Übermensch* in a mind temporarily bereft of pride and cunning. In so doing, Zarathustra the madman is no longer able, in all conscience, to bring to life Zarathustra the prophet. He discards the mask, only for it to be hastily retrieved by those who crafted it: his proud eagle and his clever serpent.

'A timeless creation of the imagination, and so more real and consistent than the changeable reality of the actor',[114] the mask of the prophet remains

---

113. Horace, Epode 16, *Altera iam teritur*, l. 38.
114. Pirandello, *Six Characters in Search of an Author*, trans. John Linstrum, Act I.

intact despite the temporary failure of the actor to animate it. Zarathustra's animals know, moreover, that the role of prophet, with its grand soliloquies and visionary rhetoric, is one with which Zarathustra, once he has mastered the role, will be loth to part. Thus, like an author in search of one of his characters, Zarathustra's animals return to teach Zarathustra the art of characterization. A hermit for ten long years, Zarathustra must now relearn the art of 'human prudence' (Z.II.21) if he is to 'go down' (*untergehen*, Z.Prol.1) into society and not "go under" (*untergehen*), for it is 'more dangerous among men than among animals' (Z.Prol.10). Dramatically speaking, Zarathustra does, initially, go under. His opening performance is quite literally an *abysmal* failure. At the critical moment, he listens to his conscience, forgets his part, and acts *out of character*: the proud and skilful ropedancer 'lost his head and the rope, he threw away his pole and, faster even than this, shot into the depth, a whirl of legs and arms' (Z.Prol.6). Abject and disillusioned, Zarathustra the actor vows to leave the theatre of delusion, where death masquerades as life, and shame as pride. 'I need companions', he cries, 'living ones - not dead companions and corpses which I carry with me wherever I want [...] Zarathustra shall not speak to the people but to companions! Zarathustra shall not be a sheep-dog to the herd' (Z.Prol.9). But even a more select audience cannot possibly be appealed to without a certain degree of herd subtlety and dissimulation, and so it is that, in spite of himself, Zarathustra requires the assistance of his animals and their timeless creations. This assistance, we shall see, is in no greater evidence than during Zarathustra's convalescence, as recounted in 'The Convalescent' (Z.III.13).

Zarathustra's Symptom: Pessimism

'The Convalescent' is divided into two parts: the first rehearses the immediate cause of Zarathustra's collapse while the second deals with Zarathustra's self-diagnosis of his illness and the types of treatment prescribed by his animals.

In Part 1 of 'The Convalescent', we discover Zarathustra in his 'loneliest loneliness', deprived by his intellectual conscience of the company of his animals and their fabulous circus. Left entirely to his own devices, Zarathustra gamely, but somewhat rashly, essays the part of a swaggering, sabre-rattling hero. Summoning up from his entrails his most 'abysmal

Physicians as Metaphysicians 53

thought' (the content of which we are not told until Part 2 of 'The Convalescent'), Zarathustra succeeds in flushing out his dæmonic opponent from its abysmal lair. Lacking the usual costume and props (provided by his ever-obliging eagle and serpent, respectively), Zarathustra suddenly loses heart in these mock heroics and, faced by the very real danger of a life-threatening antagonist, is 'crushed' by the 'greatest weight' of his abysmal thought.

Reference to the 'moving, stretching [and] rattling' of Zarathustra's 'abysmal thought' recalls the parable of the shepherd and the tenacious serpent, as narrated in part two of 'On the Vision and the Riddle' (Z.III.2). According to this parable, a young shepherd is in danger of choking to death on a heavy black serpent which had crept into his mouth while he was sleeping. By heroically biting off and spitting out the serpent's head, the shepherd is simultaneously redeemed and regenerated. It is a 'vision' which does not, however, pose much of a 'riddle' if viewed in the light of the preceding section (Z.III.2.1) where, after a tiresome preamble in which Nietzsche flogs yet another dead metaphor (the heroic journey, symbolizing the crossing of the sea of life, the overcoming of its dangers, and finally, the attainment of perfection), the reader is given an autobiographical account of Zarathustra's interminable battle with his debilitating pessimism (here represented by the 'Spirit of Gravity' - its gravity prefiguring the heaviness of the black serpent). It is a vision, therefore, of Zarathustra's inner torment[115] and of his longed for release from such torment.

---

115. Although this vision is intensely personal, Zarathustra is not its unique author; it is a parable which can be found in Sufi mythology: 'A wise man was riding along (at the moment when) a snake was going into the mouth of a man asleep. / The rider saw that, and was hurrying to scare away the snake, (but) he got no chance (of doing so). / Since he had an abundant supply of intelligence, he struck the sleeper several powerful blows with a mace. / The strokes of the hard mace drove him in flight from him (the rider) to beneath a tree. / There were many rotten apples which had dropped (from the tree): he said, "Eat of these, O you in the grip of pain!" / He gave the man so many apples to eat that they were falling out of his mouth again. / [...] Till nightfall he (the rider) drove (him) to and fro, until vomiting caused by bile overtook him. / All the things he had eaten, bad or good, came up from him: the snake shot forth from him along with what he had eaten. / When he saw the snake outside of him, he fell on his knees before that beneficent man. / As soon as he saw the horror of that black, ugly, big snake, those griefs departed from him. / [...] "Oh, blest (is) the hour that you saw me: I was dead, you have given me new life..." ' See 'The Amir and the sleeping man into whose mouth a snake had crept'. *The Mathnawi of*

The section ends with an invocation to heroic courage with which, as the only noble alternative to Schopenhauerian self-denial, Zarathustra hopes to haul himself out of the abyss of pessimism into which a Schopenhauerian *Weltanschauung* has cast him. (An obvious parallel can also be drawn here between the Zarathustra who is locked in mortal combat with his Spirit of Gravity and the Zarathustra who is later seen flexing his heroic muscle prior to challenging his most 'abysmal thought'.)[116]

This connection between Zarathustra's sickness and his earlier vision is further strengthened by the kinship which binds Zarathustra's serpent to that of the young shepherd.[117] Both serpents clearly symbolize the strangulating effects of knowledge, but whereas the youthful shepherd (a callow Zarathustra) imagines he has the courage simply to deny his pessimism (to bite off its head), a faint-hearted and recently defeated Zarathustra now cleverly utilizes the serpent's cunning in his repeated efforts to overcome his pessimism. The subtler, more modulated shift from sickness to convalescence is, of course, far less dramatic than the crude transformation from pessimism to laughter, but the desired goal in both cases is identical: escape from pessimism. In reality, however, a terrifying abyss separates Zarathustra from his redemptive vision:

> No longer a shepherd, no longer a man, - one transformed, effulgent, *laughing*! Never yet on earth had any man laughed as he laughed!
>
> O my brothers, I heard a laughter that was no human laughter - and now a thirst consumes me, a restless longing.
>
> My longing for this laughter consumes me: oh how can I bear to go on living! And how could I bear to die now!

Jalalu'ddin Rumi Book II, trans. Reynold A Nicholson, (Cambridge: Cambridge University Press, 1982), pp. 318-9.

116. Lampert notes how part one of 'On the Vision and the Riddle' and part one of 'The Convalescent' both end 'just after courage has been summoned for a decisive encounter' (p. 211). What he fails to point out, however, is that on both occasions the summoned courage is not forthcoming.

117. The connection between the two serpents has hitherto been overlooked by critics. For example, Thatcher distinguishes between Zarathustra's serpent and the other serpents which appear in *Zarathustra*, arguing that 'Zarathustra's own serpent is clearly an agathodæmon (a good genius), but the other snakes he encounters are malign and repulsive' (Thatcher, op. cit., p. 249); similarly, Lampert stresses that 'the heavy black snake symbolizing Zarathustra's fear is clearly not Zarathustra's snake symbolizing his prudence' (Lampert, op. cit., p. 170) - a surprising remark given the naturally intrinsic connection between fear and prudence.

It is hope and imagination, rather than courage, which saves the ironic man of *ressentiment* from choking to death on the (bad) knowledge that the bridge between *Mensch* and *Übermensch* can never be crossed: 'even the greatest of men cannot attain to his own ideal' (*UM*.III.3).

The ironic man of *ressentiment* is, by nature, the most solitary of men: he is condemned to solitude because the ironic distancing of a man whose intellectual conscience not only exposes his essential nihilism but also, and more critically, his inability to overcome it, sets him at odds with both himself and mankind.[118] With respect to the latter, insofar as Zarathustra recognizes his *Übermensch* as the supreme achievement - the masterpiece, as it were - of 'the *art of metaphysical comfort*' (*AS*.7), and, by implication, his complicity in the tyrannical rule of nihilism, his intellectual conscience sets him apart from mankind: '*the vast majority [of people] lacks an intellectual conscience*. Indeed, it has often seemed to me as if anyone calling for an intellectual conscience were as lonely in the most densely populated cities as if he were in a desert' (*GS*.2). On the other hand, insofar as he admits his failure to rise above mankind, to become a laughing *Übermensch*, he is forced to recognize his kinship with decadent humanity (albeit a kinship which disgusts him). In short, '[Zarathustra] can neither accept nor fully transcend the context that produced him.'[119]

With respect to Zarathustra's contradictory relations with himself, his intellectual conscience, 'Reasoning upon its own dark Fiction',[120] scorns the cowardly subterfuge of his 'proud, deceptive consciousness'[121] and demands the courage of open combat, the 'courage that attacks' (*Z*.III.2.1) and that the prudent and cunning man of *ressentiment* by definition lacks. In both the *visionary* parable and the preamble to 'The Convalescent', the voice of conscience[122] rings out. In the former, the young shepherd heeds his inner voice:

---

118. As Beatty observes: 'Zarathustra is [...] essentially restless, wavering between his impulse to self, which is finally wearisome, and his impulse to men, which frustrates him and forces him back upon himself'. See Joseph Beatty, 'Zarathustra: The Paradoxical Ways of the *Creator*', *Man and World* 3 (February 1970), p. 65.
119. Pippin, p. 55.
120. Blake, *The Everlasting Gospel*, (d).
121. 'If the lion was advised by the fox, he would be cunning.' Blake, *The Marriage of Heaven and Hell*, 'Proverbs of Hell', Plate 10.
122. A conscience which, unlike Kant's 'categorical imperative', is intrinsically subjective.

> 'Bite! Bite!
> Its head off! Bite!' - Thus it cried out of me, my horror, my hate, my disgust, my pity, all my good and evil cried out of me with a single cry (Z.III.2.2),

as does Zarathustra in the latter:

> Zarathustra sprang up from his bed like a madman [and] cried with a terrible voice [... which] rang out in such a way that his animals approached him in terror [...] Zarathustra, however, spoke these words:
> Up abysmal thought, up from my depths! (Z.III.13.1)

So far so good: in common with the young shepherd, Zarathustra is now suitably prepared (his shrewd animals having been petrified by the 'Minotaur of conscience' *BGE*.29) for open, as opposed to covert, combat. 'Courage [...] slays dizziness at abysses' (Z.III.2.1), assures Zarathustra, but on the edge of his own abyss, courage is not forthcoming. Whereas the *visionary* shepherd bites off the serpent's head and becomes like one transformed, Zarathustra tragi(comi)cally (the entire scene is a hideous hotchpotch of mixed metaphors and crude histrionics, or what Luke would describe as 'a kind of rhetorical debauch of images')[123] chokes on the disgust engendered by direct confrontation with his abysmal thought, keels over into the abyss, and remains prostrate for 'a long time.'

In Part 2 of 'The Convalescent', Zarathustra's abysmal thought is unmasked to reveal the ghastly face of the 'eternal recurrence' of all things.

A great many theories have been put forward regarding the cosmological validity of Nietzsche's doctrine of the eternal recurrence, but these need not detain us here. It was not the scientific verifiability of this metaphysical doctrine which principally concerned Zarathustra, but rather the 'moral imperative'[124] (not to be confused with Kant's categorical

---

123. F D Luke, 'Nietzsche and the Imagery of Height' in Malcolm Pasley (ed.), *Nietzsche: Imagery and Thought: A Collection of Essays*, (London: Methuen, 1978), p. 106.
124. It is this ethical dimension of the teaching of eternal recurrence which, as Ansell-Pearson convincingly argues, does not cohere with the cosmic (in the sense of the affirmation of life in its totality and unity) dimension: 'if eternal return is to be viewed [as a kind of ethical imperative], then it cancels out the attitude of total affirmation implied in the cosmic view, and imposes on human beings the necessity, *as moral beings*, of making judgments on life: not only saying yes, I will that again

Physicians as Metaphysicians   57

imperative)[125] that he deemed it to carry.[126] The former may have interested Nietzsche, but the latter compelled him, and in section 341 of *The Gay Science*, the ancient dictum of *carpe diem*, implicit in the idea of eternal recurrence, is made explicit:

> *The greatest weight.* - What if some day or night a devil were to steal after you into your loneliest loneliness and say to you: "This life as you now live it and have lived it, you will have to live once more and innumerable times more; and there will be nothing new in it, but every pain and every joy and every thought and sigh and everything unutterably small or great in your life will have to return to you, all in the same succession and sequence - even this spider and this moonlight between the trees, and even this moment and I myself. The eternal hourglass of existence is turned upside down again and again, and you with it, speck of dust!" Would you not throw yourself down and gnash your teeth and curse the devil who spoke thus? Or have you once experienced a tremendous moment when you would have answered him: "You are a god and never have I heard anything more divine." If this thought gained possession of you, it would change you as you are or perhaps crush you. The question in each and every thing, "Do you desire this once more and innumerable times more?" would lie upon your actions as the greatest weight. Or how well disposed would you have to become to yourself and to life *to crave nothing more fervently* than this ultimate eternal confirmation and seal?

To will eternal recurrence, the highest expression of *amor fati* and the highest affirmation of life, is, for Nietzsche, man's greatest test of courage.[127] Only he who is able to affirm life in all its aspects - who is able

---

and again, but also saying, no, never again.' See Keith Ansell-Pearson, *An Introduction to Nietzsche as Political Thinker* (Cambridge: Cambridge University Press, 1994), p. 115.
125. For an account of this distinction see Bernd Magnus, *Nietzsche's Existential Imperative* (Bloomington: Indiana University Press, 1978), pp. 139-40.
126. As Magnus argues: 'Of the two versions of the doctrine of eternal recurrence which we have distinguished, normative and empirical, no sustained argument for the cosmological status of eternal recurrence exists in any work published by Nietzsche or authorized by him for publication. References to the empirical requirements of the doctrine are to be found only in the *Nachlaß*' (p. 74).
127. Although, as Soll persuasively argues: 'what appears to be the momentous human import of the doctrine is negated by its supra-historical character, which removes its consequences beyond the possible limits of the individual human consciousness and the cumulative historical consciousness of mankind'. See Ivan Soll, 'Reflections on

to will the past (Z.II.20), the present (Z.III.2.2) and the future (Z.III.4) - can embrace the doctrine of eternal recurrence. The *Schwerpunkt* of this doctrine resides in the present, for every 'moment' contains within it the infinity of past and future (Z.III.2.2). Both the doctrine and its emphasis on the present are ideas which Nietzsche most probably appropriated from Schopenhauer. In *The World as Will and Representation*, Schopenhauer argues that: 'the present alone is that which always exists and stands firm and immovable.'[128] He then goes on to claim that 'whoever is satisfied with life *as it is*, whoever affirms it in every way, can confidently regard it as endless' (emphasis added).[129] Zarathustra, however, is not only dissatisfied with life as it is, but disgusted with it to the point of asphyxiating despair. Would not his answer to the devil's question be 'the answer of Empedocles' (*UM*.III.3)? Does not Zarathustra share Schopenhauer's suspicion that 'perhaps at the end of his life, no man, if he be sincere and at the same time in possession of his faculties, will ever wish to go through it again. Rather than this, he will much prefer to choose complete non-existence.'?[130] It is not surprising, therefore, to find Zarathustra's animals fashioning the exquisite mask of the *Übermensch* (a non-existent figure) in order to conceal, among other things, the grim countenance of the eternal recurrence of all things.

Zarathustra's Physic: Self-Deception

In Part 2 of 'The Convalescent', Zarathustra finally regains consciousness and with it his incurable pessimism, and for seven days thereafter languishes under the paralyzing weight of his affliction. During this critical period, we are told that Zarathustra's animals never leave his side. This is because Zarathustra requires their help in devising for himself and his own peculiar illness, the type of 'comfort' and 'convalescence' most likely to effect a speedy recovery. Particulars of the remedy which Zarathustra and his animals concoct, can be found in section 25 of *Beyond Good and Evil*:

Recurrence: A Re-examination of Nietzsche's Doctrine, *die ewige Wiederkehr des Gleichen*' in Solomon (ed.), p. 342.
128. Arthur Schopenhauer, *The World as Will and Representation* Vol I, trans. E F J Payne (London: Dover, 1969), p. 279.
129. Ibid., p. 280.
130. Ibid., p. 324.

> Flee into concealment! And have your masks and subtlety, so that you may be mistaken for someone else! Or feared a little! And do not forget the garden, the garden with golden trelliswork! And have people around you who are as a garden - or as music on the waters in the evening, when the day is turning into memories. Choose the *good* solitude, the free, wanton, easy solitude, which gives you too the right to remain in some sense good! How poisonous, how cunning, how bad every protracted war makes one, that cannot be waged with open forces. These outcasts of society, these long-pursued, wickedly persecuted ones - also the enforced recluses [...] - always finally become sophisticated vengeance-seekers and brewers of poison, even if they do so under the most spiritual masquerade ... (*BGE*.25)

Once again, Nietzsche alludes to the serpent's dual nature, to the intrinsic and insidious connection between bad and good, between the enforced, detested, impossible solitude and 'the free, wanton, easy solitude', between cunning reason and proud imagination. For man is 'the proudest animal under the sun and the cleverest animal under the sun', and when Zarathustra's pride succeeds in fending off the categorical and pernicious demands of his intellectual conscience, prudence is free to make wanton display of her self-preservative skills:

> As a means of preserving the individual, the intellect unfolds its principal powers in dissimulation, which is the means by which weaker, less robust individuals preserve themselves - since they have been denied the chance to wage the battle for existence with horns or with the sharp teeth of beasts of prey. This art of dissimulation reaches its peak in man: here is deception, flattery, mendacity and delusion, talking behind the back, posturing, living in borrowed splendour, masquerading, hiding behind convention, play-acting before oneself and others, in short, the continuous fluttering around a flame of vanity ... (*TL*.1)

Vanity is, of course, one of the dominant traits of the man of *ressentiment*, who would rather be 'mistaken for someone else' than taken for *who* he really is; shame before oneself and others quickly learns the prudent art of dissimulation.

Zarathustra's Physician: Poetic Imagination

Upon regaining consciousness, and mindful of the principal cause of his collapse - an untimely meditation to which his animals were not privy - Zarathustra is eager to draw his animals back into his confidence and so benefit from their restorative skills. On the seventh day Zarathustra completes the work of creating what he and his animals have been busily engaged in.[131] On this holy day of rest, Zarathustra is determined to enjoy the fruits of their joint labour: the world transfigured into an Elysian garden 'with golden trelliswork' - hung, no doubt, with lusciously Edenic clusters of the vine with which to cure the 'purple melancholy' (Z.III.14) of Zarathustra's soul. His animals indulge him with a rhapsodic evocation of their new creation, and under the burning sun of a prudent "wisdom", which casts a golden light over these enchanted 'Isles of the Blest' (Z.II.2), Zarathustra 'bathes his nakedness' in the refreshing waves of his animals' gay chatter.

For Zarathustra and 'the poet of *Zarathustra*' (*EH* '*Thus Spoke Zarathustra*' 4), the lyricism of language is man's greatest creation and his greatest comfort:

> 'O my animals' replied Zarathustra, 'chatter on like this and let me listen! Your chatter is so refreshing to me: where there is chatter, there the world lies before me like a garden.
> 'How sweet it is that there are words and sounds: are not words and sounds rainbows and illusory bridges between eternally-separated things? [...]
> 'Are things not given names and sounds, so that man may refresh himself with things? Speaking is a beautiful folly: with it man dances over all things.'[132] (Z.III.13.2)

---

131. Adapted from Gen. 2:1-3.
132. Lampert, however, (mis)interprets the last sentence of this citation as a *sincere* eulogy to the beautiful folly of speech which enables man to dance over all things: 'These words in praise of speech assert man's responsibility to name all things, including the animals; speech thus enacts, in a way, man's dominion over all things, but now as man's dance over all things, as the justice done to things by the most spiritual of things. In this way, all being comes to word through Zarathustra, and all becoming learns from him how to speak (III.9)' (p. 214). There are two problems with this reading: in the first place, Lampert appears to be unaware of the heavy irony - signalled by the word 'folly' - with which Zarathustra here speaks of language (cf. Nietzsche in 'On the Truth and Lies in a Nonmoral Sense'). Second, he exalts Zarathustra to the transcendent heights of sublime wisdom (an exaltation evidenced

With language, man 'dance[s] over all things', because language empowers him to create out of the chaos of existence a beautiful, harmonious, unified whole: it transforms tropes into truths, descriptions into explanations, interpretation into meaning, similarity into identity and the 'eternally-separated' into unity. In this way, and only in this way, language represents man's 'most spiritual will to power'; as the proudest and cleverest (but by no means the wisest) animal under the sun, man arrogates to himself the right not only 'to name all things' but to imagine that this act of naming entitles him to 'dominion over all things'. As Nietzsche points out in one of his earliest essays, 'On the Truth and Lies in a Nonmoral Sense', so-called 'truths are illusions which we have forgotten are illusions; they are metaphors that have become worn out' (*TL*.1). Far from doing 'justice' to things,[133] therefore, this most spiritual will to power is audaciously *unjust* both in its nihilistic denial of the chaos which constitutes the world and in the prodigious deception which it thereby perpetrates.

The masterfully deceptive power of the intellect 'is never more luxuriant, richer, prouder, more skilful and more daring' (*TL*.2) than when it succeeds in deceiving itself. According to Nietzsche, man has 'an invincible inclination to let himself be deceived and, as it were, enchanted with happiness when the rhapsodist tells him epic fables as if they were true, or when the actor in the play appears more regal than a real king' (*TL*.2). It is in such an entranced manner that Zarathustra - 'a sick man made weary by his terrible torment' (*Z*.III.2) - listens to the rhapsodic tones of his animals' voices, for 'only by forgetting that he himself is an *artistically creating* subject, does man live with any repose, security, and consistency' (*TL*.1).[134] Far from imparting wisdom to his unenlightened animals, Zarathustra is the needy pupil of his animals' proud and clever "wisdom". With a wry smile

---

by Lampert's numerous references to the 'highest' and 'most spiritual will to power' of 'the wisest and most powerful of men' - see pp. 213-15, 220 and 223), and consequently equates Zarathustra's relationship to his animals with that of the "wise" philosopher-king to his subjects. But as we have already seen, Zarathustra is neither truly wise nor truly powerful, his "wisdom" being merely an imaginative construct designed to counter the crippling effects of knowledge. Indeed, the so-called divine attributes of omniscience and omnipotence are no more than the 'colourful rainbows' of fools and poets (*Z*.IV.14.3) to which Zarathustra alludes in the citation in question.

133. See previous footnote.
134. In this light, the order of rank between Zarathustra and his animals is the reverse of that formulated by Lampert.

and an uneasy sense of dependency, Zarathustra allows his animals to charm him into blissful self-forgetfulness.

Dancing attendance on their patient, eagle and serpent continue to humour Zarathustra with their chattering dance over all things. Now privy to the cause of the convalescent's seizure (terror at the thought of the eternal recurrence of all things) and principally responsible (as healing agents) for the rehabilitation of their charge, Zarathustra's sick-nurses set about their tranquilizing task. With soothing 'words' and harmonious 'sounds', they fashion a benign and alluring mask with which to cover the sickening face of Zarathustra's most abysmal thought. Physicians metamorphose into metaphysicians: the 'moral terrorism'[135] of the interminable 'Round of Existence' (*Ring des Seins*), and the unendurable pressure which it places on the 'moment', are adroitly excised by Zarathustra's animals and the wound treated by 'a cosmic therapy'[136] which transforms this vicious circularity into a wheel of innocent becoming, renewal, and rebirth. Zarathustra is delighted by these remedial skills of his animals but, unfortunately, with all their talk of wheels and rings and cycles - a circumlocution which cleverly avoids any mention of the noxious 'eternal recurrence' - Zarathustra is reminded of his illness:

> 'O you rogues and barrel-organs!' replied Zarathustra and smiled again, 'How well you know what had to be fulfilled in seven days: -
>
> 'and how that monster crept into my throat and choked me! But I bit its head off and spat it away.
>
> 'And you - you have already made a hurdy-gurdy song out of it? But now I lie here, still weary from this biting and spitting away, still sick from my own redemption.
>
> '*And you watched it all?* O my animals, are you also cruel? Did you want to watch my great pain, as men do? For man is the cruellest animal.'

He is also the pettiest animal. Having enlisted the help of his animals to redeem him from the *sickness* of his own redemption (for, unlike the parabolic shepherd who sprang up - 'transformed, effulgent, *laughing*!' - after his victory over the serpent, Zarathustra 'fell down like a dead man and remained like a dead man for a long time'), Zarathustra, the irredeemable

---

135. Daniel Halévy, p. 274.
136. Erich Heller, 'Nietsche's Terrors: Time and the Inarticulate', *The Importance of Nietzsche* (London: The University of Chicago Press, 1988), p. 185.

man of *ressentiment*, now avenges himself on his animals: 'Whoever is dissatisfied with himself is constantly ready to avenge himself [...] for the sight of what is ugly makes one bad and gloomy' (*GS*.290). He rebukes them for watching him suffer (reasoning, no doubt, that had they not deserted him in his hour of need - which was, paradoxically, also to be his finest hour - he would not be in his present bathetic state). All men of *ressentiment* need a scapegoat and Zarathustra, like all 'enforced recluses [... who] always finally become sophisticated vengeance-seekers' (*BGE*.25), is no exception. He blames his animals for not intervening when he precipitately, and now regretfully, decided to cast in his lot, albeit temporarily, with his intellectual conscience. It is a case of sour grapes, but what begins as peevishness soon escalates into a wholesale accusation of man. The vicious circle of Zarathustra's nihilism repeats its eternal cycle: shame breeds self-disgust, self-disgust burgeons into disgust at man, and disgust at man explodes into an all-consuming pessimism: 'There are days when I am afflicted by a feeling blacker than the blackest melancholy - *contempt for man*' (*A*.38). Once again, Zarathustra finds himself reeling on an emotional precipice:

> 'The great disgust at man - *that* choked me and had crept into my throat: and what the soothsayer prophesied: "Everything is the same, nothing is worthwhile, knowledge chokes".
>
> 'A long twilight limped in front of me, a mortally-weary, death-intoxicated sadness which speaks with a yawn.
>
> ' "The man of whom you are weary, the little man, recurs eternally" - thus my sadness yawned and dragged its feet and could not fall asleep.
>
> [...] ' "Alas, man recurs eternally! The little man recurs eternally!"
>
> 'I had seen them both naked, the greatest man and the smallest man: all-too-similar to one another, even the greatest all-too-human!
>
> 'The greatest all-too-small! - That was my disgust at man! And eternal recurrence of even the smallest! - That was my disgust at all existence!
>
> 'Ah, disgust! Disgust! Disgust!' Thus spoke Zarathustra and sighed and shuddered; for he remembered his sickness.

At this point, Zarathustra's life-preserving animals - still smarting, no doubt, from their recent scolding, and not wishing to provoke a repetition of the same - intervene and hastily administer to their patient the placebo which all three had spent seven days perfecting. Waxing lyrical and repeating the 'same old tunes', Zarathustra's 'hidden barrel-organs' (*HH*.II 'Opinions and Maxims' 155) try to entice Zarathustra back from the brink of abysmal pessimism, but not one of their pastoral 'rainbows' - neither 'gardens' nor 'roses', 'bees' nor 'doves', 'song-birds' nor 'songs' - succeeds in charming Zarathustra out of his depression. Not even a special reference to the *Übermensch* - normally guaranteed to uplift Zarathustra's spirits - can distract him from his gloomy thoughts:

> he lay still with his eyes closed, like one sleeping, although he was not asleep: for he was conversing with his soul. The serpent and the eagle, however, when they found him thus silent, respected the great stillness around him and softly withdrew.

'The Convalescent' ends with the animals' withdrawal, but this in no way marks the end of Zarathustra's convalescence. On the contrary, as Zarathustra's proud and deceptive consciousness gives way to thrusting and inexorable instinct, the full extent of his sickness becomes glaringly apparent. Conversing with his soul in the succeeding chapter, the convalescent continues to lament and whine over the incurable melancholy of his recalcitrant soul, and in the last four chapters (13-16) of Part III, Zarathustra bears the unmistakable marks of romantic pessimism.

Unable to ' "overcome" this time in himself', he continues to suffer precisely 'from this time, his untimeliness, [and] his *romanticism*' (*GS*.V.380). Decadent modern culture - represented by the soothsayer (pessimistic philosophy), the two kings (political misrule), the conscientious man of spirit (scholastic science), and the sorcerer (theatrical/histrionic art) - and decadent Christian culture - represented by the last pope (faith, hope, and love), the ugliest man (bad conscience, shame, and pity), and the voluntary beggar (meditation, benevolence, and philanthropy) - infest Zarathustra's soul. The decadence of contemporary man prevents him from willing the eternal recurrence of all things (Z.III.13) and from alleviating the 'purple melancholy' of his decadent soul (Z.III.14). Irreversible and inextinguishable decadent deeds seduce him into a dance of death with life (Z.III.15) and compel him to concede that *if* and only *if* he were not a modern man, but rather an *Übermensch*, he would be able to 'lust after eternity and the wedding ring of rings - the ring of recurrence!' (Z.III.16).

By the end of Part III, the doomed prophet still more closely resembles a tragic hero than a fool. The tragic myth, recording the inexorable fate of all higher men from Prometheus and Oedipus (*BT*.10) down to Schopenhauer, Wagner, and finally Zarathustra, denies the tragic hero any possibility of 'transcendental buffoonery'. Part III closes with Zarathustra's

Apollonian vision of the *Übermensch* positively lusting after eternity: 'Dionysus [still] speaks the language of Apollo' (*BT*.21). In Part IV, the Dionysian hero finally avails himself of the cap and bells: Apollo (in the figure of the buffoon) finally speaks 'the language of Dionysus; and so the highest goal of tragedy and of art in general is attained' (ibid.). But is it?

PILGRIMAGE

The Higher Men and Zarathustra's Shadow

5 The Art of Self-Overcoming

Decadent Deeds and Redemptive Satire

> Once in a while we harvest love and honour for deeds or works which we have long since cast from us like a skin: and then we become easily tempted to play the comedians of our own past and throw the old hide once again over our shoulders. (*HH*.II 'Opinions and Maxims' 393)

Having affected the 'artistic distance' of the 'transcendent buffoon' and the art of mocking self-reflection, Zarathustra is now able to 'look down upon himself and laugh and weep over 'the hero no less than the fool' (*GS*.107) performing in the drama of his soul. But a performance is all it is. For if, in Part IV, the rebirth of tragedy as tragi-comedy (prefigured in the parable of the ropedancer) is finally realized, the Dionysian wisdom that speaks through the mask of Apollo is intrinsically tragic. 'Dionysian wisdom [...] is an unnatural abomination [... and he] who by means of his knowledge plunges nature into the abyss of destruction must also experience in himself the disintegration of nature' (*BT*.9). It is precisely the fragmentary nature of Zarathustra's psyche and its dramatic attempts at reintegration that is staged in Part IV. But Zarathustra's past is so poignant and his old hide so well-preserved that the 'comedian', like the circus clown, remains more tragic than comic.

Burdened by the past and driven by the 'spirit of revenge' (*Z*.II.20), 'the cruel wheel of [Zarathustra's] restless, morbidly lascivious conscience' (*GM*.III.20) backtracks along the irreversible rut of time. Time's gateway is Janus-faced,[137] and if that aspect facing the forward-looking traveller bears the inscription 'Moment' (*Z*.III.2.1), then that facing the backward-looking traveller bears the epitaph 'It was' (*Z*.II.20). Unable to reverse the past, Zarathustra rehearses it, albeit with harrowing consequences. For while the

---

137. Like the two aspects of Zarathustra's psyche: the madman who looks behind and the prophet who looks ahead.

hearse known as memory stages the passion play, its 'rolling Ixionian wheel'[138] cleaves ever-deeper the rut of recollection. Recalling the 'accidents' of his past, Zarathustra recycles them into a tragi-comic satire: '[for] that is all my art (*Dichten*) and aim, to compose (*dichten*) and gather into one what is fragment and riddle and dreadful accident' (ibid.). The repetition here of '*dichten*' underscores Zarathustra's aesthetics[139] of redemption, that is, his attempt to resurrect (re-present) the past by refashioning (re-casting) the bloody spectres of illusory truth and passionate regret into parodic higher men; for it is 'only artists, and particularly those of the theatre [... who] have taught us the art of viewing ourselves as heroes [...] the art of staging ourselves in front of ourselves. Only in this way can we get over some of the base details in ourselves' (*GS*.78).

Self-Contempt and Self-Pity

At the start of Part IV, we find Zarathustra *still* convalescing in his alpine sanatorium and *still* being ministered to by his two assiduous sick-nurses. We are to infer from Zarathustra's white hair and 'dark' looks that his convalescence has been a long and melancholy one. The seemingly terminal illness from which he is suffering is the decadence of 'modern culture' - 'Who of us has not dirtied his hands and heart in the disgusting[140] service of the idols of modern culture? Who is not in need of the waters of

---

138. Alfred, Lord Tennyson, *Lucretius*, l. 260.
139. Notwithstanding the promissory note sounded in the title of Alexander Nehamas' book, *Nietzsche: Life as Literature* (London: Harvard University Press, 1985); the particular relevance of Nietzsche's partially autobiographical work *Zarathustra*; and Nehamas' central interpretative claim concerning 'Nietzsche's effort to create an artwork out of himself' (p. 8); this aspect of what Nehamas refers to as Nietzsche's 'aestheticism' is poorly argued and, with the exception of *Ecce Homo*, lacks persuasive textual support. His correlative claim that Nietzsche showed not only 'that writing is perhaps the most important part of thinking', but 'also the most important part of living' (p. 41), is implicitly refuted by Nietzsche himself in *UM*.III.3, *GS*.93 and *BGE*.296. For a convincing rejection of Nehamas' anachronistic ascription to Nietzsche of a specifically post-modern form of aestheticism whereby one looks at the world 'as if it were a literary text' (Nehamas, p. 3), see Brian Leiter, 'Nietzsche and Aestheticism', *Journal of the History of Philosophy* 30, (2 April 1992), 275-90.
140. This adjective (*widerlich*) is absent from Hollingdale's translation.

purification?' (*UM*.IV.1) - while nausea and pity at the sight of modern man are the persisting symptoms which preclude his long-awaited return to society. Long years of solitude, away from 'the madhouses and hospitals of culture [...] away from the nauseating stench of inner corruption and the hidden infestation of disease', have shielded Zarathustra from his 'great disgust at man' but not, as we are soon to discover, against his 'great pity for man' (*GM*.III.14). His nausea at the thought of the 'eternal recurrence of even the smallest of men' (*Z*.III.13) - the cause of his initial breakdown - has, with the healing powers of 'active forgetfulness' (*GM*.II.1) and the passage of time, abated considerably; old age has dimmed the sickening memory of the 'all-too-human' pride and complacency of the 'last man' (*Z*.Prol.5), and his former 'contempt for man' (*A*.38) has now mellowed into pity.[141]

This mellowing process has been artificially accelerated by a superabundance of 'honeyed' illusion - produced by the 'Apollonian artifice' (*BT*.22) of 'transfiguring mirrors' (*BT*.3) - administered to Zarathustra by his complaisant eagle and serpent. But, in the same way that Dionysus would find a surfeit of 'honey offerings'[142] (*Z*.IV.1) cloying and ultimately indigestible, Zarathustra finds his increasing dependence upon 'hermit-phantasmagoria' (*HH*.I.Pref.2) - the ingenious artwork of 'hermits' pets' (*Z*.IV.1) - a morally insupportable burden. Paradoxically, weighty illusion is Zarathustra's 'specific gravity' (*GS*.V.380). Thus, in response to his animals' facetious question, 'Do you not lie in a sky blue lake of happiness?' Zarathustra wryly remarks upon the aptness of their metaphor,[143] knowing, of course, that they 'also know that my happiness is heavy and not like a rolling wave (*flüssige Wasserwelle*): it oppresses me and will not leave and acts like molten pitch' (*Z*.IV.1).

---

141. White also notes the absence of disgust from the Zarathustra of Part IV, but attributes this to Zarathustra's transformation at the end of Part III: 'After embracing the thought of the eternal recurrence, Zarathustra can pass by even the rabble' (p. 103). As will become apparent in the chapters which follow, however, the Zarathustra of Part IV not only fails to 'pass by' his higher men - all of whom, despite their eminence, harbour within themselves rabble values - but actively pities them.
142. In Greek mythology, honey is the food of the gods.
143. Given the collusion of hermit and hermit's pets, the latter well know how the former 'like to sit in the abyss below a perfectly clear sky: they need different means than other men for enduring life; for they suffer differently (namely, as much from the profundity of their contempt for man as from their love for man). - The most suffering animal on earth invented for itself - laughter' (*KSA*.11.576).

Having 'murdered all gods [...] for the sake of morality' (GS.153), Zarathustra is left with the once nauseating but now pitiful sight of unregenerate and diminutive man. In this indiscriminate "reduction" of man ('The greatest all-too-small!'), self-identification is inescapable: the pity which Zarathustra feels for man - a form of Schopenhauerian compassion engendered by empathic identification[144] - morally compels him to hold the fool's mirror up to his own face. There he sees self-contempt mingled with self-pity. 'Through knowing ourselves and regarding our own nature as a moving sphere of opinions and moods, and consequently learning to despise oneself, we restore our proper equilibrium with others' (HH.I.376); contemptuous pity for man turns into pitiful self-contempt and his fool-reflection grows ever darker. 'Upon the best personalities of our time,' writes Nietzsche in his early essay 'Schopenhauer as Educator', 'there lies a certain gloominess and torpor, an eternal frustration over the struggle between dissimulation and honesty which is being fought out in their breast, an uneasy self-confidence - whereby they become totally incapable of being signposts and at the same time taskmasters for others' (UM.III.2).

Signposts and Gravestones

Discomforted by the ill-fitting masks of prophet (taskmaster) and 'individual higher exemplar' (UM.III.6) (signpost), and torn between the fool's mirror and his animals' 'transfiguring mirror', Zarathustra disingenuously employs the latter's reflection of fraudulent happiness as 'bait' for the 'queerest fish' (signposts and taskmasters are necessarily strange and untimely creatures) that he hopes to catch in the 'rich sea'[145] of humanity (Z.IV.1).[146] But, without the self-confidence injected by his sick-nurses, and their imperial ('a thousand year empire' ibid.) art of metaphysical comfort, the signpost

---

144. Schopenhauer, p. 295.
145. Sea traditionally represents the 'primordial waters; chaos; formlessness; material existence; endless motion; it is the source of all life, containing all potentials; the sum of all possibilities in manifestation; the unfathomable'. It also symbolizes 'the sea of life which has to be crossed' (Cooper, p. 121). In other words, the sea represents the locus of the will to power.
146. Bennholdt-Thomsen points out that this image of Zarathustra as the fisher of men is 'less like the disciples of Jesus (Mark 1:17) than the philosophical fisher in Lucian's *Fisherman*'. See Anke Bennholdt-Thomsen, *Nietzsches* Also sprach Zarathustra *als literarisches Phänomen - Eine Revision* (Frankfurt am Main: Athenäum, 1974), p. 128.

bearing the name Zarathustra loses its exemplary *sense* of direction and remains but a sign: 'a question mark for such as have the answers' (*DD* 'The Fire-Beacon [*Feuerzeichen*]'). This question mark is the fish-hook of 'irritable honesty' (*GS*.107) which had long ago cast up its answers from the tumultuous sea of life and which now confines itself to Zarathustra's 'sorrowful, black' (Z.III.1) inland sea. As in the macrocosm, so in the microcosm: such as have the answer will be reeled in and closely scrutinized. Their rare and splendid brilliance will be marvelled at and admired, but in the final analysis these 'fairest human fish' will be deemed all-too-nauseatingly-human and cast out once again into 'the belly of all black affliction' (Z.IV.1).

In these dirty waters of truth (Z.I.13), Zarathustra's fish-hook of integrity discovers no '*historical* future [of] paradise regained',[147] but of paradise irredeemably lost. Buried deep within him lies Zarathustra's 'grave-island' (Z.II.11), the land of his father and forefathers: 'the land of [modern] culture' (Z.II.14).

On this deathly island, Zarathustra finds neither 'creators' nor 'harvesters', merely 'the graves of [his] youth' (Z.II.11). But whereas, in Part II, he made a pilgrimage to this sacred land and, 'as life and youth, sat there upon yellow grave-ruins, hoping' (ibid.); and, in Part III, painfully recalled how such hope had later turned into despair and his 'sighs sat upon all human graves and could no longer rise up' (Z.III.13); in Part IV, Zarathustra ironically reflects upon his folly.[148] As his 'irritable honesty' had turned his contempt for man into self-contempt, it had also redirected his magnanimity away from 'the [afterworldly] convalescent [who] glances tenderly at his illusions and, at midnight, creeps around the grave of his god' (Z.I.3), towards his own graveyard vigils when he too had cast 'loving glances' at the all too fleeting 'visions and apparitions of his youth' (Z.II.11).

---

147. Erich Heller, 'Zarathustra's Three Metamorphoses: Facets of Nietzsche's Intellectual Biography and the Apotheosis of Innocence' in *The Importance of Nietzsche* (London: The University of Chicago Press, 1988), p. 83.
148. 'Folly is an endless maze, / Tangled roots perplex her way, / How many have fallen there! / They stumble all night over bones of the dead, / And feel they know not what but care, / And wish to lead others, when they should be led'. Blake, *Songs of Experience*, 'The Voice of the Ancient Bard'.

Self-Knowledge and Self-Parody

Zarathustra is 'a hero of his time' and, like Lermontov's hero, is a portrait 'not of a single person' but rather 'of the vices of [his] whole generation in [its] ultimate development.'[149] As one of those 'who have to be the *conscience* of the modern soul and as such have to possess its *knowledge*, in whom all that exists today of sickness, poison and danger has come together - whose lot it is to have to be sicker than any other individual because [they] are not "*only* individuals" ' (*HH*.II.Pref.6), Zarathustra can either, like Pechorin, succumb to the poison or, like the 'transcendent buffoon', struggle to rise above it. Unlike Pechorin, however, the "hero" of Part IV of *Zarathustra* - like all great men, a 'genuine child of his time' (*UM*.III.3) - is not only acutely aware of his cultural vices, as symbolized by his higher men, but, by employing this self-knowledge as material for malicious and relentless self-parody (*GS*.Pref.1), is able 'to skin, exploit, expose [and] "portray" '(*HH*.II.Pref.6) the afflicitions of his time from which he so keenly suffers.

A compassionate contempt like that which characterizes Zarathustra's state of mind in Part IV is born, according to Hume, of a not unlikely coupling: 'the misfortunes of our fellows often cause pity, which has in it a strong mixture of good-will. This sentiment of pity is nearly allied to contempt, which is a species of dislike, with a mixture of pride.'[150] Like Lear's exuberant, dancing and childish Fool, Zarathustra playfully mocks the folly of his master(s). But his 'simultaneous commitment to exalted visions and to a renegade impulse which mockingly dissolves them',[151] forces Zarathustra both to scorn the ghosts of his 'dead companions' who haunt the manifold 'hiding places' (*Z*.IV.2) within his soul, and to offer them indefinite 'refuge' (*Z*.IV.6) there.

Possessing a soul which thirsted to experience 'the entire range of values and desiderata to date' and to sail around 'all the coasts of this ideal "mediterranean" '; a soul which wanted to know 'from the adventures of his own most authentic experience how a conqueror and discoverer of the ideal

---

149. Mikhail Lermontov, 'Author's Preface' to *A Hero of Our Time*, trans. Paul Foote (Middlesex: Penguin, 1987), p. 19.
150. David Hume, *An Enquiry Concerning the Principles of Morals*, Section VI, Part II:202, footnote 1.
151. Morton Gurewitch's depiction of the ironist, cited in D C Muecke, *The Compass of Irony*, p. 186.

feels, like [for example] an artist, a saint, a legislator, a wise man, a scholar, a pious man, a soothsayer, and an old style divine esoteric'; Zarathustra had sailed for many years in the company of the 'Argonauts of the ideal' (*GS*.V.382). Zarathustra's pilgrimage in Part IV recounts, and to a certain extent relives, this voyage. The higher men whom Zarathustra encounters - the soothsayer, the two kings (legislator), the conscientious man of spirit (scholar), the sorcerer (artist), the last pope (pious man), the ugliest man (wise man), and the voluntary beggar (saint) - are in small part caricatures of those cultural figures whom Zarathustra has at some time 'honoured and revered', and in large part allegorical representations of the decadent values and nihilistic ideals which these figures body forth and which continue to take refuge in the innermost recesses of Zarathustra's soul.

In short, Zarathustra himself becomes the 'monster of parodic material' which finally attracts him, and which he transforms, if not transfigures, into a 'downright wicked and malicious' (*GS*.Pref.1) self-portrait. Unlike most self-portraits, however, Zarathustra accomplishes his own by means of not one mirror but a series of 'ghostly' mirrors (namely, his seven higher men and his shadow), the shadowy outlines of which he fleshes out in the *primary* colours of self-knowledge, for 'the great poet dips *only* from his own reality.' (*EH* 'Why I am so clever' 4).[152]

---

152. Cf. '*Painting in writing.* - An object of significance will be best represented if, like a chemist, one takes the colours for the painting from the object itself, and then uses them like a painter: so that the portrayal is allowed to grow out of the boundaries and shadings of the colours. Thus the painting will acquire something of the ravishing element of nature which makes the object itself significant' (*HH*.I.205).

6 The Decadence of Modernity

Schopenhauerian Pessimism: The Soothsayer

> To live with tremendous and proud composure; always beyond -. To have and not to have one's affects, one's for and against, at will, to descend to them for a few hours; to seat oneself on them as on a horse, often as on an ass - for one must know how to make use of their stupidity as well as of their fire. To preserve one's three hundred foregrounds; also the dark glasses: for there are times when nobody may look into our eyes, still less into our "grounds". And to choose for company that roguish and cheerful vice, courtesy. And to remain master of one's four virtues: of courage, insight, sympathy and solitude. (*BGE*.284)

The above citation constitutes Zarathustra's *ironic* form of ironic distance; and in Part IV, 'philosophical pessimism', a symptom of romanticism (*GS*.V.370), is the first cultural 'vice' to which Zarathustra condescends. Schopenhauer and his philosophy of the will is a 'fact' of Zarathustra's life, one of those 'accidents of people and books' (*BGE*.44); but to suffer incurably from '*romantic pessimism*, that is to say the pessimism of the renunciators, [of] the failed and defeated' (*HH*.II.Pref.7), from 'the last *great* event in the fate of [his] culture' (*GS*.V.370), is his fate. If Zarathustra, a true child of his time, cannot elude the fate of all higher men, he can, however, with the immensely 'proud composure' - so proud, in fact, that one is forced to doubt its immensity - of a consummate actor, affect an ironic distance to it. 'Six thousand feet above' (*EH* 'Why I am so wise' 4), but not quite 'beyond', modern man, Zarathustra pensively traces 'the shadow of his [undeniably modern] figure in the ground', while his industrious animals are away fetching fresh supplies of honey - 'for Zarathustra had wasted and squandered the old honey down to the last drop' (*Z*.IV.1). Low on illusion and thus brought low by heightened integrity, Zarathustra finds himself face to face with his romantic pessimism. But just as in tragedy 'the Apollonian snatches us out of Dionysian universality and charms us with the individual' (*BT*.21), so in Part IV Zarathustra objectifies the *Weltschmerz* of modern man. In the interest of self-preservation, the tolerable face of an historical figure, a representative individual, is preferable to the unbearable face of inexorable fate - 'for only if [the failed genius] is thought of as being entirely distant from us [...] does he not wound us' (*HH*.I.162). Zarathustra's ironic distance is, however, a fragile Apollonian artifice and the 'Dionysian flood and excess' (*BT*.21) of tragic insight eddies beneath 'a sky-blue lake of happiness'; Zarathustra's proud composure, like his happiness, is oppressive and 'acts like molten pitch.'

Schopenhauer, as the 'objective correlative' of Zarathustra's romantic pessimism, is referred to throughout *Zarathustra* as 'the soothsayer'. This is a significant appellation, and one which needs to be distinguished from 'prophet'.[153] Whereas a prophet (*Prophet*) is an *inspired* teacher, a soothsayer (*Wahrsager*) speaks the truth. The former is eager to bestow upon mankind the "gift" of his "wisdom" (*Z*.Prol.2), while the latter, like Tiresias in Sophocles' *Oedipus Tyrannus*, is reluctant to utter the truth of his terrible knowledge. The inspired teaching of the prophet inspires discipleship and hero-worship among those who would sooner believe in someone other than themselves (*Z*.I.22.3) and who would rather 'flow out into a god' (*GS*.285) than create a god out of themselves (*Z*.I.17), whereas the soothsayer, with his 'plain, harsh, ugly, repellent, unchristian, immoral truth' (*GM*.I.1), simply alienates. Schopenhauer's 'truth' is of the latter variety: according to Nietzsche, 'the ungodliness of existence was, for Schopenhauer, regarded as something given, palpable, indisputable [...] His whole integrity rests on this point: unconditional, honest atheism is simply the *presupposition* of his way of looking at the problem [of existence]' (*GS*.V.357). For Schopenhauer, as for Nietzsche, 'the decline of faith in the Christian God [and] the triumph of scientific atheism' (ibid.) gave rise to the pessimistic *Weltanschauung* endemic in post-Enlightenment Europe. Indeed, this cataclysmic moment in history is perhaps nowhere more fearfully and ominously evoked than in Nietzsche's famous 'madman scene' (*GS*.125) in which the madman's lantern symbolizes, on the one hand, man's need of warmth in the cold 'age of reason', and on the other, a flicker of hope to preserve him in the grim wake of God's death.

Thus, when Zarathustra confronts the soothsayer and looks into his eyes, it is the reflection of his own romantic pessimism that he perceives

---

153. Hollingdale misleadingly translates '*Wahrsager*' as 'prophet'.

there. The 'bad tidings and ashen lightning-flashes' that he sees run across the soothsayer's face are not the lightning-flashes of the *Übermensch* prophesied by an ecstatic Zarathustra in the market square (Z.Prol.4), but the terrible tidings which the madman, one year before, had felt constrained to yell out in the same market square with the same contumelious results (GS.125).[154] Too truthful to be a prophet, and not truthful enough to be a soothsayer, Zarathustra 'recognizes' (Z.IV.2) in the soothsayer ('the soothsayer, who had perceived what was taking place in Zarathustra's soul, wiped his hand across his face, as if he wanted to wipe it away; Zarathustra did the same. And when both had thus silently composed and fortified themselves, they shook hands as a sign that they wanted to recognize one another' ibid.) that which will forever preclude his return to the market square - tragic insight. As Zarathustra learnt in his stillest hour, his 'fruits are ripe but [he is] not ripe for [his] fruits' (Z.II.22). Having once 'looked truly into the essence of things [and] *gained knowledge*, [...] true knowledge, an insight into the terrible truth' (*BT*.7), neither the soothsayer nor Zarathustra, both 'Argonauts of the ideal' (*GS*.V.382), can block their ears to the Sirens' song intoned by Byron's Manfred: 'Sorrow is knowledge: they who know the most / Must mourn the deepest o'er the fatal truth.'[155] This 'immoral truth', which proclaims the eternal flux of existence (a Heraclitean truth which Schopenhauer formulated as 'will' and Nietzsche as 'will to power'), is quintessentially tragic.

That both the soothsayer and Zarathustra are afflicted by the same disease is attested to in Part II of *Zarathustra*. In a chapter entitled 'The Soothsayer', the narrator recalls how the pessimistic teaching of the Schopenhauerian cypher - 'All is empty, all is the same, all is past! [...] Truly, we have grown too weary even to die; now we are still awake and live on - in sepulchres!' - had pierced 'Zarathustra's heart and transformed him' (Z.II.19). Standing before his disciples in the approaching twilight of the gods, the private voice of the madman speaks through the public mask of the prophet: 'Truly, this long twilight is very nearly upon us. Alas, how shall I preserve my light through it? May it not be extinguished by this sadness!' A few days later, the madman once again gives voice to his pessimism. Upon waking from a deep sleep, he relates to his disciples the content of his

---

154. See 'The Parable of the Ropedancer'.
155. Lord Byron, *Manfred*, I.i.10-11. This 'immortal verse' is cited by Nietzsche in *HH*.I.109.

nightmare: 'I dreamed I had renounced all life. I had become a night-watchman and grave-watchman' (not unlike his disciples, in fact, who had 'sat around him in the long watches of the night and waited anxiously to see whether he would awaken and speak again and be cured of his sorrow'). Keeping his midnight vigil over the living dead, he is suddenly startled by three loud knocks on the door of the vault. Shortly thereafter, a roaring wind rips the wings of the door apart and hurls at him a black coffin which suddenly 'burst asunder and spewed forth a thousand peals of laughter.' Terrified, Zarathustra screams as he never screamed before, and wakes up. Zarathustra gradually recovers from the shock of his nightmare and, while his favourite disciple indulges him with a benign (mis)interpretation[156] of his dream (in *Zarathustra*, the prophet's disciples serve the same function as the hermit's pets), finally grasps its import. It is not Zarathustra - as his disciple would have it - who laughs at night-watchmen and grave-watchmen, but rather his 'dearest dead ones' (*Z*.II.11) whom he buried long ago (*Z*.Prol.8); it is the ghosts of his youthful illusion who now mock Zarathustra's compulsive graveyard vigils. Thus enlightened by self-knowledge, Zarathustra 'gazed long into the face of his disciple who had interpreted the dream, and shook his head.'

In Part IV, the soothsayer returns to mock Zarathustra, but with less devastating effect than in Part II. The Gothic has mellowed into the tragi-comic: sinister laughter dissolves into gentle irony, and the Munchean scream into mute fear and, finally, 'benevolent dissimulation' (*HH*.I.293).[157] A more mature, more ironic Zarathustra is now much better equipped to deal with the eternal 'resurrection' of 'predilection and prejudice, youth [and] origin', from those 'agreeable musty nooks' (*BGE*.44) 'buried' deep in the 'caves' (*Z*.IV.2) of his soul. After the initial shock of recognition, Zarathustra replaces his 'dark glasses', as it were, and greets the soothsayer with 'that roguish and cheerful vice, courtesy' (*BGE*.284). Notwithstanding this disguise, however, Zarathustra and the soothsayer understand each other perfectly: they know only too well that cheerfulness often masks a deep-seated melancholy, and that for such a creature to fish for happiness in 'the

---

156. Cf. '*Misunderstood sufferers*. - Magnificent natures suffer very differently from what their admirers imagine: they suffer most keenly from the ignoble and petty agitations of some evil moments - briefly, from their doubts about their own magnificence - but not from the sacrifice and martyrdom which their task demands from them' (*GS*.251).
157. 'In traffic with man a benevolent dissimulation is often necessary, as though we do not see through the motives of their actions.'

belly of all black sorrow' is indeed an incredible 'stupidity' (Z.IV.1). 'There is for everyone a bait which he must take' (*HH*.I.359), and just as Zarathustra had fittingly baited the soothsayer with (ill-concealed) pessimism, so the soothsayer now equally fittingly uses the same bait to 'seduce' Zarathustra to his 'ultimate sin' - the sin of pity.

Pity and pessimism are, of course, the twin poles in Schopenhauer's philosophy: given man's shared experience of the horrors of existence and, in particular, the subtle machinations of an egoistic and malicious will, his sole redeeming inclination, albeit a rare one, is pity. Nietzsche, however, sees this sympathetic magnetism in the ethical sphere as a dangerous double negative. For him, pity born out of a hatred of suffering is the stigma ('our morality of pity, against which I was the first to warn, that which one might call *l'impressionisme morale*, is one more expression of the physiological over-excitability pertaining to everything *decadent*.' *TI*, 'Expeditions of an Untimely Man' 37) and the stigmata ('Is not pity the cross upon which he who loves man is nailed?' Z.Prol.3) of Schopenhauerian morality. Pity affords the decadent not only an escape from personal suffering, but also from '[t]his strange disease of modern life',[158] and, ultimately, from life itself. According to Nietzsche, pity is the seedbed of nihilism in all its forms:

> What was at stake was the *value* of morality [...] the value of the "unegoistic", the instincts of pity, self-abnegation, self-sacrifice, which Schopenhauer had gilded, deified, and idealised (*verjenseitigt*) for so long that at last they became for him "value-in-itself", on the basis of which he *said No* to life and also to himself. But it was precisely against *these* instincts that there spoke from me an ever more fundamental suspicion, an ever more entrenched scepticism! It was precisely here that I saw the *great danger* to mankind, its most sublime enticement and seduction - but to what? to nothingness? - it was precisely here that I saw the beginning of the end, the dead stop, a retrospective weariness, the will turning *against* life, the tender and melancholy signs of the last illness: I understood the ever-spreading morality of pity that had seized even on philosophers and made them ill, as the most sinister symptom of our European culture that had itself become sinister, perhaps as its detour to a new Buddhism? to a European Buddhism? to - *nihilism*? (*GM*.Pref.5)

---

158. Matthew Arnold, *The Scholar Gypsy*, l. 203.

In the revaluation of moral values, the stakes are unspeakably high: 'He who deviates from the conventional is the sacrifice of the extraordinary; he who remains in the conventional is the slave of the same. In either event he perishes' (*HH*.I.552). Life itself is at stake: on the one hand, in Schopenhauer's 'enticement' to, at best, a devaluation of the self and, at worst, a European strain of Buddhistic nihilism; and, on the other, in the increased suffering from life and its attendant pessimism consequent upon Nietzsche's ethical imperative to murder all gods 'for the sake of morality' and so 'live alone "without God and morality"' (*KSA*.11.571). The former is nihilism, but the latter is also nihilism - nihilism of a far more fatal kind.[159]

Although Schopenhauer's will to asceticism suggests a denial of life, it does in fact express a fundamental will to life: '*the ascetic ideal springs from the protective and redemptive*[160] *instinct of a degenerating life*, which seeks by all means to sustain itself and to fight for its existence' (*GM*.III.13). Conversely, Nietzsche's moral 'cleanliness' - which compelled him to renounce the teaching of his mentor and idol by 'taking sides *against* myself and *for* everything that was painful and hard especially for *me*' (*HH*.II.Pref.4) - demanded of him 'that courageous pessimism that is the antithesis of all romantic mendacity' (ibid.) and that alone could nobly preserve him from the fatal consequences of extreme pessimism. It is precisely courageous pessimism, however, that Nietzsche lacked in the moral war he nobly but misguidedly waged against himself. Once this deficiency is acknowledged, the question needs to be asked: at what price morality? When life and morality hang in the balance and romantic pessimism precludes courageous pessimism, the moral either/or: ' "Either abolish your reverences or - *yourselves*!" ' (*GS*.V.346) is necessarily outweighed by the existential either/or: "Either abolish your reverences *and* (consequently) yourselves or transcend moral fastidiousness by means of artistic distance." Discretion is the better part of valour, and faced with a *vital* moral dilemma - namely, Schopenhauer's "unegoistic" morality of egoistic pity which impoverishes life but nonetheless preserves it, or his own "egoistic" morality of unegoistic self-contempt which increases the moral value of life but at the (possible) cost of life itself - Nietzsche saves himself from almost certain death by leaping into amoral aestheticism.

---

159. This sentence is an intentional misappropriation of *GS*.V.346.
160. This adjective is overlooked in Kaufmann and Hollingdale's joint translation.

From an artistic distance, Zarathustra laughs and weeps over the irony of his "transcendence": hovering high *above* 'good and evil' (that is, Christian morality), he is yet far from being *beyond* his own ultimate "sin" of pity. A protracted convalescence has deluded him into believing that he is now strong enough for a rediscovery of 'the *hero* no less than the *fool* in [his] passion for knowledge', and for a pure morality that goes 'beyond good and evil'. Consequently, and in the absence of his diverting animals, he decides to entertain himself with a dramatic extemporization of his long-repressed inner strife. It proves to be a foolhardy decision, for his desire to rediscover the foolish heroism of his past is itself motivated by an equally foolish and heroic passion for self-knowledge and, by implication, moral rectitude. In Part I, he had taught that 'the thought is one thing, the deed another, and the image of the deed yet another' (Z.I.6). The hero must be superior to pity: 'resolute for the fray, but unattached to the result',[161] but in struggling to overcome the old morality within himself (*KSA*.10.180), the hero in Zarathustra, like that in the 'pale criminal', was 'equal to the deed when he did it: but he could not bear its image after it was done' (Z.I.6).

In spite of, or perhaps because of, his cap and bells, Zarathustra's irritable honesty continues to embroil him in moral warfare 'for the sake of over-severe demands' (*GS*.107) which his heroic folly makes upon him. 'To have and not to have one's affects, one's for and against, at will' (*BGE*.284), from however great an artistic distance, is to become a 'virtuous monster and scarecrow' (*GS*.107). And to 'remain master of one's four virtues, courage, insight, sympathy, solitude' (*BGE*.284) is to recognize that these *reappraised* virtues - virtues which do not spring from the nihilistic root of Christian *ressentiment* - are, in all honesty, not those possessed by Zarathustra. His *courage* is not of the kind which 'destroys giddiness at abysses' and which thereby 'also destroys [the] pity' which accompanies tragic *insight* - for 'pity is the deepest abyss, as deeply as man sees into life, so deeply does he also see into suffering' (Z.III.2.1); nor is his *sympathy* of the kind which 'conceal[s] itself under a hard shell' (Z.I.14); nor his *solitude* an Elysian haven where 'the godly are offered auspicious escape'[162] and where, 'with warm feet', Zarathustra purportedly runs 'hither and thither upon [his] mount of olives', and in a 'sunny corner [...] sing[s] and mock[s]

---

161. Ananda Coomeraswamy, paraphrasing the teaching of the *Bhagavad Gita* in his book, *The Dance of Shiva* (London: Peter Owen, 1958), p. 144.
162. As prophesied by Horace (Epode 16, 41 *et seq.*).

all pity' (*Z*.III.6). On the contrary, it is precisely Zarathustra's contemptuous pity for man which robs him of the 'courageous pessimism' and the '[*in*]active sympathy for the ill-constituted and weak' (*A*.116), which together will enable him to return to society and thus bring to an end his wintry and interminable solitude.

In Part II, from the icy peaks of his solitude (which Apollonian illusion disingenuously transforms into a sunny 'mount of olives'), Zarathustra had taught that 'for one person, solitude is the escape of an invalid, for another, solitude is escape *from* invalids' (*Z*.III.6); but in Part IV, the erstwhile prophet has learnt that his solitary convalescence is the ignominious escape of an invalid from like invalids. Far removed from the pitiful ugliness of the human face (*HH*.I.320) - which acts as a constant reminder of the disease of decadence afflicting all modern men, but from which the 'greater' modern man suffers 'more acutely than the smaller' (*UM*.III.3) - Zarathustra cannot escape the ugliness of his own features mockingly reflected in his fool's mirror.

In tempting Zarathustra to his ultimate sin, all the soothsayer need do is hold up this ironic mirror before his victim, who, temporarily bereft of his pets' transfiguring mirror, can no longer evade the piercing gaze of his own thinly veiled torment. Beneath the calm surface of his 'sky-blue lake of happiness', Zarathustra clearly discerns the surging 'waves of great distress and melancholy': concealed behind the mask of 'a cheerful old man' (*Z*.IV.2) is the 'whole inner "hopelessness" of the higher man' (*BGE*.269). 'It is high time!' comes the soothsayer's parodic cry; high time for the 'great event' (*Z*.II.18) of Zarathustra's self-unmasking. This great event is prefigured in Part II, in a chapter entitled 'Of Great Events'. A mariners' tale recounts how Zarathustra was seen flying through the air, 'like a shadow', in the direction of a smoking volcano situated on an island not far from 'Zarathustra's Isles of the Blest'.[163] Just as Empedocles, afflicted by excessive self-consciousness and an acute sense of his spiritual 'untimeliness', hurled himself into the crater of Mount Etna, so, in similar fashion, Zarathustra's shadow hurtles towards the crater of nihilism.[164] But

---

163. The idea of the Isles of the Blest 'perhaps reflected *the tales of mariners* who had reached islands off the West coast of Africa' (emphasis added). See *The Oxford Companion to Classical Literature*, compiled by Paul Harvey (Oxford: Oxford University Press, 1986), p. 224.
164. Nietzsche himself felt a certain affinity to Empedocles: 'My ancestors: *Heraclitus, Empedocles, Spinoza, Goethe*' (*KSA*.11.134).

who or what is Zarathustra's 'shadow'? It is the reflection of his (distressed and melancholy) soul - a shadowy reflection which he fears 'will ruin [his] reputation' (Z.II.18).[165] On his so-called 'Isles of the Blest' - where, according to Greek mythology, 'the blessed among the dead live again in bliss'[166] - an ungodly Zarathustra lives among the buried remains of his past, only to keep reverential and nostalgic watch over them in a distressed, and in any case far from blissful, state. 'It is high time!' mocks the soothsayer; high time for Zarathustra to stop the absurd pretence of happiness and finally heed the human 'cry of [inner] distress' which escapes from the melancholy depths of his 'black sea':

> 'Do you hear? Do you hear, O Zarathustra?' cried the soothsayer. 'The cry is meant for you, it calls to you: Come, come, come, it is time, it is high time!'
> Hereupon Zarathustra was silent, confused, and deeply shaken; at last he asked like one undecided: 'And who is it that calls me?'
> 'But you know who it is,' answered the soothsayer vehemently, 'why do you conceal yourself? It is the *higher man* that cries for you!'
> 'The higher man?' cried Zarathustra, horror-stricken. 'What does *he* want? What does *he* want? The higher man! What does he want here?' - and his skin was covered with sweat.
> The soothsayer, however, did not respond to Zarathustra's anguish, but listened intently towards the depths. But when it had remained quiet there for a long time, he turned his gaze back and saw Zarathustra standing and trembling.
> 'O Zarathustra,' he began in a scornful voice, 'you do not stand there like one made giddy by happiness: you will have to dance if you are not to fall over!
> 'But even if you were to dance before me and indulge in all your tricks, no one could say: "Behold, here dances the last happy man!"
> 'Anyone who sought *him* here would visit these heights in vain: he would find caves, certainly, and caves behind caves, hiding-places for the hidden, but not mines of happiness and treasure-houses and new gold-veins of happiness.
> 'Happiness - how could man find happiness with such buried men and hermits!'

---

165. The 'shadow' will be dealt with at length in the final section of Chapter 7.
166. Paul Harvey, p. 224.

Drowning in the flood of pessimism which has, through his own agency, burst through his dam of repression, Zarathustra staunches the flow by silencing the soothsayer and resuming his former cheerfulness. Thus 'concealed', Zarathustra can with a good (Christian) conscience go in search of the distressed higher man whose cry has reawakened his latent and ineluctable pity for 'higher men into whose rare torment and helplessness some accident allowed us to look' (*BGE*.41). His pity is indisputably of the Christian variety: just as *agape* is, according to Nietzsche, a "moral" means of escaping from one's 'personal necessity of misfortune' (*GS*.338),[167] so too is Zarathustra's need to wage war with representative higher men a way of escaping the cry of personal distress which emanates from his own inner being. In common with his creator, Zarathustra's incisive critique of Christian pity (and of solitude) owes its insight to self-knowledge, to which latter insight, however, Zarathustra attains only in his declining years. Thus, whereas in Part I, Zarathustra taught: 'One man runs to his neighbour because he is looking for himself, and another because he wants to lose himself' (*Z*.I.16); in Part IV, Zarathustra learns that in attempting to lose himself in his pity for objectified higher men, he has succeeded only in finding himself - his own contingent, historical creation - and thereby the Christian source of pity: empathic identification. His attempt to escape the higher men within him, to deny his own inner reality, is merely another form of nihilism; a 'roguish' ruse which, like his cheerful mien, can neither *fool* nor long evade the exigencies of his romantic pessimism:

> 'O Zarathustra, you are a rogue! [said the soothsayer]
> 'I know it already: you want to get rid of me! You would rather run into the forests and hunt evil beasts![168]
> 'But what good will it do you? In the evening you will have me back; in your own cave I shall be sitting, patient and heavy as a millstone (*Klotz*) - and waiting for you!'

---

167. *Contra* Nietzsche, Scheler differentiates between *agape* and "altruism" and, with elegance and persuasiveness, argues that whereas the latter is symptomatic of *ressentiment*, the former springs from 'a powerful feeling of security, strength, and inner salvation, of the invincible fulness of one's own life and existence'. See Max Scheler, '*Ressentiment*', in Solomon (ed.), pp. 249-51.
168. Cf. '*Appearance of heroism.* - To throw oneself into the midst of the enemy can be a sign of cowardice' (*D*.299); and 'Asceticism is the right way of thinking for those who have to exterminate their sensuous drives because the latter are raging beasts of prey' (*D*.331).

86 *Zarathustra contra Zarathustra*

Upon regaining his artistic distance, Zarathustra ironically invites the soothsayer to make himself at home in his cave and to help himself to any honey he might possibly find there, in preparation for an evening (the time of the day when Zarathustra's pessimism is at its most oppressive) of revelry. Ironic distancing and mocking self-reflection enable Zarathustra to resign himself to his fate. With the high spirits vouchsafed to him by irony (when honey is lacking), he trips off in philanthropic search of the distressed higher man who, it transpires, is a type - more precisely a 'decadent' type - rather than a specific individual.

Political Abdication: The Two Kings and an Ass

'A journeyman to grief',[169] Zarathustra sets off on his pilgrimage in search of the lost, but still cherished, illusions of his youth: beloved higher men who now cry out for deliverance from prolonged and brutal repression. His first encounter is with two biblical refugees leading their symbolic ass out of Matthew 21 and onto the Zarathustran stage. 'There is a point in every philosophy', writes Nietzsche, 'when the philosopher's "conviction" appears on stage: or, to put it in the words of an ancient Mystery: *adventavit assinus / pulcher et fortissimus*'[170] (*BGE*.8). The ass symbolizes what one might call pragmatic method[171] as applied in *all* areas of science,[172] and 'the conscience of *method* demands' that the only reality is 'our world of desires and passions' (*BGE*.36). Accordingly, he who sits 'with immense and proud composure' upon his *own* ass symbolizes sovereignty, that is, the ability 'to have and not to have one's affects, one's for and against, at will, to condescend to them for a few hours; to *seat* oneself on them as on a horse, often as on an ass: - for one must know how to make use of their stupidity as well as their fire' (*BGE*.284). Just as an ass was brought to Jesus by two of his disciples so that the philosopher-king[173] might ride triumphantly into

---

169. Shakespeare, *Richard II*, I.iii.274.
170. 'The ass arrived, beautiful and most brave'.
171. In the words of Blake: 'As the true method of knowledge is experiment, the true faculty of knowing must be the faculty which experiences'. (*All Religions are One*).
172. *Wissenschaft*, in the broadest sense of the word.
173. I use this Platonic term to differentiate between those who rule in the realm of thought (philosopher-kings) and those who rule in the realm of politics (kings). The two are not, of course, mutually exclusive.

Jerusalem, so too an ass is now brought to Zarathustra by two of his disciples, 'for the highest man should also be the highest lord on earth' (Z.IV.3). But pragmatic method further demands that the highest lord should also be the highest beast - that is to say, a dynamic synthesis of 'creature and creator' (BGE.225) - and so, with the courage of his convictions,[174] Jesus mounts the ass of his "wisdom" and rides to his death at Golgotha where he finally suffers into truth: 'My God, my God, why hast thou forsaken me?' (Matt. 27:47).[175] Similarly, it is Zarathustra's convictions which lead him down from the mountain and, heedless of the hermit's warning (Z.Prol.2), into the market square where he makes, as it were, a complete (but edifying) ass of himself (Z.Prol.3-6).

There are, however, two important distinctions to be made regarding the relative status of the philosopher-king and the two disciples as represented in both "pragmatic" parables. With respect to the philosopher-king, whereas Jesus, 'flooded with the light of certain delusions' (HH.I.144), believed unequivocally in his teaching, an aged Zarathustra has recanted (but not fully relinquished) much of *his* earlier teaching.[176] By Part IV, Zarathustra has become 'a sceptic', whose 'grand passion' for knowledge (cf. GS.107) has 'used and used up' his convictions as a means to this knowledge (A.54). Having finally attained a degree of ironic distance, Zarathustra will now only seat himself upon the ass of his former passions and convictions as a satirical device, for in every successful self-parody, 'one must know how to

---

174. 'A very popular error: having the courage of one's convictions; rather it is a matter of having the courage for an *attack* on one's convictions!!!' (Musarion edition, Vol. XVI, p. 318). Cited in Walter Kaufmann, *Nietzsche, Philosopher, Psychologist, Antichrist* (Princeton, New Jersey: Princeton University Press, 1974), p. 354.
175. '*On the knowledge acquired through suffering* - [...] He who suffers intensely looks *out* at things with a terrible coldness [...] he himself lies there before himself stripped of all colour and plumage. If until then he has been living in some perilous world of fantasy, this supreme sobering-up through pain is the means of extricating him from it: and perhaps the only means. (It is possible that this is what happened to the founder of Christianity on the cross: for the bitterest of all exclamations "My God, why hast thou forsaken me!" contains, in its ultimate significance, evidence of a general disappointment and enlightenment over the delusion of his life; at the moment of supreme agony he acquired an insight into himself of the kind told by the poet of the poor dying Don Quixote.)' (D.114).
176. Zarathustra views Jesus' false convictions in the same way as he views his own youthful follies: '[Jesus] died too early; he himself would have recanted his teaching had he lived to my age! He was noble enough to recant! / But he was still immature' (Z.1.21).

make use of [one's] stupidity as much as of [one's] fire.' With respect to the two disciples, whereas in the biblical story they are simple men who by nature are more inclined to learn from a prophet than from the vagaries of their own instincts and who accordingly lead the ass to one who, unlike them, has the courage of self-determination; in *Zarathustra*, they are kings who, above all others, are expected to rule in their own right and to seat themselves upon their *own* ass rather than scour the land in search of a surrogate ruler. What this juxtaposition of kings and disciples reveals is the levelling effect of two thousand years of Christianity. 'Without the *pathos of distance*, which arises out of inveterate (*eingefleischten*) class-distinction' (*BGE*.257), plebeian values have been allowed to usurp the authority of noble values: disciples have become kings and kings disciples.

Nietzsche's principal purpose in re-presenting this biblical parable is, I would suggest, an ethical one. He aims to show that life itself *should be* a means to knowledge (*GS*.324); that only by 'living dangerously' can man attain to any kind of knowledge, particularly self-knowledge: 'Build your cities on Vesuvius! Send your ships into uncharted seas! Live at war with people like yourselves and with yourselves! Be robbers and conquerors as long as you cannot be rulers and possessors, you seekers of knowledge!' (*GS*.283). According to Nietzsche, 'the higher nature is more *irrational*: - for those who are noble, magnanimous, and self-sacrificial[177] do succumb to their instincts', as opposed to 'common natures [to whom] all noble, magnanimous feelings appear inexpedient' (*GS*.3). It is precisely this masterful exploitation of the beast[178] within - 'the *monstrum in animo*' (*TI* 'The Problem of Socrates' 9) - which distinguishes 'master morality' from 'slave morality' (*BGE*.260). Whereas the noble values of the former promote warlike virtues so that man may have the strength and the courage to unfetter the beast, for 'this hidden core (*Grund*) needs to erupt from time to time' (*GM*.I.11), the decadent values of the latter advocate pity and repression so that the ' "creature in man" ' (*BGE*.225) may be castrated and domesticated rather than gainfully employed. One's 'morality', writes Nietzsche, 'bears decided testimony to *who [one] is* - that is to say, in what order of rank the innermost drives of [one's] nature stand in relation to one

---

177. Nietzsche means here those who sacrifice themselves to themselves and not to others and the values of others.
178. In Greek mythology, the ass is sacred to Dionysus and Typhon as a brutish aspect (Cooper, p. 16).

another' (*BGE*.6). Jesus' morality (*not* to be confused with "Christian" and thus 'slave' morality) is decidedly of the 'master' variety, bearing witness to an order of rank and a system of government analogous to liberal feudalism as opposed to tyrannical repression. Enthroned upon an ass, Jesus symbolizes the noblest form of, as it were, *esprit de corps*: the proud freedom of sovereign man who enjoys within himself the symbiotic unity of 'creature and creator'.

In *The Everlasting Gospel*, Blake claims that 'There is not one Moral Virtue that Jesus Inculcated but Plato and Cicero did Inculcate before him'.[179] If this is the case, then Jesus' crucifixion marks the demise of master morality and the rise of slave morality: it marks the death not only of Jesus, "*King* of the Jews" - representing the last in a long and illustrious line of Hebrew kings, prophets and judges, who traditionally rode on white asses[180] - but of all great philosopher-kings. After the death of Jesus and the rise of the Church (fashioned by Paul out of the "crafted" timber of Jesus' wooden cross), the tragic fate of all higher men was (irrevocably?) fixed: the 'gruesome superlative' of the paradoxical crucifixion (*BGE*.46) would henceforth symbolize the 'gruesome' paradox of great-souled men who would never become truly great or who, becoming great merely by some stroke of luck, would never be acknowledged as such, because the concept of greatness had been nailed to the cross (*BGE*.269). According to Nietzsche, Paul was the arch-enemy of Jesus: he converted an historical figure into the "meaning" of Christ; homily into theology; and a vague ethic into doctrinaire moral precepts. Moreover, it was Paul who systematically inverted Jesus' teaching and rendered his noble values ignoble. Pauline precepts required those of "Christian" faith - a faith which guarantees "salvation" (Rom. 5:1-3) - to trade life for death, to sacrifice 'all freedom, all pride, all self-confidence of the spirit' (*BGE*.46) on the doctrinal altar of 'the Church, that form of mortal enmity to all integrity, to all *loftiness* of soul, to all discipline of spirit, to all frank and gracious humanity' (*A.37*). Freedom of thought and action was henceforth to be enslaved to an immoral - immoral, that is, from a non-Christian perspective - system of morality, which dictates that honest pride[181] is evil and humility good, and that spiritual self-confidence is "egoistic" and evil whereas self-mutilating spiritual repression is "altruistic"

---

179. Blake, *The Everlasting Gospel*, Supplementary Passages.
180. Cooper, p. 16.
181. 'The noble soul has reverence before itself' (*BGE*.287).

and good. 'One seeks in vain', writes Nietzsche, 'a grander form of *world-historical irony*' than that of 'mankind falling on its knees before the opposite of the source, the meaning, the *right* of the gospels'. Christianity, as 'sanctified in the concept "Church" ' (*A*.36), is a travesty of its genesis; the 'Evangel', Nietzsche tells us, the first and last true Christian, died on the cross (*A*.39).

The 'paradoxical "formula" god on the cross' represents for Nietzsche the stigma of truly "fallen" man; the sign of the cross (like that which betokened plague victims) marks the disease of Christianity. This turning point in the history of humanity Nietzsche sees reflected in the Bible. Whereas in the Old Testament he finds 'great human beings, a heroic landscape, and something of the very rarest quality in the world, the incomparable naïveté of a strong heart; what is more, I find a people'; in the New he finds 'nothing but petty sectarianism, mere rococo of the soul' (*GM*.III.22). After the cataclysmic crucifixion a noble people slowly but inexorably degenerated into a contemptible "mass" of pious mediocrity. Sectarian indoctrination in the manner, say, of Paul's *Epistle to the Romans* - with its 'exhortations' to self-sacrifice, humility and charity (Ch.12); with its appeals for neighbourly love and Christian unity (Ch.15) - led to the diminution and devaluation of man (*BGE*.203) and disseminated the seeds of modern democracy.[182] 'With the aid of a religion which has indulged and flattered the most sublime herd-animal desires', writes Nietzsche, 'it has got to the point where we find even in political and social institutions an increasingly evident expression of this morality: the *democratic* movement is the heir of the Christian movement' (*BGE*.202).

The most sublime expression of this "demoralization" of man is to be found in the French Revolution and in the 'moral fanaticism' (*D*.Pref.3) instinct in Robespierre's perversion of revolutionary and religious ideals: dictatorship masquerading as the "common interest", and a bloody appropriation of the divine right of kings masquerading as "virtue". Nietzsche claims that 'with the French Revolution, Judea once again triumphed over the classical ideal: the last political *noblesse* in Europe, that of the *French* seventeenth and eighteenth century, collapsed beneath the popular instincts of *ressentiment*' (*GM*.I.16). Debilitated by a long and gradual decline, the old nobility - in particular, kings and philosopher-kings,

---

182. For a refutation of the indebtedness of socialist and democratic principles to Christianity, see Scheler, pp. 255-6.

as representatives of political control and self-control - finally perished under the weight of an ideological paradox exemplified in Rousseau's concept of the 'general will'.[183] Individual *liberty* (in Nietzsche's sense of 'the *sovereign individual*', liberated from 'the morality of mores and the social straitjacket' *GM*.II.2) was now to be sacrificed to collective liberty. Both in the political and in the moral sphere the will to power of the ignoble man would henceforth flaunt its vulgar victory in the 'mottled' (*Z*.II.14) livery of mob-rule and 'slave morality'.

Notwithstanding the savage splendour of Napoleon ('a last signpost to a *different* route' *GM*.I.16), who briefly revived not only some of the nobler values of the *ancien régime*,[184] but also some of the more barbaric[185] (hence Nietzsche's ambivalent characterization of Napoleon as the personification of the 'ideal of antiquity itself [...] the problem of the *noble ideal in itself* made flesh [...] Napoleon, this synthesis of the *inhuman* (*Unmensch*) and *Übermensch*' ibid.),[186] the eventual corruption and ruination of 'the more profound and comprehensive men of [the nineteenth] century' (*BGE*.256) had become the rule. Neither kings nor philosopher-kings would be seen sitting triumphantly astride an ass because 'herd' values had effectively precluded the synthesis of 'creature and creator'. Man was no longer to exploit and master the beast within, but to yoke himself to the collective beast of burden. Yoked thus to the "sinner", who is fearfully weighed down by the concepts of 'guilt, punishment and immortality' (*A*.58), the noble and independent of spirit cannot but suffer from being the 'bad conscience of their time' (*BGE*.212). Gradually, the "untimely" are vitiated and worn down by the "timely", and empathic identification of one individual with another ultimately mutates into a monstrous and nauseating collective identity.

Kings have become courtiers and courtiers kings. Rulers must now swear allegiance to the mob and pretend to serve the *common* interest: ' "I serve, you serve, we serve" - so here too the hypocrisy of the rulers intones - and woe, if the first ruler is *merely* the first servant!' (*Z*.III.5.2). Even philosopher-kings - 'creative men' who initiate a change in values (*Z*.I.15) - are constrained by the popular demands of the new ideology. Those who

---

183. Jean Jacques Rousseau, *The Social Contract*, Bk 1, Ch VII.
184. For example, a commitment to humane and enlightened policies in government.
185. For example, a ruthless and savage pride in military glory.
186. As White (p. 55) stresses: 'Nietzsche explicitly identifies Napoleon as incarnating the *problem* of the noble ideal, *not* its solution'.

condescend to play to the gallery[187] do so at the cost of artistic purity and intellectual integrity, while those who steadfastly refuse to debase themselves in such a fashion suffer at best notoriety and at worst anonymity. Both wait: the former upon the new bourgeois "nobility" and the latter upon the world's oldest nobility, "Lord Chance" (Z.II.4). The nobler courtier plays a perverse kind of waiting game which almost invariably defeats its own objective:

> *The problem of those who wait* - It requires strokes of luck and much that is incalculable if a higher man in whom the solution of a problem lies dormant is to act - "to erupt", one might say - at the right time. Usually it does *not* happen, and in every corner of the earth sit men who wait, who hardly know to what extent they wait, but even less that they wait in vain. From time to time the awakening call, that chance event which gives "permission" to act, comes but too late - when the best part of youth and strength for action has already been used up through sitting still; and how many a man has discovered to his horror, just as he "sprang up" that his limbs had gone to sleep and his spirit was already too heavy! "It is too late" - he has said to himself, having lost faith in himself and henceforth forever useless. - Could it be that in the realm of genius, 'Raphael without hands', taking this phrase in the widest sense, is perhaps not the exception but the rule? (*BGE*.274)

Among those who wait on "Lord Chance", and wait in vain, is Zarathustra. Old and grey, and well past his prime, Zarathustra sits in solitary exile awaiting "permission" to return to man: 'Here I sit and wait, surrounded by old shattered law-tables and also new, half-written law-tables. When will my hour come? / - the hour of my going down and going under: for I want to go among men once more!' (Z.III.12.1). But in what capacity and to what end will he return to the people? To whom will Zarathustra the lawgiver dictate his tables, those same unfinished laws which in Part III he could only recite to himself (Z.III.12)? Just as Jesus had destroyed in vain Moses' Tables, inscribed by the finger of God,[188] so Zarathustra has to little

---

187. As in (Nietzsche's perception of) the case of Wagner: 'The theatre is a form of demolatry in matters of taste; the theatre is a revolt of the masses, a plebiscite *against* good taste' (*CW*.Postscript).
188. 'What was the sound of Jesus' breath? / He laid His hand on Moses' Law: / The Ancient Heavens, in Silent Awe / Writ with Curses from Pole to Pole, / All away began to roll / [...] "Good & Evil are no more! / "Sinai's trumpets, cease to roar! / "Cease, finger of God, to write! / "The Heavens are not clean in thy Sight.' (Blake, *The Everlasting Gospel*, (e), ll.10-24.

or no purpose shattered the Christian Tables, inscribed by Paul and recently appropriated by 'the new idol'. This godless monster, the state, confuses 'the language of good and evil', and to the impotent, idolatrous mob perfidiously roars: ' "On earth there is nothing greater than I: I am the ordering finger of God" ' (Z.I.11). The people have their new idol and a new set of worldly values, what need have they of an iconoclast who can guarantee neither material nor spiritual salvation, merely the 'madness' of trying to create an *Übermensch* out of the creature in man (Z.Prol.3)?[189]

Upon whom, then, will Zarathustra bestow the "gift" of his "wisdom" (Z.Prol.2)? Certainly not upon the people, who do not even deserve a king (Z.III.12.21), much less a philosopher-king; and certainly not upon precursory *Übermenschen*, in whose miraculous *coming*, to be heralded by the sign of 'the laughing lion with the flock of doves' (Z.III.12.1), Zarathustra has absolutely no reason to believe. No, the sole beneficiaries of Zarathustra's "gift" will be those doomed higher men who, in common with their benefactor, share the bequest of a higher culture which has been vitiated by the increasing prevalence of 'slave' values. Not the laughter of the lion but the cry of distressed higher men - 'men of great longing, of great disgust, of great weariness, and that which [his higher men] called the remnant of God' (Z.IV.11) - is the real, as opposed to the ideal, *sign* of the times.

These higher men, in whom the 'hidden mob' still lurks, come to Zarathustra not 'as signs that higher men are already on their way to me' (ibid.) - a wil[l-to-power]ful flight of fancy taken by his 'wild wisdom' - but as a sign of "gravity"; a "timely" reminder that in the age of reason what goes up must come down. Just as it is the soothsayer who first hears the cry of distress, and who later mocks Zarathustra's fanciful talk of 'laughing lions', Edenic gardens, Isles of the Blest, and a 'beautiful new race' (ibid.) of *Übermenschen*, so it is Zarathustra's Schopenhauerian 'Spirit of Gravity' which mocks the soaring pride and imagination of his wild wisdom: ' "You have thrown yourself so high, but every stone that is thrown - must fall!" ' (Z.III.2.1). Indeed, each higher man whom Zarathustra encounters is one more millstone round his neck, sinking him further and further into his abysmal 'black sea', into 'the abyss where the glance plunges *downward* and the hand grasps *upward*' (Z.II.21): downward towards the real world of

---

189. '... the happiness which the madman enjoys from his *idée fixe* proves [nothing] with regard to its rationality' (*HH*.I.161).

suffering and upward towards an ideal world of redemptive gods and *Übermenschen*.

In the abysmal depths of Zarathustra's heart lies his 'twofold will', his will to honesty and his will to artifice: 'That my glance plunges into the heights and that my hand wants to hold on to the depths and count upon them - that, that is *my* precipice and my danger' (Z.II.21). From out of this abyss the more nauseating aspects of Zarathustra's own repressed 'hidden mob' gaze pathetically and searchingly up at him, because 'when you gaze long into an abyss, the abyss also gazes into you' (*BGE*.146). But his involuntary pity for the creature in man forces his hand to caress and comfort (Z.III.9) where it should smash and re-create (*BGE*.225).

Disgust and pity constitute Zarathustra's fundamental ambivalence: his dual need for solitude and humanity. If the soothsayer comes to seduce Zarathustra to pity, the choleric king's[190] pathological disgust for his 'rabble kingdom' (Z.IV.3) reflects Zarathustra's own apoplectic disgust at mob-rule. What distinguishes the latter's disgust from that of the former, however, is ironic reflexivity. Zarathustra knows how pervasive and deep-rooted 'slave' values are, and his will to honesty everywhere discerns, particularly within himself, the ubiquitous 'small man'. It is this tragic and pitiful insight which compels Zarathustra to life-preserving artifice, to the fantastic invention of free spirits and *Übermenschen*; and it is precisely this *lack* of insight which serves to disclose the kings' partial kinship with those whom they once governed and now despise.

Once one has lost the 'pathos of distance' it becomes harder to differentiate between contrivance and creation, guile and genius. As Zarathustra taught in Part I, 'The people have little understanding of greatness, that is, of creativeness. But they have a taste for all performers and actors of great things' (Z.I.12). Thus, because Zarathustra speaks to his pupils differently than he does to himself (Z.II.20); because he 'performs' well; the kings mistakenly believe not only in the greatness of Zarathustra but also in his rhetoric of redemption. They further mistake - on account, perhaps, of the violence of his 'theatrical rhetoric' (*CW*.8) - Zarathustra's address to 'War and Warriors' (Z.I.10) as an apostrophe to the bloody wars of the past and as an urgent call to arms to those who feel threatened and spiritually impoverished ("demoralized") by the current predominance of

---

190. Of the two kings, the sedate 'king on the left' merely acts as a sounding-board for the loquacious and irascible 'king on the right'.

mob-rule. But when Zarathustra teaches, 'You should seek your enemy, you should wage your war - a war for your opinions' (ibid.), he is exhorting one not to civil war, but to internal warfare. It is a call to the battlefield of pragmatic method, where one must have the courage to attack one's convictions.[191]

What these two figureheads fail to understand is that when Zarathustra proclaimed that 'The age of kings is past: what today calls itself a people deserves no kings' (Z.III.12.21), he had hoped that the loss of *political* sovereignty would incite erstwhile kings and (enlightened) subjects to assume *personal* sovereignty. But, instead of riding their own ass and trying to attain a higher degree of self-governance, the two kings lead to Zarathustra 'the ass of [his] wisdom' (*KSA*.10.448).[192] Repelled by the mercantile "nobility", the two kings seek to find in Zarathustra the precursor of a 'new nobility': a nobility of the future which, by being 'the adversary of all mob-rule and all despotism, and [by writing] anew upon new law-tables the word "noble" ' (Z.III.12.11), shall 'redeem all that is past' (Z.III.12.12). But in common with the two kings Zarathustra is tainted by modern culture and its rabble values and thus lacks not only the classically inspired nobility which alone has the right to inscribe the word "noble" on new law-tables, but the divinely inspired (*übermenschliche*?) conviction which alone will guarantee the completion of Zarathustra's law tables (after all, even Moses required a providential hand in the writing of his law [Ex. 34]).

Zarathustra's "nobility" is just as false as that displayed by the two kings, 'cloaked (*überhängt*) and disguised in the old, yellow pomp of [their] grandfathers' (Z.IV.3), and their common desire for a 'new nobility' is fundamentally atavistic. Both Zarathustra and the 'king on the right' dream not only of 'redeeming' but also of reviving the past: the latter wishes to revive the bloodthirsty bellicosity of his ancestors and - even more retrogressively, yet part of the same continuum - the romantic myth of the noble savage; while Zarathustra's future nobility of 'higher, stronger, more victorious, more cheerful men, such as are upright in body and soul' (Z.IV.11), of beautiful heroes who 'stand with relaxed muscles and unharnessed will' (Z.II.13), bears a striking resemblance to the sublime nobility of homeric and other lion-hearted heroes of antiquity on the one hand, and of quixotic heroes of the romantic period on the other.

---

191. See footnote 174.
192. 'And kings shall still lead the ass of my wisdom'.

Irony alone induces Zarathustra to mount the ass which has been brought to him by two of his disciples. Seated upon the ass of his wisdom, Zarathustra ironizes his past follies which have yet brought him to knowledge. He knows that what he once *present*ed as convictions of his wild wisdom are in truth no more than 'hermit phantasmagoria'; he knows that his future nobility of neo-classical and neo-romantic heroes, upon whom the two kings wait, is a vain fantasy. It is with mocking irony, therefore, that Zarathustra tells his two regal disciples: 'My cave will be honoured if kings would sit and wait in it; but to be sure, you will have to wait a long time!' (Z.IV.3).

Scholastic Science: The Conscientious Man of Spirit

Pressing on 'through forests[193] and past bogs', Zarathustra penetrates 'farther and deeper' (Z.IV.4) into the abyss of that 'unknown sage' called 'self' (Z.I.4). *En route*, he stumbles over the body of the ropedancer which he had tenderly laid to rest, many years before, 'in a hollow tree' hidden deep in the forest (Z.Prol.8). As we saw in Chapter 2, the fatal fall of the ropedancer symbolizes the destructive powers of critical reflexivity and the consequent failure and concomitant decline into nihilistic pessimism of 'an audaciously daring, magnificently violent, high-flying and high-climbing type of higher man' (*BGE*.256). The law and the spirit of *gravity* dictate that soaring spirits fall to earth as a result of the gravitational pull of the critical spirit: as Zarathustra teaches, 'Spirit is the life that itself cuts into life' (Z.II.8). Fear of what Zarathustra calls ' "the beast within" ' (Z.IV.15), of man's wild and voracious passions, causes the ropedancer to falter on the tightrope stretched between the real 'world of desires and passions' (*BGE*.36) and the ideal world of heroic perfection. As the representative of the inner beast (otherwise known as 'will to power'), and the ironic mediator between the prophet and the madman (the public and the private), the buffoon is at once the fearful voice of tragic insight and the means of ironic suspension above the inexorable 'reality of our drives' (ibid.).

---

193. The forest commonly symbolizes the realm of the psyche; it is 'a place of testing and initiation, of unknown perils and darkness' (Cooper, p. 71). To bury something in the forest is therefore a metaphor for repression.

The Decadence of Modernity 97

Zarathustra's act of burial symbolizes his renunciation of idealism - 'all idealism is mendaciousness in the face of what is necessary' (*EH* 'Why I am so clever' 10) - and leads him to reflect seriously upon the "wisdom" and "virtue" of becoming a popular leader or, as he puts it, 'a sheep-dog' (Z.Prol.9). To adopt Zarathustra's trope: the sheep-dog, realizing that all the while he has been barking up the wrong tree, finally abandons the herd and withdraws with his tail between his legs. The clumsiness and abysmal failure of Zarathustra's rhetorical acrobatics is bodied forth in the ropedancer's inept and tragi-comic *spectacle*; and, to return once again to Zarathustra's metaphor, the sheep-dog's compassion for 'the dead dog' - the buffoon's contemptuous sobriquet for the ropedancer (Z.Prol.8) - is clearly much more than a case of empathic identification. Zarathustra *buries* the 'dead dog' deep in the *forest* because the pitiful sight of the 'whole inner hopelessness of the higher man', and thus of his *own* tragic destiny, 'may perhaps cause him one day to turn bitterly against his own lot and to make an attempt at self-destruction' (*BGE*.269).

With the 'self'-confidence of one whose hovering irony has given rise to a false sense of security, and toying, perhaps, with the idea of a brief but complacent vigil at the symbolic burial site of the ropedancer, Zarathustra returns to the same dark and perilous forest. Stumbling over the prostrate but very much alive *figure* of the ropedancer, Zarathustra jumps clean out of his 'lion-skin' (the 'spotted skin of the beast of prey and the matted hair of the inquirer, seeker, conqueror', being the sham and shabby mantle of would-be 'famous wise men' Z.II.8). Tired, no doubt, of his prolonged and solitary exile, and eager to rewrite his own history with a Kantian emphasis on the good rather than the thwarted intentions of the will,[194] the ropedancer undergoes a figurative metamorphosis and reappears as 'the conscientious man of spirit' (Z.IV.4). In this guise, the broken and twisted remains of Zarathustra's former insatiable passion for knowledge and for a life lived in fearless celebration of this knowledge - *'amor fati'* (*GS*.276) - crawl out of hiding and now lie defiantly across Zarathustra's path.

Amor fati is Nietzsche's 'formula for greatness in a human being' (*EH* 'Why I am so clever' 10). But it would appear that that is all it is: a formula, an ideal, a pretty lie 'in the face of what is necessary' (ibid.). The violent reaction of the erstwhile prophet of 'self-overcoming' - 'in his fright he

---

194. Immanuel Kant, *Groundwork of the Metaphysic of Morals*, trans. H J Paton (London: Harper & Row, 1964), pp. 61-2.

raised his stick and brought it down on the man he had trodden on' (Z.IV.4) - testifies to a failure to overcome fearfully repressed drives (to let sleeping dogs lie) and to a patent lack of *amor fati*. No sooner, however, has Zarathustra registered the alarming magnitude of his vulnerability than he regains the equanimity of his former ironic distance and, in a supreme effort to distance himself even further from this resurgence of fear, proceeds to regale the man he has just 'trodden on' and beaten down (but not stamped out) with the following parable:

> How a wanderer dreaming of distant things, unexpectedly stumbles over a sleeping dog on a lonely road, a dog lying in the sun:
> how they both started up and let fly at one another like mortal enemies, these two, frightened to death - thus it happened to us.
> And yet! And yet! - how little was lacking for them to caress one another, this dog and this lonely man! For they are both - lonely!

Fear of 'the beast within' and the loneliness of those who inquire and seek after a scientific framework within which to cage the conquered instinctual beast, bind the 'dreamy wanderer' to the 'sleeping dog [...] lying in the sun'. Whether, as in the latter case, one blinds oneself to the glaring truth - 'the blindness of the blind man and his seeking and groping shall yet bear witness to the power of the sun into which he gazed' (Z.II.8) - or, as in the former, averts one's gaze and dreams of distant things, one is dealing in the same counterfeit currency of idealism (*GM*.III.26).

Wissenschaft (science) and *gewissenhaft* (conscientious) share more than a merely formal resemblance; etymologically, they are rooted in the same infernal element - *wissen* (to know). Scholastic, scientific, and philosophical seekers after knowledge - 'the conscientious of spirit' - are alike constrained by an 'unconditional will to truth' (*GM*.III.24): 'It is still a *metaphysical faith* that underlies our faith in science - and we enlightened men of today, we godless men and anti-metaphysicians, we, too, still take *our* flame from the fire ignited by a millennia-old faith, the Christian faith, which was also Plato's faith, that God is truth, that truth is *divine*' (ibid.). But what is the precise nature of this "truth" after which the conscientious of spirit thirst? If we take the method of 'backward inference' one step further - that is, 'from the ideal to those who *need* it' (*GS*.V.370) - we will find that a 'metaphysical faith' arises out of a need for 'metaphysical comfort' (*BT*.7). In other words, the "truth" which the conscientious of spirit *need* is a 'picturesque' (*A*.13) one: they need *absolute* reassurance that 'despite all changes of appearance, life is at bottom indestructibly powerful and joyful' (*BT*.7). But, as Zarathustra teaches, 'all deep knowledge flows cold', and the ice-cold, 'innermost wells of the spirit' (*Z*.II.8) extinguish all too soon the metaphysical fire. Once it is discovered that the indestructibly powerful source of life is will to power ('*The world is will to power - and nothing besides*' *KSA*.11.611), and that endless flux is the distressing manifestation of this will (*Z*.III.12.8), the value of truth is immediately called into question. 'A life-threatening, destructive principle [...] 'will to truth' [...] that could be a concealed will to death' (*GS*.V.344), compels one to ask: at what price truth? In a bid for survival, the conscientious of spirit begin to turn truth on its head, and an inexorable will to truth gradually and paradoxically mutates into an equally compelling will to artifice, illusion, and fraudulent idealism.[195] '*Freez[ing]* to death on the ice of knowledge' (*Z*.III.6), the conscientious of spirit are those most in need of anæsthetizing idealism: this 'fieriest water of the spirit' (*UM*.III.26) is the nihilistic but life-preserving intoxicant to which those benighted by enlightenment and frozen by fire are addicted.

'All great things', writes Nietzsche, 'bring about their own destruction through an act of self-transcendence (*Selbstaufhebung*)' (*GM*.III.27), and just as doctrinaire Christianity destroyed itself by its own moral dogmatism (ibid.), so science is hoist with its own petard. It is the rigour of scientific method which discloses the limitations of its own discourse: 'spurred on by its [own] powerful illusion, science rushes inexorably to its limits where its optimism, concealed in the essence of logic, perishes' (*BT*.15). At the heart of the phenomenal world, science discovers a mysterious lacuna,[196] and it requires the 'extraordinary courage and wisdom of Kant and Schopenhauer' to mark out distinctly and definitively 'the boundaries and relativity of knowledge in general, and thus to deny decisively the claim of science to universal validity' (*BT*.18).

Placed within this post-Enlightenment context, the scientific drive of the conscientious of spirit must, at the very least, be viewed with scepticism. 'Is

---

195. Cf. Hume: 'Truths which are *pernicious* to society, if any such there be, will yield to errors which are salutary and *advantageous*' (*Principles of Morals*, Section IX, Part II:228).

196. Or what Quine describes as a 'blurring of the supposed boundary between speculative metaphysics and natural science'. See Willard Van Orman Quine, 'Two Dogmas of Empiricism', *From a Logical Point of View* (New York: Harper & Row, 1963), p. 20.

the scientific drive (*Wissenschaftlichkeit*) perhaps merely a fear of, an escape from, pessimism? A cunning self-defence against - *truth*?' asks Nietzsche. Is it, 'morally speaking, something like cowardice and falseness? Amorally speaking, a ruse?' (*AS*.1).[197] Similarly, one might ask of Nietzsche's Zarathustra whether his will to the *Übermensch* is not also 'a fear of, an escape from, pessimism? A cunning self-defence against - *truth*?' To pursue an 'aesthetic' (*A*.13) and transfiguring "truth" as a redemptive ploy against the 'plain, harsh, ugly, repellent, unchristian, immoral truth' (*GM*.I.1) evidenced by the senses (*BGE*.134),[198] is the ultimate idealist activity. If science is 'an artifice for the *preservation* of life' (*GM*.III.13) then, notwithstanding Nietzsche's efforts to distance the philosopher, who is 'a real human being' (*UM*.III.7), from the 'theoretical man' (*BT*.15), who purportedly is not, the conscientious of spirit - insofar as they seek an *ideal* solution to the very *real* problem of being human - must be classed among those 'decadents [who] *need* the lie - it is one of the conditions of their preservation' (*EH* '*The Birth of Tragedy*' 2).

Thus, notwithstanding a difference in means, Zarathustra and the conscientious man of spirit pursue the same end: to construct a redemptive raft out of the tree of knowledge so as not to be 'swept away and lost' (*TL*.2) by the truth of reality as manifested in the chaotic flux of existence. Of what significance is the fact that the conscientious man of spirit fishes for his species of metaphysical comfort - objective "truth" - in the 'swamps' which surround him on all sides, or that Zarathustra, with his 'golden fishing-rod' (*Z*.IV.1), fishes for his subjective "truth" in the 'unfathomable rich sea' (ibid.) of his unconscious? Neither of them is deceived or comforted by his solitary, scientific endeavours. An expert on the *brain* of the leech, the former is bled dry by the conscientious rigour - 'hard, severe, narrow, cruel, inexorable' (*Z*.IV.4) - of his *rational* inquiry: 'For the sake of the leech I have lain here beside this swamp like a fisherman, and already my outstretched arm has been bitten ten times' (ibid.); while the latter, well aware of the 'stupidity' (*Z*.IV.1) of his enterprise, vainly persists in baiting freshwater fish, as it were, in the black sea of humanity.[199] The groundless optimism of Zarathustra's 'wild wisdom', crossing the sea (to use another

---

197. Does this, perhaps, explain the impulse behind Nietzsche's so-called "positivistic period"?
198. 'All credibility, all good conscience, all evidence of truth come only from the senses'.
199. 'I cast my net into [the poets'] sea and hoped to catch good fish; but I always pulled out an old god's head. (*Z*.II.17).

Zarathustran metaphor) 'like a sail, trembling before the impetuosity of the spirit' (Z.II.8), will suffer shipwreck on the bedrock of reality just as surely as the equally groundless optimism of Socratic rationalism will run aground in its own shallow waters.

The leech symbolizes the spirit of inquiry, the spirit that 'cuts into life' and increases its own knowledge through its agony (Z.II.8): 'The Tree of Knowledge is not that of Life.'[200] Knowledge is 'a form of asceticism' (A.57), and the conscientious of spirit are paradigmatic ascetics. In Part II of *Zarathustra*, this form of asceticism is sanctified and glorified: 'to be anointed and through tears consecrated as a sacrificial beast' is, Zarathustra assures us, 'the happiness of the spirit' (Z.II.8). But after many years of ascetic indulgence and the ever-increasing danger of 'bleed[ing] to death from knowledge of truth' (HH.I.109) the 'beauty' and 'delight' of self-sacrifice (GM.II.18) begin to pall and by Part IV Zarathustra's former "ascetic idealism" has become another lost illusion and the butt of cruel self-mockery. Neither Zarathustra nor the conscientious man of spirit is blessed with either happiness of spirit or holiness of spirit: the "holiness" of the scientist is not a beatific state of self-transcendence, but rather an emergency state of self-avoidance (GM.III.8). Repressive measures may succeed in sustaining life, but only at the cost of denaturalization: 'Science is related to wisdom as virtuousness is related to holiness; it is cold and dry [... and] is as useful to itself as it is harmful to its servants, insofar as it transfers its own character to them and thereby ossifies their humanity' (UM.III.6). Although an artifice for self-preservation, the leech of asceticism cuts into the full-blooded life of the senses and sucks it dry.

Zarathustra's re-encounter with his resurrected idealism serves to demonstrate that he is 'still midway between a fool and a corpse' (Z.Prol.7). Just as in the Prologue he had shown compassion for 'the dead dog', so in Part IV he is drawn once again to 'the sleeping dog [...] lying in the sun'. This time, however, the identification is conscious and ironic. For whereas in the Prologue Zarathustra had glimpsed his tragi-comic reflection in the face of the jeering crowd, in Part IV it peers insolently out of the fool's mirror with which he cruelly torments himself. The older, ironic Zarathustra is half-corpse because he has learnt that 'the ascetic ideal' - a form of death in life - 'springs from the protective and redemptive instinct of a degenerating life which', having peered into the abyss of knowledge, 'seeks

---

200. Byron *Manfred*, I.i.10-12.

by all means to sustain itself and to fight for its existence' (*GM*.III.13); and half-fool because the recently acquired, but somewhat precarious, 'artistic distance' of the 'transcendent buffoon' enables him to mock with bitter irony the divine folly of his youth.

This tragi-comic figure calls himself Zarathustra ('I call myself Zarathustra' Z.IV.4), but, as he and his *conscientious* reflection well know, Zarathustra is more tragic than comic, more "saint" than fool, more ascetic than corpse. A fool certainly; but not fool enough. Thus, when called 'a fool' by his mocking reflection, Zarathustra replies with much gravity, much irony, and not a little deterministic resignation: 'I am what I must be' (Z.IV.4).

Wagnerian Melodrama: The Sorcerer

Boldly retracing his steps still further along the beaten(-down) path of decadence, Zarathustra espies 'not far below him on the same path a man who was throwing his limbs around like a maniac and who finally belly-flopped to the ground' (Z.IV.5.1). This is the stuff melodrama is made on, and 'the incomparable *histrio*' (*CW*.8) whom Zarathustra sees is 'the modern artist *par excellence*' (*CW*.5). But if from a distance Zarathustra perceives the historical figure of Wagner, at close quarters he sees only 'the psychologically picturesque' (*CW*.8) figure of his own most insidious disease. Situated only a few paces above 'the artist of decadence' (*CW*.4), Zarathustra can squint his eyes and make believe that he 'beholds the entire fact of man at a tremendous distance - below' (*CW*.Pref). At the same level of decadence, however, he cannot fail to see - short of closing his eyes[201] - the full extent of his own cultural contamination. Running to the spot where 'the Cagliostro of modernity' (*CW*.5) lay, Zarathustra finds 'a trembling old man with staring eyes' (Z.IV.5.1), and a reader would be forgiven for (mis)taking this pathetic old man for Zarathustra the convalescent who not long before had also lain 'pale and trembling' (Z.III.13.2) like a fading romantic artist. Just as in 'The Convalescent' a desolate and solitary Zarathustra had shamelessly played to the gallery, had crashed to the ground like a dead man, and had looked to his 'sick-nurses' for (albeit transient and self-delusory) redemption from his suffering; so in 'The Sorcerer' the 'first-

---

201. See final paragraph of this section.

rate acting' (*CW*.8) of the grand seducer, having successfully lured a cruelly caricatured Zarathustra, resumes its 'wicked and malicious' parody (*GS*.Pref.1) by 'continually looking around with pathetic gestures, like one forsaken by and isolated from all the world' (*Z*.IV.5.1). It is, of course, a self-parody and one which reveals that 'the sorcerer's apprentice' is still caught in his master's spell.

But if ironic distance keeps Zarathustra 'five steps from the hospital' of modernity (*CW*.9) and thus from the nauseating sight of his own diseased soul, then once he has taken those five critical steps and thereby lost 'the pathos of distance' (*BGE*.257), his 'diagnosis of the modern soul' (*CW*.Epilogue) loses its objectivity and betrays its pathological roots in introspection and projection. It is, therefore, simply a matter of perspective as to whether Nietzsche's 'vivisection of the *most instructive* case' (*CW*.Epilogue) of modern decadence begins with the case of Zarathustra or with the case of Wagner. In either case, the overall result will be the same because Zarathustra, 'no less than Wagner, is a child of [t]his time; that is, a decadent' (*CW*.Pref). If we return, then, with our hermeneutic scalpel to the convalescent's bedside (*Z*.III.13), and take the liberty of treating the less confident, more vulnerable Zarathustra as an authorial extension, we will discover that Nietzsche's picture of Wagner is merely one more self-portrait hanging in his own 'pathological gallery' (*CW*.5) of decadent higher men.

Klugheit,[202] judging by the relative frequency of its application in *The Case of Wagner*, is, from Nietzsche's perspective at least, one of Wagner's most prominent character traits. Whether this is the case or not, it is decidedly one of Zarathustra's. As we have seen in Chapters 3 and 4, *Klugheit* is Zarathustra's principal tool of redemption and one which he utilizes to full effect in 'The Convalescent'. If, as Nietzsche claims, 'subtlety (*Raffinement*) [is] the expression of *impoverished* life' (*CW*.Second Postscript), then it is not to be wondered at if a debilitated Zarathustra - 'a spirit who understands the serpentine cleverness (*Schlangenklugheit*) of *changing one's skin*' (*HH*.II.Pref.2) - employs 'the cleverest animal under the sun' (*Z*.Prol.10) to be his chief sick-nurse. For it is precisely when his intellectual conscience has forbidden him the fruits of self-deception that Zarathustra is most keenly at the mercy of his sickness and most desperately in need of his ministering angels. It is then that any valiant attempt at authenticity paradoxically smacks of dissimulation - because 'there is a

---

202. *klug*: *CW*.9 and *CW*.Postscript; *Klugheit*: *CW*.9 and *CW*.10.

wicked falseness among those who will beyond their capabilities' (Z.IV.13.8) - and inevitably leads to ignominious moral defeat. As 'The Convalescent' amply demonstrates, changing one's (yellow) skin without the necessary serpentine art is simply *'clever* stupidity' (*CW*.9), resulting in 'grotesque comedy' (*UM*.IV.3).[203]

Lacking the courage for his 'most abysmal thought' and so failing in his endeavour to purge himself of the "morality" of *ressentiment*, Zarathustra falls victim to the extreme 'contrast between his desires and his capacity to fulfil them' (ibid.). 'Hollowed out and consumed by failure' (*UM*.IV.2),[204] Zarathustra looks to his proud and deceptive consciousness for redemption through art, because 'art is there *to prevent the bow from snapping*' (*UM*.IV.4). For Zarathustra, however, there is one art in particular 'which most profoundly cheered and consoled him in his need [and] which most soulfully accommodated [t]his need' (*UM*.IV.8): the magical elixir of 'myth and music [...] such as Wagner has dispensed as the most delicious of draughts to all who have suffered profoundly from life' (ibid.). Accordingly, it is in the 'psychological magic' of Elysian myth and the lyricism of language, dispensed to him by his sick-nurses, that Zarathustra 'bathed and healed his soul' and returned to life 'with the smile of convalescents' (ibid.).

It is, however, a wry smile, for whereas '[t]he Wagnerian, with his believer's stomach, is actually sated by the fare which his master conjures up for him' (*CW*.8), this 'most corrupted Wagnerian' (*CW*.3)[205] knows that - notwithstanding the incomparable talent of his *'clever* hosts [...] for representing a lavish table at modest expense' (*CW*.8) - the mythical 'rainbows' (Z.III.13.2) which his animals conjure up for him are merely the 'dramatic emergency measures, [...] designed to deceive only for a moment'

---

203. 'Seen from close to and without love, Wagner's life has, to recall an idea of Schopenhauer's, much of the comedy about it, and markedly grotesque comedy at that'.
204. 'Even among those who only pursue their own moral purification, among hermits and monks, there are to be found [the] savage and disease ridden, men hollowed out and consumed by failure'.
205. In his superlative essay on Nietzsche's relationship to Wagner, Furtwängler argues that 'right to the end of his days Nietzsche remained the Wagnerian that he had been from the beginning. Nor could it be otherwise. Whatever else may evolve in the course of one's life, one can do nothing to change one's fundamental relationship to art, embedded, as it is, in the depths of our subconscious.' ('The Case of Wagner' in *Furtwängler on Music*, ed. and trans. by Ronald Taylor (London: Scolar Press, 1991), p. 78.

(*UM*.IV.3), of an ironic and penitent 'Cagliostro of modernity'. If loving hands are needed to warm the coldness of his heart and lofty idealism to counter the shame of tragic insight; 'if iron, leaden life should lose its gravity through golden, tender, unctuous melodies' and his 'melancholy [... find] rest in the hiding-places and abysses of *perfection*' (*NCW* 'Where I raise objections'), Zarathustra must needs repent, for 'it is our alleviations for which we have to atone the worst!' (*HH*.II.Pref.4). Thus, when the magical moment has passed, Zarathustra must once again reckon with his relentless intellectual conscience: 'a merciless spirit that knows all the hideouts where the ideal is at home - where it has its secret dungeons and, as it were, its ultimate safety' (*EH* '*Human, All Too Human*' 1). Whether wearing motley (*Z*.Prol.6) or *cutting* a more sinister figure as 'half dwarf, half mole' (*Z*.III.2.1), Zarathustra's intellectual conscience is the spirit that 'cuts into life' (*Z*.II.8); and Zarathustra, whether *thrown* by the buffoon (*Z*.Prol.6), weighed down by 'the spirit of gravity' (*Z*.III.2.1) or 'torn piecemeal by some Minotaur of conscience' (*BGE*.29), is forever being made to repent his restorative flights of fancy. It is this penitential relationship between Zarathustra and his 'hangman-god' (*Z*.IV.5.1) which the sorcerer cruelly parodies in his lament.

In this dithyrambic[206] *cri de coeur*, not one of Zarathustra's allegories of intellectual conscience escapes 'the magical eye of the dramatist, who can read souls as easily as the most familiar writing' (*UM*.IV.8). In the first stanza of the sorcerer's poetic parody, we re-encounter no less than three transmogrifications: first, Zarathustra's wintry guest (*Z*.III.6), who causes his host to shake with 'unknown fevers' and to shiver 'with piercing icy-frost arrows' (*Z*.IV.5.1); second, the soothsayer, whose 'bad-tidings and ashen lightning flashes' (*Z*.IV.2) strike Zarathustra down, and whose 'mocking eye' (*Z*.IV.5.1) stares at him from the dark abyss of tragic insight; and finally, the 'crippled and crippling' (*Z*.III.2.1) spirit of gravity, under whose weight Zarathustra contorts himself, 'tortured by every eternal torment' (*Z*.IV.5.1). The second stanza re-introduces Zarathustra's 'conscientious spirit' (*Z*.IV.4) which, 'with blunt arrows' strikes deeper and deeper (*Z*.IV.5.1) into Zarathustra's heart. The parasite that 'grow[s] fat on

---

206. A slightly, but significantly, modified version of the sorcerer's lament was to appear three years later in the guise of a *Dionysus-Dithyramb* entitled 'Lament of Ariadne'. For an inspired and profoundly religious account of this renaming, see Karl Reinhardt, 'Nietzsche's Lament of Ariadne', trans. Gunther Heilbrunn, *Interpretation* 6 (October 1977), 204-24.

[Zarathustra's] sick, sore places' (Z.III.12.19) worms its way into the third stanza and, with the aid of 'the longest ladder [which] can descend the deepest' (ibid.), into Zarathustra's heart and his 'most secret thoughts' (Z.IV.5.1). Zarathustra's conscientious spirit of inquiry 'strikes' again in the fourth stanza, spurred on by Zarathustra's 'cruellest spur' (ibid.) - his inexorable will to honesty. Finally, in stanzas five, six and seven, in a devilish inversion of the Mephistophelean myth, the buffoon reappears to demand a *philosopher-king*'s 'ransom' (ibid.). Not content with Zarathustra's soul, the buffoon returns to extract his pound of sovereign flesh. Since the true philosopher-king is a perfect synthesis of 'creature and creator' (*BGE*.225), of 'self and ego' (Z.I.4); and since, as Zarathustra claims, 'there is more reason in your body than in your best wisdom' (ibid.); the buffoon will not rest content until, so far as concerns Zarathustra, he has the full measure of both philosopher *and* king. Having all too easily cut down in the market square and held up for public contumely the philosopher's soaring pride and cunning rhetoric, the buffoon is now *hell*-bent on cutting into the private chambers of the regal self, the self which 'rules and is also the ego's ruler' (ibid.). Only then will the *raison d'être* of Zarathustra's creative partnership - that is, whether it is 'hunger or superabundance that has here become creative' (*GS*.V.370) - be fully exposed; only then will the buffoon's ironic victory be complete.

Unlike the other figures of intellectual conscience, the buffoon, with his light feet and hovering irony (clearly a foil for the crippled spirit of gravity with his 'heavy feet and sultry heart' Z.IV.13.16), actively displays a positive dimension[207] (albeit one which emanates from a negative principle). Whereas the other figures exhibit the negative aspect of the spirit that cuts into life or, as in the case of those who are 'virtuous beyond [their] own strength' (Z.IV.13.13), cuts life down, the buffoon symbolizes the process of *Bildung*, from the acute pain of discipline (*Zucht*) to the nostalgic ache of growth (*Züchtung*). 'The discipline of suffering, of *great* suffering', writes Nietzsche, is the discipline which 'alone has created all the enhancements of man hitherto' (*BGE*.225). On this showing, suffering is the spur to self-knowledge and subsequently to the creative activity of self-development. But cultivating one's garden, as it were, requires more than horticultural expertise for, while pruning finds its human analogue in 'the discipline of suffering', memory is wholly resistant to the cultural process and thus

---

207. See chapters 1 and 2.

altogether indifferent to man's bold claims of improvement (*BGE*.179); 'not far below'[208] man's veneer of culture resides the pain of lost innocence and the disillusionment that such loss brings. In an endeavour to deal with this pain, Zarathustra, having denied himself both Schopenhauer's and Wagner's particular brands of anæsthetizing idealism, seeks in ironic buffoonery a more honest but evidently less effective form of redemption. As the tragicomic voice of Dionysian insight and subsequently of ironic reflexivity, the buffoon is the closest Zarathustra ever gets to a practical and practicable 'Dionysian theodicy'.[209]

As a potentially redemptive figure, the buffoon represents Zarathustra's most *authentically* positive projection. Hovering precariously above the tightrope stretched between beast and god, the buffoon demonstrates how, with a *good* conscience, one can deal with the 'tension of the soul in unhappiness' (*BGE*.225). By means of ironic suspension above the rack of human suffering, above the tension between self-doubt and self-aggrandisement, between man's will to honesty and his will to illusion, between intellectual conscience and bad conscience, between shame and pride, pride and shame, the Zarathustra of Part IV is able to save himself from falling off the human tightrope. And so an ironic Zarathustra relentlessly mocks the violent vacillations of this 'most solitary' (*Z*.IV.5.1) and most divided of men, a man at once scientific and religious whose 'solitary and agitated mind' seeks to drown the voice of bad conscience in a surge of divine madness, in the vain hope that 'epilepsies [... will become] indistinguishable from epiphanies'.[210] 'Ah, give me madness, you heavenly powers! Madness that I may at last believe in myself! Give deliriums and convulsions, sudden light and darkness, terrify me with frost and fire such as no mortal has ever felt, with deafening din and prowling figures, let me howl and whine and crawl like a beast: that I may only come to believe in myself!' (*D*.14). For when intellectual conscience - striving towards self-legislation, self-creation and self-determination - fails to become instinct, let alone 'the dominating instinct' (*GM*.II.2), it turns against itself and becomes the self-flagellating scourge of bad conscience. Half-corpse, half-fool, Zarathustra is a man who, '[f]reezing to death on the ice of knowledge' (*Z*.III.6), is at one

---

208. See opening sentence of this section.
209. Georges Goedert, 'The Dionysian Theodicy,' trans. Robert M Helm, in O'Flaherty, Sellner and Helm (eds.), *Studies in Nietzsche and the Judæo-Christian Tradition*, (London: The University of North Carolina Press, 1985), 319-34.
210. Miller, p. 140.

moment (stanza 1) 'Stretched out, shuddering / Like a half-dead man' and begging for the 'hot hands' of love (Z.IV.5.1), and at another (stanza 5) standing 'on all the stilts of [his] pride' (*DD* 'Amid Birds of Prey'); or, inversely, now "playing" the fool on his precarious stilts and now tumbling into the abyss, 'All footing lost'[211] (Z.Prol.6 and Z.III.13); or, having finally (stanza 8) been spared by his 'cruellest enemy' (Z.IV.5.1), intellectual conscience, perversely beseeching his return (stanza 9) together 'with all your torments' (ibid.). In short, the soul of Zarathustra, 'convulsed with fire and icy fevers' (*HH*.I.141), with wild wisdom and savage self-loathing, is seen to be indistinguishable from the hungry soul of the so-called saint. And with this disclosure, the buffoon's victory is complete.

According to Nietzsche's typology of the "saintly" soul, this ritual torment of crime and punishment, of voluptuous self-indulgence and ascetic self-denial, is the perverse pastime of bored "saints" and hermits. To parody this rousing ritual, however, is the sublime recreation of an ironic 'saint of immoralism.'[212] The same rules, however, hold for both games: whether self-indulgence is reflexive or non-reflexive, the penitential flagellation - 'he scourges his self-idolization with self-contempt and cruelty' (*HH*.I.142) - follows with equal force and equal necessity. 'Every such orgy of feeling has to be *paid* for afterwards, that goes without saying - it makes the sick sicker: and that is why this kind of remedy for pain is, by modern standards, "guilty" ' (GM.III.20). Viewed in this light, the buffoon's victory is pyrrhic: cutting too deeply into Zarathustra's 'sick, sore places' and thereby reopening the 'festering wounds' of memory (*EH* 'Why I am so wise' 6), the buffoon looses his footing, and hovering irony plunges into bitter reflection. Failing 'to redeem the past and to re-create' - through his ruthless, retrospective caricature - 'every "It was" into a "Thus I willed it!" ' (Z.II.20), Zarathustra resorts to repression. Not fool enough to retain his ironic distance nor corpse enough to admit defeat, Zarathustra 'took his stick and began to beat the wailing man with all his might' (Z.IV.5.2). It is the powerful will, the dominating instinct, of bad conscience that wields Zarathustra's splenetic stick of revenge, and the same 'imprisoned will' that, fettered to time and thus unable to 'will backwards' (Z.II.20), so

---

211. Sophocles, *Oedipus Tyrannus*: 'swollen with ill-found booty, / From castled height Pride tumbles to the pit, / All footing lost', ll. 873-881 (first antistrophe of the second stasimon).
212. Thomas Mann, 'Nietzsche's Philosophy in the Light of Contemporary Events' in Solomon (ed.), p. 365.

meticulously guides Zarathustra's stick of *ressentiment* around the ragged contours of his decadent shadow (Z.IV.2 and Z.IV *passim*).

In Parts I and II, Zarathustra had sought redemption from his 'romantic pessimism' in 'wrathful' counteraction (*HH*.II.Pref.4): he had 'take[n] sides against everything sick in me, including Wagner, including Schopenhauer, including all of modern "humaneness" ' (*CW*.Pref). He had railed against the (Wagnerian) 'poet's spirit' which is 'the peacock of peacocks and a sea of vanity!' (Z.II.17); against the (Schopenhauerian) 'spirit of revenge' which emanates from the belief that 'No deed can be annihilated' (Z.II.20); and against 'the compassionate [...] who cannot surmount their pity' (Z.II.3). But this 'special' kind of 'self-discipline' (*CW*.Pref) is self-defeating. Greater than the sum of his parts, man does not conform to the laws of bookkeeping: off-setting one affect with another is to settle accounts but always with recollective remainder. Like 'the pale criminal', Zarathustra 'was equal to his deed when he did it: but he could not endure its image after it was done' (Z.I.6). Repression will never cure Zarathustra of his decadent diseases because memory ensures the ultimate impotence of cold reason in its struggle against ardent passion. He may claim to have 'grown weary' of the 'poet's spirit [that] wants spectators' at any cost (Z.II.17), but his easy seduction by the sorcerer's poetic spirit, and the alacrity with which he runs to the old 'counterfeiter's' (Z.IV.5.2) side, belies the weariness to which he lays claim. He may prefer to be compassionate 'from a distance' (Z.II.3), but, at the sight of the sorcerer's apparent suffering, his compassion is driven inexorably towards its pitiful object (Z.IV.5.1). Finally, he may wish to believe that the causal connection between deed and guilt, pride and shame, intellectual conscience and bad conscience, is not a necessary one (Z.II.20), but it is his 'spirit of revenge', hardened by bad conscience, that metaphorically beats 'his actor's genius' (*CW*.8; Z.IV.5.2), and thus his penitential breast, into temporary submission.

When 'put to the test', Zarathustra proves himself to be a 'penitent of the spirit [... that is, a] poet and sorcerer who finally turns his spirit against himself' (Z.IV.5.2). His poetic spirit has turned penitent (Z.II.17) and his conscientious spirit has mutated into the spirit of revenge (Z.II.20): Zarathustra has 'reaped disgust as [his] single truth' (Z.IV.5.2). The violence with which the 'wise Zarathustra' strikes the decadent artist testifies to the '*hard*'-hitting truths of the latter's savage caricature, and with every blow, the depth of his 'bad knowledge' and the tyranny of his 'bad conscience' strikes home more and more forcefully (ibid.). Whereas in Part

If Zarathustra's intellectual conscience had been spared by the serpentine arts of bad conscience, in Part IV it suffers at the hands of the latter the severest of beatings. A more naïve Zarathustra had been unaware of his animals' vast sphere of influence, of how his bad conscience had changed even its own skin so as not to frighten to death his intellectual conscience ('You would even mask your disease if you showed yourself naked to your physician' ibid.) and thereby enabled an affronted intellectual conscience to retain enough pride[213] and good conscience for redemptive flights of fancy ('A terror came over me when I saw these best of men naked: then I grew wings to soar away into distant futures' Z.II.21). By Part IV, however, Zarathustra has seen through the preservative arts of his eagle and serpent, but still lacks the strength to dispense with them completely. His wings have been clipped by the spirit of irony, and that which once soared is now leapt over by the art of transcendental buffoonery: his Schopenhauerian pessimism (Z.IV.2) wears the (thorny) 'rose-wreath crown' of (ironic) laughter (Z.IV.13.18); the ass of his wisdom (Z.IV.3) is mounted by a (Pretender) philosopher-king whose 'lame foot' of *ressentiment* will, when alighting from the seat of irony, 'stumble' upon the rock of bad conscience (Z.IV.13.10); his 'wild wisdom' is cured by the 'leech of conscience' (Z.IV.4), but at the risk of killing the patient; and finally, the spell of Wagnerian illusion (Z.IV.5.2) is broken, but only by the vengeance of disillusion.

At the moment of truth, however, when bad conscience drops its mythical (but deciduous) fig-leaves and intellectual conscience blushes beneath the rod of *ressentiment* ('To our strongest drive, the tyrant in us, not only our reason but also our conscience submits' BGE.158), Zarathustra has 'no lie and no cunning left - [he is] disenchanted with [him]self' (Z.IV.5.2). He had sought mythical higher men but found only his own higher men. They in turn had sought a mythical Zarathustra but found only themselves: the soothsayer had sought 'one made giddy by happiness' but found only romantic pessimism (Z.IV.2); the two kings had sought 'the highest man' but found only the hero-worship of one who dreams of the highest man (Z.IV.3); the conscientious man of spirit had emulated 'the great leech of conscience' but discovered only bad conscience; and now the sorcerer seeks 'one who is genuine, right, simple, unambiguous, a man of all honesty, a repository of

---

213. Coiled around the eagle's neck (Z.Prol.10), the serpent can be seen as a kind of amulet - the eagle, of course, having long been a protected species.

wisdom, a saint of knowledge, a great man', but finds instead one who is false, complex, ambiguous, and disingenuous; a penitential saint of bad knowledge and thus a repository of wildly prudent wisdom. In short, a man of *ressentiment*.

Ressentiment is the mainspring of redemption, and whether or not Zarathustra avenges romantic pessimism with repression, or vice versa, he will never manage to free himself from the shackles of residual rancour and bad conscience. In seeking redemption from himself through 'art and philosophy' - that is, through the agency of cunning and pride - the ironic saint knows that he is in fact seeking 'revenge against life itself' (*NCW* 'We Antipodes'). It is this bad knowledge that gnaws at Zarathustra's intellectual conscience. 'A mighty striving conscious of repeated failure makes one bad' (*UM*.IV.2), and at the moment of unendurable self-knowledge, when failure weighs heavily upon the heart and *ressentiment* eclipses every best endeavour, intellectual conscience submits to the metaphysical needs of bad conscience. Consequently, when the sorcerer conjures up the noble Zarathustra of mythical origin, the decadent Zarathustra of romantic origin closes his eyes[214] and surrenders to the enchanting fiction of the great man "Zarathustra".

---

214. See footnote 201.

7 The Decadence of Christianity

Faith, Hope, and Love: The Last Pope

The priestly bearing of the last pope and the ascetic idealism which that connotes mark a thematic shift in Zarathustra's picaresque drama of the soul. With the last pope, Zarathustra's aesthetics of redemption moves on from an exploration of cultural paradigms (dealt with in the preceding chapter) to an excavation of the latter's genealogical roots in, as it were, the ascetics of redemption (to be dealt with in this chapter). These "pious" higher men, whose faith in the ascetic ideal is merely a 'believer's need to believe', are all guilty of pious fraud;[215] for enveloping this *'need* for faith' is the fog of 'a certain pessimistic gloom, something that smells of weariness, fatalism, disappointment, and fear of new disappointments' (*GS*.V.347).[216] Bound upon his conscientious wheel of fire and ice, illusion and disillusion - a vicious circle of death and resurrection - Zarathustra is stopped in his tracks by his (former) 'rock of salvation' (Ps. 89:26; 95:1): the *Übermensch*. It is with deep integrity and even deeper irony that Zarathustra, an 'out of work' (Z.IV.6) prophet, reflects upon his (former) apostolic ministry - undertaken in 'Zarathustra's Prologue' - and its implicit ascetic articles of 'faith, hope and love' (I Cor. 13:13) or what Nietzsche calls 'the three Christian shrewdnesses' (*A*.23).

Faith

Having proclaimed the death of God, the madman withdrew from the market square and 'carried [his] ashes to the mountains' (*Z*.Prol.2), the ashes, that

---

215. 'The free spirit, the "pious man of knowledge" - finds *pia fraus* even more offensive to his taste (to *his* "piety") than *impia fraus*' (*BGE*.105).
216. Cf. Edmund Burke's assessment of pious frauds as 'much better calculated for the private advantage of the preacher than the edification of the hearers' *Observations on a Publication,* 'The present state of the nation'.

is, of 'great longing, great disgust, great weariness' - in short, the "remains" of God (Z.IV.11). But just as in Christian mythology the ashes of man betoken the 'sure and certain hope of his resurrection',[217] so too do the madman's ashes carry intimations of immortality. Indeed, after ten years in '*azure* solitude' (*EH 'Thus Spoke Zarathustra'* 6), the madman has rekindled his ashes and in the fire of his "wisdom" (Z.Prol.1) forged anew both himself and the remnant of God within him. Faith in the sun of his "wisdom", and in the 'gold'[218] which it will pour out into the sea of humanity (Z.III.12.3), has alchemically transformed the madman into a prophet: 'His breath exhales gold and golden rain: thus his heart *wants* it. What are ashes and smoke [...] to him now!' (Z.II.18, emphasis added). It is the madman turned prophet - his eyes ablaze (fueled by longing and 'leaden-eyed despairs'),[219] his mouth tight-lipped (thinly concealing its disgust), and his easy, dancer-like gait (belying its weary Dance of Death)[220] - who in section 2 of 'Zarathustra's Prologue' is observed carrying his 'fire into the valleys'. His hand having 'welded the furthest to the nearest, and fire to spirit and joy to sorrow' (Z.III.16.4), having welded an incandescent midday to 'an ash-grey dawn' (Z.III.6) and the *Übermensch* to the remains of God, the resurrected and re-cast madman returns to the market square to proclaim in 'tongues of fire: It is coming, it is near, the *great noontide*!' (Z.III.5.3). His new-found faith in the great noontide - 'when man stands in the middle of his course between beast and *Übermensch* and celebrates his journey to the evening as his highest hope: for it is the journey to a new morning' (Z.I.22.3) - is quintessentially faith in the ascetic ideal, for '*this* is precisely what the ascetic ideal means: that something was *lacking*, that man was surrounded by a dreadful *void*, - he did not know how to justify, to explain, to affirm himself; he *suffered* from the problem of his meaning [...] *and the ascetic ideal gave him a meaning!*' (*GM*.III.28).

---

217. *The Book of Common Prayer, 1559, Burial of the Dead*, First Anthem.
218. Gold here symbolizes the glad tidings of the *Übermensch*: '...*the heart of the earth is of gold*' (Z.II.18), and 'the *Übermensch* is the meaning of the earth' (Z.Prol.3).
219. Keats, *Ode to a Nightingale*, 1. 28.
220. Cf. 'Wanderer, who are you? I see you walking on your way without mockery, without love, with unfathomable eyes; moist and sad like a sounding lead that has emerged into the light unsatisfied from every depth [...] with a breast that does not sigh, with a lip that hides its disgust, with a hand that now only reaches out slowly: who are you? what have you done?' (*BGE*.278).

Hope

In common with that of the first pope (I Pet. 1:3-12), Zarathustra's first address to the people opens with the ("stressed") hope of salvation: '*Behold, I teach you the Übermensch*' (Z.Prol.3). Their putative saviours are different, of course, but it is a difference in degree not in kind. For although Peter's redeemer is the moral Christian God, and Zarathustra's redemptive *Übermensch* an immoral anti-Christian god, the same nihilistic[221] trinity constitutes both deities: *suffering* - 'This [salvation] is a cause of great joy for you, even though you may for a short time have to bear being plagued by all sorts of trials' (I Pet. 1:6) - cf. 'Who alone has good reason to *lie his way out* of reality? One who suffers from it' (*A*.15); *self-contempt* - 'Do not behave in the way that you liked to before you learnt the truth' (I Pet. 1:14) - cf. 'Behold, I teach you the *Übermensch*: he is this sea, in him your great contempt can drown (*untergehen*). What is the greatest experience you can have? It is the hour of the great contempt. The hour in which even your happiness arouses your disgust and also your reason and your virtue' (Z.Prol.3); and *faith in the ideal* - 'you are sure of the end to which your faith looks forward, that is, the salvation of your souls' (I Pet. 1:9) - cf. 'The *Übermensch* is the meaning of the earth. Let your will say: The *Übermensch shall be* the meaning of the earth' (Z.Prol.3).

In prophesying the coming of the *Übermensch* (Z.Prol.4), Zarathustra takes his place among those 'prophetic men [who] are greatly afflicted men' (*GS*.316). For although Peter's God inspires 'superterrestrial hopes' and Zarathustra's *Übermensch* is 'the meaning of the earth', both superhuman figures represent the salvation from life's miseries 'that the prophets were looking and searching so hard for' (I Pet. 1:10). And so far as both these gods and the minds of their makers inhabit a fictive future world (whether temporal or atemporal) - an ideal future against which the very real present is judged and condemned - Christian and anti-Christian prophet alike are '*decadents* [who] *need* the lie [of the ideal] - it is one of the conditions of their preservation' (*EH 'The Birth of Tragedy'* 2). In sacrificing an insupportable present to an equally insupportable future, in their 'counterfeiting of transcendence and the beyond' (*CW*.Postscript), both Peter and Zarathustra reveal their common roots in *ressentiment*. As Zarathustra teaches, it is suffering, impotence and weariness that 'create[s] all gods and afterworlds'

---

221. We are, of course, dealing here with the optimistic and idealist nihilist.

(Z.I.3). For all his atheism, scepticism, immoralism and impiety, the latest pope (Zarathustra of the Prologue) no less than the earliest pope is one of 'those gruesome hybrids of sickness and will to power that one calls founders of religions' (*EH*.Pref.4); founded on impotence, suffering (Z.I.3) and the 'fear of pain', the religion of the former no less than that of the latter is 'a religion of love' (*A*.30).[222]

Love

'I love man' (Z.Prol.2): these are the first words spoken by Zarathustra after ten years of solitude. The significance of this declaration lies not only in its being the reason Zarathustra gives for his return to man, nor yet in its being the reason for Zarathustra's former flight from man, but above all in its being a *confession* of (nihilistic) faith - faith in the ascetic ideal. Zarathustra's faith in the higher, *übermenschliche* self and his 'highest' hope that this 'hero in [man's] soul' (Z.I.8) will one day be realized, spring from a spiritual love of man. This love for the ideal in man,[223] for the 'creator, educator, hammer-hardness, spectator-divinity, and seventh-day' (*BGE*.225), is the kind of love which comes easily to the solitary who has retired far from the madding crowd, and arouses what one might term a *creative* pity for what in man 'must be formed, broken, forged, torn, burnt, made incandescent and purified' (ibid.). This type of pity longs to 'descend to earth like a god and "with fiery arms raise up to heaven" all that is weak, human and lost' (*UM*.IV.7). But, for the social animal in constant contact with the 'creature in man', with that which is 'matter, fragment, excess, clay, filth, nonsense, chaos' (ibid.), such an ideal type of love gives rise to a *degenerative* pity for the all-too-human in man. This type of pity can be so overwhelming that it precipitates a self-preservative flight into solitude, which is a paradoxical act of self-denial: 'The *desert* [...] an avoidence of one*self*' (*GM*.III.8), the self, that is, as perceived through the (all-too-human) other.

Midway between solitude and society, 'mountain' and 'valley' (Z.Prol.2), Zarathustra oscillates between these strong and weak forms of

---

222. 'The fear of pain, even the infinitely small in pain, - *cannot* end otherwise than in a *religion of love*'.
223. It is interesting to note that Scheler, in his defence against Nietzsche's attack on *agape*, maintains 'that love in the Christian sense is always primarily directed at man's ideal spiritual self', p. 256.

pity. The saint, whom Zarathustra meets in the forest[224] (situated between mountain and valley), represents that weak, degenerative pity which had previously driven the madman into solitude: 'Why', said the saint, 'did I go into the forest and the desert? Was it not because I loved man all too much? Now I love God: man I do not love. Man is too imperfect a thing for me. Love of man would kill me' (Z.Prol.2). This 'saint's pity' for man is, according to Nietzsche, 'pity for the dirt of the human, all-too-human. And there are degrees and heights at which he feels pity itself as pollution, as dirt' (BGE.271). The prophet Zarathustra, who masks the madman in the same way as the madman's faith in the ascetic ideal 'masks the feeling of a profound weakness, of weariness, of old age, of declining powers' (GS.V.377), represents that strong, creative pity which wants to 'bring man a gift' (Z.Prol.2), a gift that will (miraculously) transform dirt into gold and the human into the suprahuman. This 'benevolent' pity of the stronger for the weaker is, according to Nietzsche, 'a pleasant stirring of the acquisitive drive at the sight of weakness' (GS.118). But, whether strong or weak, creative or degenerative, so far as each is the product of an ideal (otherworldly) love of man and thus symptomatic of faith in the ascetic ideal, both types of pity constitute '*practical* nihilism' (A.7).

Faith in the ascetic ideal is that which binds the first pope to the last pope and the last pope to the latest pope. Under the penetrating gaze of the old Zarathustra of Book IV, the credulous Zarathustra of the Prologue appears as one of those 'ambitious artists who like to pose as ascetics and priests but who are at bottom only tragic buffoons' (GM.III.26). And if, in the priestly figure of the last pope, Zarathustra sees only 'disguised affliction' (Z.IV.6), it is precisely in the 'refracted light' (GS.311) of this casuistic counterfeiting that the ironic Zarathustra sees in the prophetic Zarathustra not a great man, but 'only the actor of his own ideal' (BGE.97): the ascetic ideal. Just as the sceptical last pope, as 'a good servant' of his Lord, 'knows everything, and a number of things, also, that his master hides from himself' (Z.IV.6), so too does an ironic Zarathustra - at once master and servant of his ascetic idealism - know exactly what his animals artfully seek to hide from him.[225] He knows that adulterous relations between sly reason and promiscuous imagination, between 'sickness and will to power', stand at the door of his

---

224. See footnote 193.
225. See chapters 3 and 4.

faith in the *Übermensch* just as 'adultery stands at the door of [the last pope's] faith in [his god]' (ibid.).

When faith is lost, however, illusion slides into disillusion. In the same way as the last pope - unfree, unhappy, and redundant - sinks back into a meaningless void after the death of his god, the disenchanted latest pope languishes in cavernous despair after the godliness of his "godless" *Übermensch* is painfully, if ironically, discerned. How pertinent, therefore, is the last pope's query as to whether he or the latest pope has the greater claim to godlessness. On the grounds that '[h]e who loved and possessed him most [...] has now also lost him the most', the last pope argues that he is 'the more godless of us two' (Z.IV.6). But was not the latest pope *so* possessed of and *by* his love for the ideal in man that he felt compelled to descend to earth not simply as a prophet of idealism but rather as a god - an *übermenschliche* 'God of life, and poesy, and light'?[226] Like the setting sun, Zarathustra 'must descend into the depths [...] and bring light to the underworld' (Z.Prol.1), but no sooner has he arrived in the underworld than the divine sun of his "wisdom" is eclipsed by pity and the prophet Zarathustra unmasked to reveal, as 'the actor of his own ideal', the benighted madman. Like the young 'god from the orient [who] was hard and revengeful' (Z.IV.6), Zarathustra entered the underworld 'full of wrath; / His flaming robes streamed out beyond his heels, / And gave a roar, as if of earthly fire'.[227] But then, like the 'old and soft and mellow and pitying' god from the orient, who 'saw how *man* hung on the cross and could not endure it, [and whose] love for man became his hell and at last his death' (Z.IV.6), the prophet Zarathustra 'choked' on his 'saint's pity' for the "fallen" ropedancer, that is, for *man* who hangs by the rope 'stretched between beast and *Übermensch*' (Z.Prol.4).

This (elective) affinity between the latest pope and the late Christian god is made even more specific in 'The Last Pope' (Z.IV.6). Both were 'hidden god[s], full of secrecy'. Both judged man by an ideal 'of transcendence and the beyond' - for in spite of Zarathustra's earnest, if unrealistic, desire *not* 'to be the accuser of man' (ibid.), his tirades are those

---

226. Byron, *Childe Harold's Pilgrimage*, canto iv, l. 1442.
227. Keats, *Hyperion, A Fragment*, Book I, ll.213-15. Cf. the Zarathustran 'fire dog, which really speaks from the heart of the earth' (or so Zarathustra would have it), but which *really* is indistinguishable from that other fire dog: 'the hypocrite dog [... which] likes to speak with smoke and bellowing - to make believe [...] that it speaks out of the belly of things' (Z.II.18).

of '[t]he small man, *especially the poet* - how zealously he accuses life in words' (Z.III.13, emphasis added). Both 'snorter[s] of wrath' were 'indistinct' - 'They do not understand me', bemoaned the latest pope (Z.Prol.5). But most significantly, both 'had too many failures'. Indeed, in the light of these common weaknesses, which the old Zarathustra arguably perceives, one begins to grasp not only the decadence underlying the latest pope's emulation of the Christian god, but, more significantly, the ironic subtext of the tragic buffoon's declamation: 'Rather no god [than the Christian god], rather make destiny on one's own, rather be a fool, rather be a god oneself!' (Z.IV.6).

And if the last pope seeks comfort for his loss in 'a festival of pious memories and divine services' (Z.IV.6), is not Zarathustra's loss and consequent need for metaphysical comfort that much greater? Not only does Zarathustra stage his own nostalgic revue of his (former) piety and ascetic idealism, but, when his festival of impious pious memories has failed to exorcise his 'great longing, great disgust [and] great weariness', he then begs his needy higher men - who have come to *him* for comfort - to humour him with talk of 'my gardens, of my Isles of the Blest, of my beautiful new race' (Z.IV.11). To disparage the need for 'metaphysical comfort' - in Part I, an older, and supposedly wiser, Zarathustra had chided the young Zarathustra for having once 'cast his delusion beyond man, like all otherworldlings' (Z.I.3) - *and then* plead with his fellow decadents to satisfy precisely this vilified need for the 'holy lie' of otherworldly idealism, is blatant hypocrisy. This wilful act of self-deception discloses a loss so profound that self-denial[228] (the "cardinal sin" in Zarathustra's morality of life), with its implicit denial of the 'will to suffer' (GS.338) and the Dionysian 'will to life' (*TI* 'What I owe to the ancients' 5),[229] is the terrible price of immorality that Zarathustra is prepared to pay for relief (however brief) from suffering.

In this refracted light of 'faults and blunders, [... of] my delusion, my bad taste, my confusion, my tears, my vanity, my owlish seclusions, my contradictions' (GS.311), the latest pope no doubt sees himself as possessing a far greater claim to "godlessness" than the last pope. By playing fast and loose with the "shades" of piety and impiety - which, like the heavy clouds of

---

228. 'It is intoxicating joy for the sufferer to look away from his suffering and to forget himself' (Z.I.3).
229. '... the will to life rejoicing in its own inexhaustibility through the *sacrifice* of its highest types.'

a 'certain pessimistic gloom', hover ironically around the adjective 'godless' - Zarathustra commits a pious fraud when, notwithstanding his 'love [of] everything that is clear-eyed and honest of speech' (Z.IV.6), he refers to himself as 'the godless Zarathustra' (ibid.). Thus, if the latest pope is 'too weak' to lift the melancholy from the last pope's shoulders (Z.IV.6), it is simply because the melancholy and impotence of the former ('His is the melancholy of incapacity' *CW*.Postscript.2) is far greater than that of the latter. For the last pope is expected not only to resign himself to the death of *his* god, but (in "loving" memory, perhaps, of his late Christianity) to play the good Samaritan and resurrect with a litany of lies the god of him who is most godless: 'Speak to me of my gardens', begs Zarathustra, 'of my *Isles of the Blest*, of my beautiful new race' (Z.IV.11).

Bad Conscience, Shame, and Pity: The Ugliest Man

Upon entering the valley known to the shepherds as 'Serpent's Death', Zarathustra is 'plunged into dark recollections' (Z.IV.7). He recalls, no doubt, how during his former sojourn there he had discerned in the 'deathly-grey twilight' the pitiful face of 'the most solitary man' (Z.III.2.1); and we, the readers, recall how in the parable of the shepherd and his serpent the most solitary man had dramatized his longed-for victory over suffocating sorrow (Z.III.2.2). As legend teaches, sorrow is the bitter fruit of an hubristic lust for knowledge. 'The tree of knowledge [robs] us of the fruit of life':[230] just as Eve's desire to 'be as Gods, / Knowing both Good and Evil as they know', fails to 'leade, / To happier life';[231] just as Ulysses' 'grey spirit yearning in desire / To follow knowledge, like a sinking star, / Beyond the utmost bound of human thought' - a noble desire 'Not unbecoming men that strove with Gods' - finds itself smouldering in Dante's *Inferno* (canto xxvi) rather than effulgent in 'the Happy Isles';[232] just as Manfred's aspirations 'beyond the dwellers of the earth' teach him only what the Fates already know: 'That knowledge is not happiness';[233] just as Faust, 'the modern man of culture, [...] storms unsatisfied through all the faculties' until

---

230. Hamann, letter to Thomas Wizenmann, 22 July 1786, in Smith, p. 260.
231. John Milton, *Paradise Lost*, Book IX, ll. 708-9 and 696-7 respectively.
232. Tennyson, *Ulysses*, ll. 30-32, 53 and 63 respectively.
233. Byron, *Manfred*, II.iv.58-61.

finally 'he yearns for a shore in the wide and barren sea of knowledge' (*BT*.18); so Zarathustra, 'who lives so that he may know and who wants to know so that one day the *Übermensch* may live [... thereby] wills his own destruction' (Z.Prol.4)[234] - for 'he will yet *freeze to death* on the ice of knowledge!' (Z.III.6).

' "Why have knowledge at all?" ' (*BGE*.230). This is the riddle which lies behind the riddle posed by 'the vision of the most solitary man' (Z.III.2.1) and by the ghastly vision of the 'ugliest man' (Z.IV.7). As the dramatic encounters of the last five sections amply demonstrate, an audacious spirit of inquiry leads inexorably to a rancorous spirit of gravity. There we saw how the age of reason degenerates into the age of romantic pessimism (Z.IV.2); noble disgust for man into ignoble pity for man (Z.IV.3); a conscientious spirit into a penitential spirit (Z.IV.4); intellectual conscience into bad conscience (Z.IV.5); and faith into disillusion (Z.IV.6). Leaden-limbed and leaden-tongued, the *ressentiment*-riddled spirit of gravity stalks the pages of *Zarathustra*. He is the hunter who, 'hung with ugly truths, the *spoil* of his hunt, [...] return[s] gloomily from the forest of knowledge' (Z.II.13, emphasis added). He is the 'solemn [...] penitent of the spirit [... whose] ugliness' elicits from the Zarathustra of Part IV shame and pity rather than mocking laughter (ibid.). His voice is the 'gurgling, rasping' voice of bad conscience which has 'stammered for too long', and his feet are 'the biggest and heaviest feet [... which] tread all roads to death and destruction' (Z.IV.7). In short, the spirit of gravity *is* the ugliest man. And whereas, for Nietzsche, man is 'the most chronically and profoundly sick of all sick animals' (*GM*.III.13) and thus the ugliest of creatures ('It is to be doubted whether a traveller would find anywhere in the world regions uglier than the human face' *HH*.I.320), for Zarathustra, the ugliest man of all is to be found in the forest and desert regions of the world where penitents of the spirit scourge themselves with their bad knowledge and where erstwhile shepherds choke to death on the heavy, black 'serpent of knowledge' (Z.I.22.1).

Knowledge, like Christianity, is 'a hangman's metaphysics' (*TI* 'The Four Great Errors' 7), demanding of its martyrs the 'sacrifice of all freedom, all pride, all self-confidence of the spirit' (*BGE*.46). But whereas the Christian's sacrifice is imposed from without, that of the seeker after truth is self-induced. Paradoxically, it is precisely the free, proud and bold spirit of

---

234. Deliberate misconstruction of *untergehen* here.

the genuine 'hero in quest of truth' (Z.I.20), rather than the accommodating will to popular "truth" of the so-called 'famous wise men' (Z.II.8), that falls victim to the very freedom, pride and boldness that it seeks to validate. Unlike the celebrated "wise" men who, as economists of truth guided by the law of supply and demand, are revered by those whom they serve, the enlightened man, a gruesome sacrifice on the altar of truth, is 'despised and rejected by men, / a man of sorrows, and acquainted with sickness, / and as one from whom men hide their faces' (Isa. 53:3). Like Christ, prophetically 'so disfigured [...] that he seemed no longer human' (Isa. 52:14), the ugliest man, 'shaped like a man, but scarce like a man, a thing unspeakable' (Z.IV.7), symbolizes the ugliness of truth. If knowledge of truth is suffering and if 'everything that suffers, everything that hangs on the cross, is divine' (A.51), then truth is a 'hangman-god' (Z.IV.5.1) and the paradoxical symbol of Christ on the cross another formulation of the riddle lurking behind the riddle of the ugliest man: 'What is the meaning of all will to truth?' (GM.III.27). 'Despoild of Innocence, of Faith, of Bliss',[235] the crucified Christ, like the ugliest man, hangs on the cross of knowledge, and Zarathustra, who has 'reaped disgust as [his] single truth' (Z.IV.5.2), sees in the face of the ugliest man the unspeakable fate of one who had lived for knowledge and who once had faith in the blissful innocence and majestic beauty of the Übermensch. Faced with this ugliest of truths, Zarathustra's pride blushes for shame, his hope for man collapses into pity for man, and his all-consuming disgust - at man, at knowledge, but most unbearably of all, at self-knowledge - produces 'the gloominess and the related sorrow of bad conscience' (GS.53).

Bad Conscience

'What is *revenge upon the witness*?' (Z.IV.7). This is the rhetorical riddle which the ugliest man puts to Zarathustra, and which the latter has no difficulty, other than reluctance, in solving. Bad conscience is the riddle which the ugliest man represents, the bad conscience of those 'great thinkers' (GS.53) whose honest will to truth, 'foul'd in Knowledge's dark Prison house',[236] has finally taken revenge upon itself. Truth is not beauty,[237] 'for

---

235. Milton, *Paradise Lost*, Book IX, l. 411 (deliberate misappropriation of Milton's description of the fallen Eve).
236. Blake, *Then She Bore Pale Desire*.
237. Despite the "statement" made by a Grecian urn: ' "Beauty is truth, truth beauty" ', Keats, *Ode on a Grecian Urn*, l. 49.

the power of beauty will sooner transform honesty from what it is to a bawd than the force of honesty can translate beauty into his likeness.'[238] This violation of honesty out of love for the beautiful lie occurs when bad conscience takes revenge upon intellectual conscience. And when Zarathustra witnesses his own prostitution of honesty - 'that youngest of virtues' (Z.I.3) - his fate, in common with all higher men, is tragically sealed. With 'unblinking eye and the glance of eternity' (Z.I.14), this omniscient god within Zarathustra witnesses with horror its own corruption, for is not the violation of innocent purity the ugliest and most unbearable sight of all? With eyes which 'pierce like arrows thoughts and thoughts behind thoughts' (Z.II.20), riddles and riddles behind riddles, Zarathustra's intellectual conscience scrutinizes the masquerade of unadulterated pessimism: how rulers serve (Z.IV.3), and scientists lack conscience (Z.IV.4), and artists lie (Z.IV.5), and godless popes commit pious frauds (Z.IV.6). But at the sight of the unmasked ugliest man, of his own 'corruption [and] ruination' (BGE.269), Zarathustra is overcome with the pity which has been welling up within him since his first encounter with the two kings: self-pity.

Self-pity is the ultimate sin to which the ugliest man seduces Zarathustra: pity for the loss of his former freedom, pride and self-confidence. Felled by self-pity, Zarathustra 'sank down all at once, like an oak-tree that has long withstood many woodcutters' (Z.IV.7). In the Old Testament, the oak-tree symbolizes human pride,[239] and it is to this symbolism that the narrator of Zarathustra arguably refers. Honesty is the arch-enemy of human pride, and it is this purest of virtues which distinguishes the enlightened man from the "wise" man and, in a darker, more sinister fashion, the ugliest man from the higher men whom Zarathustra has thus far encountered. Unlike the soothsayer whose bad tidings flash without trace across his face; and the king on the right whose disgust is, to some extent, kept in check by the king on the left; and the conscientious man of spirit whose shallow scientific rationalism saves him from the abysmal depths of pessimism; and the sorcerer whose vanity paints over the ugliness of disease; and the last pope whose blindness in one eye impairs the divining powers of intellectual conscience; the ugliest man is the

---

238. Shakespeare, Hamlet, III.i.111-114.
239. Isa. 2:3; Zech. 11:2.

The Decadence of Christianity   123

abhorrent face of intellectual conscience - he *is* the spirit of gravity. As the personification of bad conscience come to consciousness, the ugliest man has the edge on all the other woodcutters who would seduce Zarathustra to self-pity. As the worm of bad conscience, which has eaten its way through the long-enduring oak, this particular woodcutter knows precisely where the wood is most rotten and thus where best to strike. Just as in Isaiah the felling of the oak-tree symbolizes the moment when 'human pride lower[s] its eyes [and] the arrogance of men [is] humbled' (Isa. 2:11), so the felling of the 'wise, proud Zarathustra' by the 'malicious lightning eyes' (Z.IV.5.1) of the ugliest woodcutter, marks the moment of truth when Zarathustra's pity for man collapses into self-pity, and his pride blushes for shame.

Shame

Shame is symptomatic of 'the morbid pampering and moralizing [... of] animal "man" ' (*GM*.II.7), and Nietzsche traces this emasculation of man back to Socrates and Plato. To these famous "wise" men Nietzsche attributes not the source but rather the principal agency of man's decline. For their own part, these 'declining types' are merely 'symptoms of [a] decay' (*TI* 'The Problem of Socrates' 2) which in turn can be traced back to the fall of proud reason - reason which, like Lucifer, was 'once fairer than the light.'[240] Confounded by the inscrutability of 'the dark desires' (ibid. 10), and reasoning that if 'the instincts want to play the tyrant; one must devise a *counter-tyrant* who is stronger' (ibid.9), proud reason turns tyrant and projects the shame of its rational impotence onto the irrational omnipotence of the instincts. Translated back into the history of man, Socrates' hypocritical faith in reason can be seen to be a necessary one. Thrusting with the syllogism (ibid.7) and fencing with the dialectic (ibid.8), Socrates not only revelled in a new and sophisticated form of *agon* (ibid.) from which his instincts were by their very nature excluded, but found thereby 'his means, his cure, his personal trick of self-preservation' (ibid.9). Socratic rationalism provided reason, on the one hand, with the tools of its tyranny and, on the other - via its insidious 'equation of reason = virtue = happiness' (ibid.4) - with its "moral" justification. In 'that bizarrest of equations' (ibid), reason was simultaneously defiled and deified, sacrificed and sanctified. But this diadem on the head of the ugliest of sages (ibid.3)

---

240. Blake, *Then She Bore Pale Desire*.

was designed to serve the same purpose as the crown worn by the ugliest man (Z.IV.11): to disguise the shame of self-knowledge. Revenge on the reflective witness is the meaning of all will to truth, for, like 'all great things', an audacious will to truth 'bring[s] about [its] own destruction through an act of self-transcendence' (GM.III.27). And just as bad conscience is a form of revenge directed at knowledge but in actuality wrought upon intellectual conscience, so Socratic 'dialectics [is ...] a form of revenge' (TI 'The Problem of Socrates' 7) directed at the instincts but wrought against reason.

Shame is the misbegotten and parricidal child of pride, and just as the shame of bad conscience murders the noble pride of intellectual conscience, so the 'petty shame' (Z.III.14) of the mind's proud but 'petty reason' murders the 'great reason' of the body (Z.I.4). This degeneration of Sophia into sophist, reason into rationalist, and honesty into casuistry, marks the turning point in the history of man. Henceforth, the pitiful face of the ugliest man - with its 'weary pessimistic glance, [its] mistrust of the riddle of life, [and its] icy No of disgust with life' - will increase 'man's shame *before man*' (GM.II.7). 'Shame, shame, shame', as Zarathustra teaches in his denunciation 'of the compassionate', is 'the history of man! / And that is why he who is noble bids himself not to shame: he bids himself to be ashamed before all who suffer.' (Z.II.3) And yet, as his encounter with the ugliest man seems to demonstrate, by withholding his helping hand and his pitying 'look and word' (Z.IV.7) from the ugliest man, Zarathustra simply increases his own shame and his own pity, that is to say, shame before himself and pity for himself. At what price moral integrity? To pity 'the shame of the great sufferer' (ibid.) at the moral cost of seriously wounding the latter's already 'sorely injured pride' (Z.II.3) is practical nihilism; but to feel shame before the sufferer at the even greater moral cost of paralyzed pride (Z.IV.7) and crippling self-pity is impractical nihilism. Surely, the increase in shame and loss of pride in the pitied ugliest man would be negligible in comparison to that accruing to the shamed Zarathustra. But moral integrity finally wins out and Zarathustra, taking the advice of the late saint, resolves to 'take something off [suffering humanity] and bear it with them' (Z.Prol.2) rather than bestow upon mankind his gift of the *Übermensch*. But in offering himself as *satisfactio vicaria*, Zarathustra sacrifices his noble pride to ignoble shame, his shame before man to shame before himself, and his liberating pity - 'However powerfully pity affects us, in a certain sense it nevertheless delivers us from the primal suffering of the world' (*BT*.21) - to paralyzing self-pity.

Pity

Zarathustra's 'greatest danger' (*GS*.271)[241] lies in self-pity. With the crucifixion of the higher man, and thus his own tragic fate, continually before his eyes (*BGE*.269), Zarathustra suffers from a severe case of over(empathic)-identification. This 'species of sympathy', which 'is nothing other than an illness', is akin to 'a Christian hypochondria which assails those solitary, religiously inclined people who have the suffering and death of Christ incessantly before their eyes' (*HH*.I.47). In both cases, pity is a powerful, if morally (in the non-Christian sense) deleterious, palliative: immoral because pity's will to power is a will 'to abolish suffering' (*BGE*.225), and because suffering, at least in Zarathustra's view, is something divine. Pity should be a crucifixion rather than an alleviation of pain, and pitying hands should sooner be nailed to the cross (*Z*.Prol.3) than be free to throw alms to those who suffer (*Z*.Prol.2). 'Is not pity the cross on which he who loves man is nailed?' (*Z*.Prol.3), asks Zarathustra, and is not his later pity for the ugliest man - a pity withheld - precisely such a crucifixion?

In Zarathustra's first sermon to the people, he discourses on 'the hour of the great contempt' (*Z*.Prol.3) when a new morality of integrity will vanquish the old Christian 'morality of pity' (*GM*.Pref.6). And, as he is to discover in Book IV, this morality of integrity is indeed a hangman's metaphysics. The hour of Zarathustra's great contempt and moral integrity is the hour of his crucifixion: if ironic distance has held Zarathustra's 'hypochondria' at bay and delivered him from the soothsayer's pessimism, the king on the right's disgust, the conscientious man of spirit's lack of conscience, the sorcerer's counterfeiting, and the pope's metaphysical need, the repulsive sight of the ugliest man - representing the overpowering immediacy of bad conscience - precludes any contrivance of distance. The ugliest woodcutter not only fells the lofty Zarathustra but nails the latter's pity for the 'suffering, doubting, despairing, drowning, freezing' (*Z*.IV.7) higher men to the cross of self-pity. And yet, as the ugliest man explains, Zarathustra's crucifixion by the vengeful hand of his own bad conscience

---

241. '*Where lies your greatest danger?* - In pity.'

had to happen because his proud, omniscient and ironic intellectual conscience

> ... looked with eyes that saw *everything* - he saw the depths and abysses of man, all his hidden disgrace and ugliness.
> His pity knew no shame: he crept into my foulest corners. This most curious, over-intrusive, over-compassionate one had to die.
> He always saw *me*: on such a witness I would have revenge - or cease to live myself.
> The god who saw everything, *even man*: this god had to die! Man could not endure that such a witness should live.

Thus spoke the self-pitying voice of bad conscience.

With the felling of the oak, the mighty ones are brought low. Just as in Zechariah '[t]he wailing of the shepherds is heard; their glorious pastures have been ruined' (Zech. 11:3), so too in *Zarathustra* the distressed cry of the ruined higher man resounds through the valley which the shepherds call 'Serpent's Death'. Brought low by bad knowledge and bad conscience, by disillusion and despair, the fallen higher man, like fallen reason, seeks redemption from self-knowledge; for if suffering is divine, the desire for 'absence of suffering' (*GM*.III.17) is quintessentially human. '*Redemption itself, total hypnotization and repose*', is far from being a 'liberation from all illusion', and even further from being "knowledge", "truth" and "being" (ibid.). On the contrary, redemption is a need engendered by knowledge, truth and being, and is manufactured by the artisans of illusion. Not 'through virtue and moral improvement' is redemption attained (ibid.), but through 'sly' invention and 'slippery' circumvention: only the 'fluttering' eagle of imagination, the 'crawling' serpent of reason, and the occasional buffonic 'leap' of irony can deliver man from his suffering. Accordingly, Zarathustra advises the ugliest man to seek repose in the cavernous workshop of the mind 'where *ideals are manufactured*' (*GM*.I.14):

> My cave is big and deep and has many corners: there the most hidden may find his hiding-place; and close by there are a hundred sly and slippery ways for crawling, fluttering and leaping creatures [...]
> And speak first and foremost with my animals! The proudest animal and the cleverest animal - they may well be the right counsellors for us both! (Z.IV.7)

Indeed! For an honestly reflective higher man afflicted with bad conscience, 'secret shame' (ibid.), and self-pity, what better physicians than shrewd reason and proud imagination? Between them, the eagle and serpent will transform bad conscience into good, secret shame into posturing pride, and self-pity into self-confidence.

Meditation, Benevolence, and Philanthropy: The Voluntary Beggar

And so the pilgrim's regress continues. Re-viewing yet another 'sun of humanity' (*D*.575) sink into roseate remembrance as he rounds the final cape of dashed hope, Zarathustra must wonder whether it will not be said of him one day 'that [he] too, *steering westward, hoped to reach an India* - but that it was [his] fate to be wrecked against infinity' (ibid.). For above all, Zarathustra knows 'from the adventures of his own most authentic experience how a discoverer and conqueror of the ideal feels' (*GS*.V.382). As a discoverer of the ideal, he knows how it feels to believe, with the soothsayer, in strong wines of wisdom;[242] with the two kings, in a nobility of the future; with the conscientious man of spirit, in the absolute authority of scientific explanation; with the sorcerer, in the heroic search for truth; with the old pope, in otherworldly idealism; with the ugliest man, in the zealous pursuit of knowledge to the point of martyrdom; and now, with the voluntary beggar, in the redemptive properties of the contemplative life: it feels good. But when it comes to 'conquering' the ideal, to exposing the nihilism and *ressentiment* which *lie* at the root of this optimism, then, precisely because faith in the ascetic ideal has engendered such a profound feeling of (misplaced) optimism, the correspondent feelings of disillusion, self-deception, and profound pessimism *a*ffectively reduce to pyrrhic victories every one of Zarathustra's so-called conquests of the ideal. It is this dual sense of victory and loss, of health and sickness, that characterizes what Nietzsche calls the '*new* health' (ibid.) and colours Zarathustra's blush of "health" with a decidedly hectic hue.

Rumination and self-parody are the means by which Zarathustra maintains a precarious balance between a will to illusion and a will to truth, between life-preserving nihilism and suicidal nihilism. Only the bathos of ironic distance saves him from sinking, along with each of his ideals ('Not

---

242. Is this metaphor possibly related to the dictum: '*in vino veritas*'?

only one sun had set for me' Z.III.2.1), into the abyss of nihilistic pessimism. But although this obsessive reopening and poking of old wounds - for the sake of proving the veracity of Nietzsche's oft-cited military maxim: 'What does not kill me makes me stronger' (*TI* 'Maxims and Arrows' 8) - has much of the machismo about it, doing battle with fallen heroes is less a sign of courageous strength than of 'sickness unto death'; most of all, however, it is symptomatic of *ressentiment*. And when cankerous *ressentiment* turns the 'memory [into] a festering wound' (*EH* 'Why I am so wise' 6), the psychological effects are not dissimilar to the physiological ones arising from a stomach ulcer. Thus, the patient: 'digests less well' (*EH* '*Thus Spoke Zarathustra*' 5) - his past deeds "repeat" on him; 'does not like to move' (ibid.) - apathy and despondency incapacitate him; and 'is all too susceptible to feeling chills as well as mistrust' (ibid.) - the frostbite of solitude and chilling self-doubt leading to the following self-diagnosis: 'Anybody who, in intercourse with men, does not occasionally glisten in all the colours of affliction, green and grey with revulsion, satiety, sympathy, gloominess and loneliness, is certainly not a man of higher tastes; assuming, however, that he does not take upon himself all this weight and aversion (*Unlust*) voluntarily, that he forever avoids it and remains [...] quietly and proudly hidden in his castle, then one thing is certain: he is not made, nor predestined, for knowledge' (*BGE*.26).[243]

It was while he was suffering from these symptoms - (a) a pathological preoccupation with his past deeds; (b) an inability to free himself from the rut of recollection; and (c) a hypersensitivity to the chill of loneliness and self-doubt - that Nietzsche wrote Part IV of *Zarathustra*. As he himself confesses in his "*auto*biography":[244] 'Except for those ten-day works [that

---

243. Cf. Plato's criticism of those men possessed of 'the highest forms of knowledge ... remaining in the upper world, and refusing to return again to the prisoners in the cave below and share their labours and rewards, whether trivial or serious' *Republic* 519 d.
244. I stress the Greek word 'auto' because *Ecce Homo* is a highly idiosyncratic work reflecting the many and diverse moods of the author, moods which range from the ironic, hyperbolic and "poetic" (in the derogatory Zarathustran sense - see Z.II.17) to the melancholic, sincere and confessional. Young's severe criticism of what he describes as 'in many ways a mendacious, deluded book' (p. 2), is a salutary reminder to all those who would seek a degree of scholarly objectivity in Nietzsche's purported philosophical autobiography: 'Nietzsche's retrospective self-descriptions, considered from the point of view of scholarly accuracy, are deeply unreliable [...] The aim [of *Ecce Homo*] is not to provide an accurate mirroring of the textual facts

is, Parts I to III of *Zarathustra*], the years during and above all *after Zarathustra* were [marked by] a crisis without equal' (*EH* '*Thus Spoke Zarathustra*' 5). Part IV falls within and deals specifically with that period of crisis following upon the completion of Parts I to III, and it was in such a state of mind that Nietzsche 'once sensed the proximity of a herd of cows, even before I saw it, because of the return of milder and philanthropic thoughts: *they* had warmth' (ibid.). Thus, in the opening of 'The Voluntary Beggar' (Z.IV.8), the reader finds Zarathustra not only suffering the same symptoms as his maker, but experiencing the same compensatory[245] sensations:

> When Zarathustra had left the ugliest man, he was frozen and he felt his solitude: for much that was cold and lonely passed through his mind so that even his limbs had become cold. But as he climbed on and on, now up, now down [...] all at once he became warmer and more cheerful again.
> 'What has happened to me?' he asked himself. 'Something warm and living refreshes me that must be nearby.
> 'Already I am less alone; unconscious (*unbewußt*) companions and brothers roam about me, their warm breath touches my soul.'[246]
> But as he looked about him and sought the comforter of his loneliness: behold, there were cows standing together on a hillock; their proximity and smell had warmed his heart. But these cows seemed to listen eagerly to one that spoke, and took no heed of him who approached.

---

but rather to create (by the discovery of hints, undertones, "real" intentions, almost utterances lurking between lines, and by obscuring, where necessary, what is said on the lines) a work of art, an *aesthetically* convincing account of the intellectual and spiritual life of the man behind the works [...] As Nietzsche-commentator, then, Nietzsche is to be viewed with greater distrust than most'. See Julian Young, *Nietzsche's Philosophy of Art* (Cambridge: Cambridge University Press, 1992), pp. 29-30. Williams is similarly sceptical: '[Nietzsche's] presentation of himself, of his deepest and most heart-felt emotions is contrived in a far more ambiguous and teasing way than is commonly understood'. See W D Williams, in Solomon (ed.), p. 102. See also Reinhardt, p. 219.

245. The psychological definition of 'compensate' is of particular relevance here: 'offset deficiency or frustration by developing another characteristic' (*COD*).

246. Both Kaufmann and Hollingdale substantially weaken the anagogic force of this sentence by rendering the adjective '*unbewußt*' (unconscious) as 'unknown' (*unbekannt*). On my reading, however, Zarathustra is here concerned with warm, inchoate thoughts which have not yet entered consciousness.

The man whom Zarathustra discovers preaching to the cows is, of course, the voluntary beggar; and if the cows represent 'the return of milder and more philanthropic thoughts', then the voluntary beggar arguably represents the philanthropic thinker of such thoughts. On one level, this thinker is clearly Zarathustra, but on another, the voluntary beggar who converses with animals - here referred to by Zarathustra as his 'brothers'[247] - is just as clearly a figurative allusion to St Francis of Assisi. But while the similarities between Zarathustra and St Francis are certainly striking, it is likely that Zarathustra's comparative allusion is intended more as a suggestion and aspiration than a felt and acknowledged identity. For, upon closer inspection, and with one or two exceptions, these apparent similarities are found to conceal intrinsic dissimilarities of which Zarathustra would doubtless have been aware.

Meditation

Zarathustra and St Francis both stress the importance of meditation (symbolized in *Zarathustra* by ruminating cows) for the edification of the individual soul and, by exemplary and pedagogic extension, the collective soul. But whilst, for St Francis, meditation was in some measure a means to subsequent action, for the Zarathustra of Part IV, it is an impediment to action.[248] In Zarathustra's case, chewing the cud is symptomatic of indigestion, that is, of an inability to have done with the past.

After having completed *Zarathustra*, the protagonist of Part IV suffers from 'the *rancune* of what is great: everything great, a work, a deed, once accomplished, immediately turns against the man who did it. By doing it he has become *weak*; he can no longer endure his deed, he can no longer face it' (*EH 'Thus Spoke Zarathustra'* 5). An unconditional will to truth forces into reluctant and volatile co-existence practice and theory, the real and the ideal, intellectual conscience and bad conscience. As 'physician and patient in one' (*HH*.II.Pref.5), Zarathustra must undergo the same examination as that

---

247. '[St Francis] was wont to call all created things his brothers and sisters'. See Thomas of Celano in Otto Karrer (ed.), *The Little Flowers, Legends, and Lauds: St Francis of Assisi and others*, trans. N Wydenbruck (London: Sheed & Ward, 1984), p. 43.
248. 'There is from the first something *unhealthy* in priestly aristocracies and in the habits ruling in them which turn them away from action and alternate between brooding and emotional explosions' (*GM*.I.6).

to which he subjects others, for the same will to truth that in Parts I to III disclosed the nihilism that masquerades as idealism - the *ressentiment* of the otherworldly (I), the asceticism of knowledge (II), and the escapism of solitude (III) - compels the Zarathustra of Part IV to recognize in himself the same insidious nihilism. Thus, in Part I, the 'conqueror of the ideal' denounced 'the despisers of the body' (Z.I.4) who 'hearkened to preachers of death' (Z.I.3), and exhorted man to hearken instead 'to the voice of the healthy body' (ibid.). But is not Zarathustra's masochistic scab-picking in Part IV indicative of self-loathing, is not his incessant harking-back to irrevocable past deeds merely contempt for the self that can 'no longer do that which it most loves to do: to create beyond itself' (Z.I.4)[249] In Part II, he proclaimed that although 'all deep knowledge flows cold' (Z.II.8), it must yet learn 'to smile' (Z.II.13). But is not Zarathustra so chilled to the marrow, frozen to death on the ice of knowledge, that he can no longer run 'with warm feet and warm thoughts [...] to the sunny corner of [his] mount of olives' (Z.III.6)? For unlike St Francis, who 'deliberately did not see the mob for the men',[250] Zarathustra's sunny thoughts are clouded over precisely with disgust for 'mob pride' and for 'the slow rebellion of the mob' which has produced 'mob above [and] mob below' (Z.IV.8).[251] Lastly, in Part III, notwithstanding his pæan to the still and silent mountain-air of solitude - which delivers him from the 'noise and bad breath', the 'poisonous flies', and the loneliest loneliness, of the market-place - Zarathustra maintained that his 'greatest danger always lay in indulgence and sufferance' (Z.III.9). But is not hypersensitivity his greatest danger: 'the absurd sensitivity of the skin to small stings, a kind of helplessness before everything small [...] caused by the enormous squandering of all defensive energies which is a presupposition of every *creative* deed, [of] every deed that issues from one's most authentic, innermost, nethermost regions' (*EH* '*Thus Spoke Zarathustra*' 5)?[252]

Meditation, which is a sign of health for the man of action, is for the man of inaction a sign of decadence. 'Sitting on a stone before his cave and gazing silently out' (Z.IV.1), Zarathustra appears to possess the serenity of Buddha, but behind his meditative gaze the penitential spirit rages.

---

249. See symptom (a).
250. G K Chesterton, *St Francis of Assisi* (London: Hodder and Stoughton, 1924), p. 110.
251. See symptoms (b) and (c).
252. See symptom (c).

Embroiled in interminable hostilities with 'It was', a fragmented, *ressentiment-riddled* and enfeebled Zarathustra struggles to 'will it thus! Thus shall I will it' (Z.II.20). Thwarted, however, by the resentful 'spirit of revenge', Zarathustra's 'creative will' (ibid.) suffocates on recollection (*BGE*.282) and thereby loses the ability 'to create beyond itself' (Z.I.4).

Benevolence

In a utopian vision, Nietzsche envisaged meditation as a customary daily activity that would transform every day into 'a festival of attained and attainable dignity of human reason: a new and fuller blossoming and efflorescence of the teacher-ideal, in which the priest, the artist and the physician, the man of knowledge and the man of wisdom, are blended into one, so that their separate virtues also necessarily appear as one complete virtue in their teaching itself, in their delivery [and] their methods' (*HH*.II 'Opinions and Maxims' 180). It is a vision which Zarathustra holds in common with St Francis and which both ascetics endeavoured to put into practice: St Francis, who 'looked to deeds rather than to discourses and doctrines',[253] by example, and Zarathustra, who 'sp[oke] to his pupils differently than to himself' (Z.II.20), by doctrines and discourses.

Zarathustra baptizes this consummate and 'highest virtue' the 'bestowing virtue' (Z.I.22), and its pre-eminent position in Zarathustra's table of values is evidenced by the fact that *Zarathustra* opens and closes with its putative hero overburdened with the fruit of many years' meditation and anxious to bestow the same upon the benighted multitudes below. In the Prologue, Zarathustra pictures himself as the ideal teacher 'whose soul is lavish, who neither wants nor returns thanks; for he always gives and keeps nothing for himself' (Z.Prol.4); who will 'bestow and distribute until the wise amongst men rejoice again in their folly, and the poor in their riches' (Z.Prol.1). But already in Part I, the visionary scope of Zarathustra's ideal has been greatly diminished by the people's mocking response to his sermon composed on the mount, and it is to a reduced flock that Zarathustra teaches 'the friend and his overflowing heart [...] in whom the world stands complete, a cup of goodness - the creative friend, who always has a complete world to bestow' (Z.I.16) and whose bestowing virtue 'compel[s] all things to come to you and into you, that they may flow back from your fountain as

---

253. Thomas of Celano, in Karrer (ed.), p. 48.

gifts of your love' (Z.I.22.1). By Part II, however, Zarathustra's fountain has all but dried up for want of thanks and requited love; deeply resenting 'the joy of the receiver', which he has never known ('They take from me: but do I yet touch their souls? A gulf stands between giving and receiving' Z.II.9), Zarathustra 'would like to rob those to whom I give' (ibid.) as recompense for the unkindness of man's ingratitude. By Part III, he has abandoned man altogether; and yet, that which sustains him in his solitude is the desperate hope 'That the lonely height may not always be lonely and content with itself; that the mountain may descend to the valley and the wind of the heights to the lowlands' (Z.III.10.2). Finally, at the close of Part IV, notwithstanding Zarathustra's (make-)belief that he is 'ripe' enough to return to man and to bestow upon him his "virtue"; notwithstanding 'the sign' and the glorious *vision* of a radiant Zarathustra emerging from his dark cave, 'glowing and strong, like a morning sun emerging from behind dark mountains' (Z.IV.20); the image that obstinately lingers on is the penultimate one - that of Zarathustra sitting upon 'the great stone and meditat[ing]' (ibid.) ... and meditating ... and meditating.

This desire for 'hearty help, benefaction and benevolence [combined] with the drive to clean and clear thinking' (*HH*.II 'Opinions and Maxims' 196) is satisfied in the life of St Francis. For Zarathustra, however, it remains an unfulfilled desire, expressing instead the paradoxical impulse that drives him 'now up, now down' (Z.IV.8): to solitude and society, to thought and deed, to affirmation and disgust, to the warmth of philanthropic thoughts and the silent, gloomy 'wretchedness of all givers' (Z.II.9). In the figure of the voluntary beggar - 'who was ashamed of his riches and of the rich, and fled to the poorest that he might give them his abundance and his heart. But they received him not'; who thereby learned 'how it is harder to give well than to take well, and that to give well is an *art*, the ultimate, craftiest master-art of kindness' (Z.IV.8) - Zarathustra perceives his own failure as a teacher. And this failure, marked by the scoffing crowds, recalls and reflects the difficult beginnings of St Francis' ministry: 'they covered him with insults, calling him a fool and a madman, and even throwing dirt and stones at him.'[254] But whereas the 'Little Poor Man' scorned the ridicule of the people and continued to bestow and to distribute until the poor rejoiced in their riches, Zarathustra's 'hand and heart [... grew] callous through nothing but distributing' (Z.II.9), for he craved love and gratitude more than he

---

254. Giovanni di Ceprano in Karrer (ed.), p. 10.

desired benefaction and benevolence. And whereas St Francis' separate virtues were blended into one complete virtue and were reflected in the method and delivery of his teaching,[255] Zarathustra's cup of contempt and *ressentiment* ranneth over into his discourse while 'radiant eyes and a benevolent smile [supplied] the kind of applause rendered to the whole great universal comedy of existence' (*HH*.II 'Opinions and Maxims' 24) - a black comedy in which Zarathustra's 'rose-wreath crown' of laughter (Z.IV.13.20) is set about with thorns. In short, while St Francis can arguably be seen as an almost perfect representative of the 'teacher-ideal', Zarathustra remains a teacher of the ideal.

Philanthropy

As mentioned earlier in this section, there are, however, two unequivocal points of affinity between Zarathustra and St Francis, and these concern the precise nature of their philanthropy and affirmative stance towards life. In respect of the former, there is a deep affinity between the specific type of philanthropy espoused by both missionaries. In his book, *St Francis of Assisi*, G K Chesterton distinguishes between the literal and received sense of philanthropist: 'A lover of men is very nearly the opposite of a philanthropist; indeed the pedantry of the Greek word carries something like a satire on itself. A philanthropist may be said to love anthropoids.'[256] The point that Chesterton is making here is that St Francis (like Zarathustra) was not a lover of mankind, of the all-too-human Everyman, but of that which is highest in man. It is precisely this love of the higher man - a love which lies at the root of Zarathustra's 'misanthropy'[257] - which led Chesterton to make the following analogy (which is especially, if not more, applicable to

---

255. 'How fair, radiant and glorious was the sinlessness of his life, the simplicity of his words, the purity of his heart [...] To this must be added his angelic appearance, the charm of his manner, his natural gentleness, the kindliness of his admonitions, the loyalty with which he treated anything told him in confidence, the wisdom of his counsel, the energy of his actions and his general lovableness [...] // He was a man of great eloquence; the expression of his face was gay and kindly, equally free of torpor as of arrogance'. See Thomas of Celano, in Karrer (ed.), p. 43.
256. Chesterton, *St Francis of Assisi*, p. 14.
257. 'Misanthropy is the result of an all too covetous love of man and "cannibalism"; but who asked you to swallow men like oysters, my Prince Hamlet?' (*GS*.167).

Zarathustra): 'But as St Francis did not love humanity but men, so he did not love Christianity but Christ.'[258]

With regard to affirmation, just as St Francis 'strove to live always in jubilation of heart' and, above all, to avoid 'the deadly sickness of despondency ("*accidia*")',[259] so too did Zarathustra canonize laughter (Z.IV.13.18) and strive towards 'painlessness [and] the removal of apathy' (*HH*.II 'Opinions and Maxims' 187). Theirs was no Dionysian affirmation, however, for at noontide, when the demon of *accidia* is said to tempt 'wandering monks and solitaries',[260] neither was so well-disposed either to himself or his life 'to crave nothing more fervently' than the eternal recurrence of this greatest of weights (*GS*.341). But, to be fair, neither did they hurl themselves to the ground and gnash their teeth (ibid.). Rather, they sought refuge in Apollonian artifice: St Francis in prayer,[261] and Zarathustra in whatever his hermit's pets happened to conjure up for him. And it is on the basis of this Apollonian affinity, as it were, that Zarathustra divines the voluntary beggar's love of honey - the need, that is, to sweeten the meditative life with either prayer or parody and to 'abstain from all heavy thoughts that inflate the heart' Z.IV.8). Accordingly, Zarathustra invites him to meet with his animals, to speak with them 'of the happiness of animals', and to partake thereby of his 'new [...] golden honey [...] cold as

---

258. Chesterton, p.14.
259. Thomas of Celano, in Karrer (ed.), p. 53.
260. 'Acedia, or Spiritual Tedium [... is] that which the Greeks call acedia, and which we may describe as tedium or perturbation of the heart. It is akin to dejection and especially felt by wandering monks and solitaries, a persistent and obnoxious enemy to such as dwell in the desert, disturbing the monk especially about midday, like a fever mounting at a regular time, and bringing its highest tide of inflammation at definite accustomed hours to the sick soul. And so some of the Fathers declare it to be the demon of noontide which is spoken of in the 90th Psalm.// When this besieges the unhappy mind, it begets aversion from the place, boredom with one's cell, and scorn and contempt for one's brethren, whether they be dwelling with one or some way off, as careless and unspiritually-minded persons. Also, towards any work that may be done within the confines of our own lair, we become listless and inert [...] we sigh and complain that bereft of sympathetic fellowship we have no spiritual fruit; and bewail ourselves as empty of all spiritual profit, abiding vacant and useless in this place; and we that could guide others and be of value to multitudes have edified no man, enriched no man with our precept and example.' See *The Spear of Gold: Revelations of the Mystics*, ed. H A Reinhold (London: Burns Oates, 1947), p. 119.
261. Thomas of Celano, in Karrer (ed.), p. 53.

136 Zarathustra contra Zarathustra

ice' (ibid.), chilled so as to sweeten the ascetic's bad conscience without cloying his good.

Penitent of the Spirit: The Shadow

> *Lear*: Who is it that can tell me who I am?
> *Fool*: Lear's shadow.[262]

The romantic device of *self* (as opposed to ego)-projection - which, as the last seven sections have sought to demonstrate, Zarathustra deploys to greatest dramatic effect in his psychic encounters with the seven higher men - culminates in Zarathustra's confrontation with his spectral shadow-self. An ancient symbol, revived and popularized by the nineteenth century *Schauerroman*,[263] a man's shadow was believed to represent his soul;[264] while the deathly portentous wraith of equally primitive belief was clearly a related superstition (a mythological correlation which might be deemed to find its etymological analogue in the common roots of 'shadow' and 'shade'). In any event, the connection between his shadow and imminent death, between his melancholy soul and abject despair, is one that Zarathustra arguably made. Pursued by his 'long-legged' (Z.IV.9) shadow, Zarathustra takes to his heels in a manner reminiscent of Tristram Shandy's comic flight from 'that death-looking, long-striding scoundrel of a scare-sinner'.[265] Unlike Tristram, however, Zarathustra does not fear for his material body but for his immaterial body ('our body is but a social structure composed of many souls' *BGE*.19). A hierarchy of oversouls and 'undersouls' (ibid.), of ruling passions and exploited passions, of masters and slaves, the *body politic* - governed by the will to power - has its factions and insurrections like any other; and what Zarathustra's shadow symbolizes is the vicissitudes of his many souls, the *state* of his 'entire inner world' (*GM*.II.16). Thus, when Zarathustra hungered after the ultimate *über-*

---

262. Shakespeare, *King Lear*, I.iv.250-251.
263. A genre pioneered by Chamisso's immensely popular *Peter Schlemihl* and perfected by E T A Hoffman's works which, according to Tymms, represent 'the peak in the *Doppelgänger's* development as a psychological gambit'. See Tymms, p. 107.
264. Cooper, p. 151.
265. Laurence Sterne, *The Life and Opinions of Tristram Shandy*, Vol II (London: Hutchinson & Co), p. 163.

menschliche ideal, his shadow reflected the bright hope of his soul, but when, broken and disillusioned, Zarathustra longed only for redemption from suffering, his shadow accordingly reflected his soul's grim despair. Suicidal despair is the spectre that now haunts Zarathustra, and in the sudden appearance of his shadow - 'thin, dusky, hollow, and worn out' (Z.IV.9) - Zarathustra sees the death of hope foreshadowed.

Zarathustra's shadow-self is the re-cast shadow of the 'penitent of the spirit', of the embittered, enlightened man who 'has sat all too long *in the shadow*, [and whose] cheeks [...] have grown pale; he has almost starved to death on his expectations' (Z.II.13, emphasis added). Zarathustra had sought truth but found only *Baubô* (*GS*.Pref.4). Truth is an obscenity that breeds truths so awful 'that they lose all power of truth, and lie bedridden in the dormitory of the soul, side by side with the most despised and exploded errors.'[266] Destroyer of tranquil, blissful ignorance and enemy to reverential love and friendship, truth belies the (illusory) concept of 'gay science' (Z.II.11). And just as in Shakespeare's *King Lear* Gloucester was doubtless a happier man when blind ignorant than when blinded by knowledge, so too in *Zarathustra* we hear the tragic hero lamenting the getting of wisdom: 'As a blind man, I once walked on blessed paths; then you threw filth in the blind man's path: and now the old footpath disgusts him' (ibid.). And therein lies the tragedy: lost innocence is irretrievable. Once the sun of enlightenment has cast its long, dark shadow, Zarathustra can either emulate the *Übermensch* and frolic naked in 'the burning sun of wisdom' (Z.II.21), or cower in the 'dark and comfortless'[267] shade of his shadow-self where 'doleful shades'[268] haunt and taunt him whose deathly pallor marks him out as one of their own, and whose partiality to shades and shadows betrays a lifetime of underworld trafficking.

One recalls how Zarathustra had murdered all his 'gods for the sake of morality' (*GS*.153), but 'the morality of piety' (*HH*.I.96)[269] runs deeper

---

266. Coleridge, *Aids to Reflection*, 'Introductory Aphorisms', Aphorism 1.
267. Shakespeare, *King Lear*, II.vii.85 (Gloucester).
268. 'Regions of sorrow, doleful shades, where peace / And rest can never dwell, hope never comes / That comes to all', Milton, *Paradise Lost,* Book I, ll. 65-67.
269. '... every convention continually grows more venerable the further removed its origin lies and the more this origin is forgotten; the respect paid to it increases from generation to generation, finally, convention becomes holy and evokes awe and reverence; and thus the morality of piety is in any event a much older morality than

than the morality of truth: 'What binds most tightly? Which ropes are all but inseverable? With men of a high and select kind they will be their duties: that reverence proper to youth, that awe and delicacy before all that is honoured and respected from of old, that gratitude for the soil out of which they have grown, for the hand which led them, for the holy place where they learned to worship - their supreme moments themselves will bind them the tightest, will lay upon them the most enduring obligation' (*HH*.I.Pref.3). Bound by a stygian oath made in his youth - 'All beings shall be divine to me [...] All days shall be holy to me' (Z.II.11) - Zarathustra feels compelled to follow the sacred river from its Arcadian but now godless heights, down into its stygian heart of darkness. It is precisely this ongoing dialogue with his fallen heroes - whose blood, let by Zarathustra's own hand, stains the battlefield of his soul - which has violently upset the naturally precarious balance between Zarathustra's conscious ego-self and his unconscious or half-conscious shadow-self. For, as Nietzsche cautions: 'There are many things we must leave in the Hades of half-conscious feeling, and not desire to redeem them out of their shadow-existence, otherwise they will, as thoughts and words, become our dæmonic masters and cruelly demand of us our blood' (*HH*.II 'Opinions and Maxims' 374). But, as we have seen, Zarathustra cannot leave well alone: 'a strong, weight-bearing man whose reverence is inherent: he has laden upon himself too many *extraneous* heavy words and values' (Z.III.11.2). Having lived with his shades for so long, Zarathustra is now but a slave to his 'dæmonic masters'; the shadow has become master and the master a mere shadow of his shadow.[270] Zarathustra now walks a liminal, twilit tightrope, and across his ashen face flit the 'shades of the prison-house':[271] 'His countenance is still dark; his hand's shadow plays upon it. The expression in his eyes is still overshadowed. / His deed itself is still the shadow upon him; the hand darkens the doer. He has still not overcome his deed' (Z.II.13).

One of Zarathustra's most cherished hopes had been to purge his manifold soul of 'romantic pessimism' - the pessimism, that is, of 'the failed and defeated' (*HH*.II.Pref.7) - by means of '*anti-romantic* self-treatment'

---

    that which demands unegoistic actions' (*HH*.I.96). I would argue that 'unegoistic' here carries both "moral" (Christian) and "immoral" (non-Christian) connotations.
270. Cf. Hans Christian Andersen's *The Shadow* in *Fairy Tales*, trans. H L Braekstad (London: William Heinemann, 1937), p. 411.
271. William Wordsworth, *Intimations of Immortality from Recollections of Early Childhood*, l. 67.

(*HH*.II.Pref.2). In 'Of the Great Longing' (Z.III.14)[272] - whose title testifies to the immense weight that Zarathustra attached not only to the success of his cure but, as suggested by the infinitive "mood" of the verb 'to long', to its subsequent failure - one finds both the prescriptive particulars of this 'spiritual cure' (*HH*.II.Pref.2) and a seemingly intransigent patient. The cure is clearly unsuccessful, but it is not until Part IV that one is able to observe the recurring symptoms and to draw one's own conclusions as to the cause of the cure's inefficacy.

To heal his soul of its nostalgia for the past Zarathustra prescribed the ancient virtue of *carpe diem*; but in Part IV we find Zarathustra's soul 'wandering like a heavy cloud between past and future' (Z.IV.19.2). To say 'today' as well as 'once' and 'formerly' (Z.III.14) is evidently not quite the same as performing 'today'.[273]

So that his soul might overcome its 'petty shame and corner-virtue' he persuaded it to 'stand naked before the eyes of the sun' (ibid.); but in Part IV we see Zarathustra's melancholy spirit, having wooed truth and stood naked before her, running for the shadows, his petty shame and corner-virtue banishing him 'from *all* truth' (Z.IV.14.3). To stand naked before *Baubô* would shame even the most shameless of men.

That 'strangler called "sin" ' was to be 'strangulated' by "spirit" (Z.III.14); but once again, it is Zarathustra's melancholy spirit that in Part IV writhes under the torment inflicted by his intellectual conscience-turned-bad conscience (Z.IV.5). The antinomian spirit is always in danger of being strangulated, in turn, by the penitential spirit.

To liberate his soul from 'the morality of mores and the social straitjacket' (*GM*.II.2) he returned to it its original 'freedom over created and uncreated things' (Z.III.14);[274] but instead of 'this power over oneself and

---

272. In an otherwise illuminating critique of Nietzsche's thought, White (pp. 93-5) offers a surprisingly pedestrian reading of this section, based on a misleading comparison. He argues that in contradistinction to the soothsayer, for whom alone 'God's death continue[s] to be a cause for despair', Zarathustra is able to affirm the value of life. On my reading, though, a Schopenhauerian pessimism (the soothsayaer) informed by the death of God, is even more questionable than Zarathustra's alleged affirmative stance (an allegation which this book explicitly calls into question).
273. Unlike the "self", 'which does not say 'I' but performs 'I' ' (Z.I.4).
274. Cf. '... the *sovereign individual*, like only to himself, liberated again from the morality of mores, the autonomous and supramoral individual (for "autonomous" and "moral" are mutually exclusive) [...] this master of a *free* will, this sovereign man -

over fate [...] penetrat[ing] to the most profound depths and becom[ing] instinct, the dominating instinct' (*GM*.II.2), it filled his soul with so much self-doubt and bad conscience[275] that, like a 'pale criminal' (Z.I.6) - who in Part IV we detect hiding behind 'the beautiful mask of a saint' (Z.IV.14.2) - it finally repented its "immoral" deed: 'I have killed the law, the law anguishes me as a corpse does a living man: if I am not *more* than the law, then I am the vilest of all men' (*D*.14).

His soul's 'gnawing worm' of contempt was to be replaced by 'the great, the loving contempt which loves most where it despises most' (Z.III.14); but in Part IV Zarathustra is bereft of love: 'Nothing that I love still lives - how should I still love myself?' (Z.IV.9). Without love, '*contempt for man*' remains his soul's 'blackest melancholy' (*A*.38) and all too often expresses itself as contempt for its ego-counterpart - 'My ego is something that should be overcome, my ego is to me the great contempt of man' (Z.I.6) - which in Part IV tries to escape from itself by means of mockery and self-mockery.[276]

Persuasion was prescribed as an artificial substitute for deficient example; but if his soul succeeds in dredging up from its 'sorrowful, black sea' (Z.III.1) fragmentary higher men with which to aba(i)te the loneliness of Zarathustran solitude, then - given the penumbral world of caves 'and caves behind caves' (Z.IV.2) that cluster around the shore of consciousness and into which these fragments emerge - his soul must be forgiven for being unpersuaded as to the purported 'height' and 'sun'light (Z.III.14) of Zarathustra's alpine "beyond".

To remedy his soul's diffidence and care, he dispensed tonics in the *form* of 'new names' (Z.III.14); but to call one who reaps care, a 'dispeller of care', and one who is crushed by fate, 'destiny' (ibid.), is at best cruel irony, and at worst an extreme case of *self*-delusion. Mere word-play - 'Only speaking colourfully, / Only screaming colourfully out of fool's-masks, / Clambering around on mendacious word-bridges, / On colourful

---

how should he not be aware [...] of how this mastery over himself also necessarily gives him mastery over circumstances, over nature' (*GM*.II.2).
275. 'Under the dominion of the morality of custom, originality of every kind has acquired a bad conscience' (*D*.9).
276. Cf. '... we should have to make it clear that we are artists of contempt [...] that we love nature the less humanly it behaves, and art *if* it is the artist's escape from man, or the artist's mockery of man, or the artist's mockery of himself' (*GS*.379).

rainbows, / Between false heavens / And false earths' (Z.IV.14.3) - is more placebo than antidote to sinister shadow-play.

Finally, he gave his soul 'all wisdom to drink, all new wines and also all immemorially old strong wines of wisdom' (Z.III.14); but wisdom is simply a matter of 'taste',[277] and the wine of wisdom that the Zarathustra of Part IV finds most palatable is the one with 'a perfume and scent of eternity, a rosy, russet, gold-wine scent of ancient happiness, / of drunken midnight's death-joy' (Z.IV.19.6).

Notwithstanding the 'spiritual cure', failure, defeat, and great longing continue to oppress Zarathustra's soul; melancholia, the quintessential romantic disease, is at bottom incurable. And just as 'neighbourly love' tends to benefit the neighbour less than the giver who gives so as to *steal* into the other (Z.I.16), so too does Zarathustra's ego-self stand to benefit more from its beneficence than its shadow-beneficiary; for in giving, the former likes to believe that it performs 'I' (see Z.I.4), but in truth it is the latter *who*[278] performs 'I' precisely, if paradoxically, in its non-performance. Hence the soul's rhetorical question: 'Which of us must thank the other? / Must the giver not thank the taker for taking? Is giving not a necessity? Is taking not - compassion?' (Z.III.14).

Ultimately, the inefficacy of Zarathustra's spiritual cure is due less to the infirmity of the patient than to the physician's choice of medication. By looking, idealistically, to 'the salvation of the soul', Zarathustra's mind had neglected 'the great and small needs' of the body (*HH*.II 'The Wanderer and his Shadow' 6). He had filled his soul with metaphysical panaceas, but "sun" burns, "spirit" strangulates, "freedom" imprisons, and "wisdom" intoxicates. Zarathustra had hazarded his soul for *übermenschliche* divinity but, although a higher order gain, the Faustian analogy still holds insofar as in both cases the enemy of mankind - in *Zarathustra*, idealism is the Mephistopheles to whom the tragic hero forfeits his soul - triumphantly claims its prize. Misguided though his bounty clearly was, Zarathustra had given his soul everything (Z.III.14). Not wishing to appear ungrateful, his

---

277. '... the Greeks, who were very cunning in such things, designated the wise man with a word that signifies the *man of taste*, and called wisdom, artistic as well as cognitive, frankly 'taste' (*Sophia*)' (*HH*.II 'Opinions and Maxims' 170).

278. In a conversation between Nietzsche and Dionysus and recorded by the former in his notebooks, Dionysus insists that a genealogical critique must begin with the question "Who?" rather than "What?" (*KSA*.12.178). That is to say, one must not ask *what* a word or deed signifies in itself, but rather *who* the author of that word or deed is.

soul now smiles sweetly and compassionately back at its needy benefactor. It is a smile, however, that is 'full of melancholy', that 'longs for tears', and that 'trembles' with suppressed 'sobs' (ibid.).

Like Zarathustra's hectic blush of health, his soul's melancholy smile is symptomatic of the '*new* health':[279] just as victory is tainted by loss, and health infected with sickness, so too is hope 'sicklied o'er' with failure. '[W]hen the best part of youth and strength for action has already been used up through sitting still' (*BGE*.274) or, what amounts to the same thing, through endless wandering; when the wonderer or wanderer has 'lost faith in himself' (ibid.) and consequently in all hope of self-creation; when 'golden sadness' (*Z*.IV.10) and 'purple melancholy' (*Z*.III.14) hang heavy on the vine; then the gaze of great longing turns away from its highest hope of 'tender eternities' and 'dearest wonders' (*Z*.II.11) and looks imploringly towards 'the vintager who waits with diamond vine-knife' (*Z*.III.14) to cut down the failed and defeated. And what the soul prefigures in Part III, the shadow, as its figurative analogue, shadows in Part IV. With unparalleled loyalty, willingness and innocent enthusiasm, Zarathustra's panchoesque shadow had accompanied his quixotic master on his rigorous and perilous quest for truth. But truth is a lie,[280] and Zarathustra's shadow, who 'sometimes [...] meant to lie, and behold! only then [...] hit upon the truth' (*Z*.IV.9), is now but a shadow of his former shadow-self. Lost innocence weighs heavy upon him and, with '[a] weary and insolent heart; an unstable will; fluttering wings; [and] a broken backbone', he now yearns only for extinction: ' "To live as I like or not to live at all" ' (ibid.).

The supreme irony, however, is that the shadow's 'saintly' desire - to live as he pleases or not at all - sins against the sacred law of the excluded middle. The "saintly" life is fundamentally life-denying: whether a holy fool, a prophetic saint, or a saint of knowledge, the ascetic ideal is their common creed. Only a naïve belief in 'the innocence of the good and their noble lies' (*Z*.IV.9) enables the holy fool to bless each day as holy. Only faith in the ideal sustains the prophetic saint, whose *übermenschliche* desire to live beyond man - in the rarefied air of authenticity where 'life-preserving errors' (*GS*.110) cannot breathe - is not only otherworldy, but ultimately underworldly:

---

279. See preceding section.
280. '*Ultimate scepticism.* - What, then, are man's truths ultimately? They are his *irrefutable* errors' (*GS*.265).

> Before me floats an image, man or shade,
> Shade more than man, more image than a shade;
> For Hades' bobbin bound in mummy-cloth
> May unwind the winding path;
> A mouth that has no moisture and no breath
> Breathless mouths may summon;
> I hail the superhuman;
> I call it death-in-life and life-in-death.[281]

The higher realm is no sooner reached than surrendered, and from the Arcadian heights of breathless *Übermenschen*, Zarathustra 'sink[s] down, pale, towards night' and the Hades of disillusioned *Untermenschen*:

> Thus even I sank
> Out of my truth-illusions,
> Out of my day-longings,
> Weary of day, sick of the light,
> Sank downwards, nightwards, shadow-wards:
> By one truth
> Burnt and thirsty: [...]
> That I am banished
> From *all* truth,
> Only a fool!
> Only a poet! (Z.IV.14.3)

Finally, only a yearning for *telos*, for stability, rest and security, drives the nomadic saint of knowledge inexorably on towards his eternally elusive "home".

Belief in the "good", in the "beyond", and in a metaphysical "home", are all forms of nihilism, and the pious fraud that unites this holy trinity is the myth of "being". But as Zarathustra's shadow now knows, the perfectionism aspired to by his former master is but a fond illusion,[282] and

---

281. Yeats, *Byzantium*, second stanza.
282. Cf. the following exchange in which Lucian articulates the findings of the shadow-self, and Peregrine the perfectionism preached by Zarathustra in the market square:
    Lucian: He that is born to be a man, neither should nor can be any thing nobler, greater, and better than a man.
    Peregrine: But, good Lucian, for the very reason that he may not become less than a man, he should always be striving to be more. It is undeniable that there is something dæmoniacal in our nature; we are suspended between heaven and earth;

the arduous journey to the "higher self" merely a circuitous route to fragmentary and importunate lower selves: 'how crude and sore / The journey homeward to habitual self!'[283] He now knows that 'being is an empty fiction' (*TI* ' "Reason" in Philosophy' 2) and that to be 'always journeying but without a goal [and] also without a home' is to be like 'the eternal Wandering Jew, except that I am neither eternal nor a Jew' (Z.IV.9) - a qualification which, with its breezy juxtaposition of the pertinent with the impertinent, obscures its all-important critique of the myth of eternity. For if Heraclitus is right, and 'everything is in flux' (Z.III.12.8), then the only true "being" is the being of becoming (see *EH* '*The Birth of Tragedy*' 3). Accordingly, if there is neither God nor eternity, neither goal nor home, then the mythical Wandering Jew need no longer await in dread his equally mythical Judgment Day nor Zarathustra's wandering shadow continue his endless search for eternal truths and a "homeland" (Z.II.14).

Truth cuts short eternity (Z.II.11) and asks incredulously: 'What mad pursuit?'[284] Once Zarathustra's shadow has discovered that "home" is a delusion; that 'seeking for *my* home [...] was my affliction; and that hope which springs eternal is an 'eternal vanity' (Z.IV.9); he can either look to the vintager to cut short his futile and seemingly eternal wandering with the knife that cuts into life or, at 'the noontide hour, when the sun st[ands] immediately above Zarathustra's head' (Z.IV.10), fade away into the temporal eternity of sleep and forgetfulness. But if the former is nihilism, is the latter not also nihilism?[285] As 'a doorkeeper on the threshold of the temple of human dignity' (*HH*.I.92), forgetfulness is 'an active and in the strictest sense positive faculty of repression (*Hemmungsvermögen*)' (*GM*.II.1); but, as an Ambrosian 'drop of golden happiness' (Z.IV.10), stolen by Zarathustra while his shadow-self slumbers in the noonday sun, it is a furtive foretaste of eternity. And Zarathustra's subsequent supplication - 'when, well of eternity! you serene and terrible noontide abyss! when will

---

on the father's side, so to speak, we are related to superior spiritual natures; on the side of our mother earth, we are related to the beasts of the field. If the spirit be not ever soaring upwards, the animal part will soon stagnate in the mire of the earth, and the man who does not strive to become a god, will find himself in the end transformed into a beast. (C M Wieland, *The Private History of Peregrine Proteus the Philosopher*, trans. William Tooke (2 vols), 1796). Cited in Miller, p. 92.

283. Keats, *Endymion*, ll. 275-6.
284. Keats, *Ode on a Grecian Urn*, l. 9.
285. A further allusion to *GS*.V.346.

you drink my soul back into yourself?' (ibid.) - is both a blessing and an indignity: a blessing to his soul which longs only for death, but a shameless indignity from one who not only exhorted man to *'remain true to the earth'* (Z.Prol.3), but who then led his soul a merry dance of death down to the grave of lost hope and there bade it sing its own requiem until redeemed by the comforting lie of eternity (Z.III.14).

Only if Zarathustra blocks his ears to the Sirens' song of his soul, 'only if he turns away from himself, will he leap over his own shadow - and, truly! into *his* sun' (Z.II.13). But Zarathustra's sun of 'truth-illusions' (Z.IV.14.3) has long since set, and having sat all too long in his own shadow, an older and wiser, thinner and weaker Zarathustra is now unlikely to make such a leap of faith. On the contrary, having listened to *his* shadow lament the vanity of *his* wandering, he can but gloomily acknowledge his own spiritual double and ruefully confess: 'You are my shadow!' (Z.IV.9). His shadow is his *home*: the nomadic home of becoming, of becoming what one is (Z.IV.1). 'You shall become the person you are' (*GS*.270), proclaims Nietzsche - a proclamation not, as many believe, of idealistic individualism (defined by Coomeraswamy as 'the doctrine of inner harmony'),[286] but of the brutally honest self-realization that 'in the final analysis one experiences only oneself' (Z.III.1).

---

286. Ananda K Coomeraswamy, 'Cosmopolitan View of Nietzsche' in *The Dance of Shiva* (London: Peter Owen, 1958), p. 142.

APOTHEOSIS

The Tragic Buffoon

8 Ignoble Lies and Insolent Truths

Hierarchical Anarchy

> You higher men, what do you think? Am I a prophet? A dreamer? A drunkard? An interpreter of dreams? A midnight bell?
> A drop of dew? A whiff and scent of eternity? Do you not hear it? Do you not smell it? Just now my world became perfect, midnight is also midday, -
> Peace is also a joy, curses are also a blessing, night is also a sun, - be gone, or you will learn: a wise man is also a fool.
> (Z.IV.19.10)

Who is Zarathustra? It is a question that Zarathustra himself addresses to his higher men, and is, of course, a rhetorical one. For as his higher men serve constantly and painfully to remind him, he is all these things (and a good many others besides) and none. Indeed, in a Heraclitean world of ceaseless flux, the very question "Who is Zarathustra?" - with its implicit assumption of an immutable, durable, essential self - is essentially meaningless.[287] Now wise man, now fool (Z.IV.19.10); now prophet and dreamer and midday sun, now madman and vigilant and midnight bell; now drunk and joyfully desirous of the eternal recurrence of life, now sober and cursed by the mere thought of the eternal return of woeful becoming; Zarathustra *is* the sum of his "parts".

Zarathustra is indeed 'a question mark, / a tired riddle' (*DD* 'Amid Birds of Prey'), but in the carnival of Part IV (chapters 11-19), the tired masks fall to reveal an exclamation mark hiding behind every question mark. In this carnival atmosphere of caricature and parody, of metaphor and meaning, of release and revelation, Zarathustra unburdens his soul, and the

---

[287]. To remark that Zarathustra 'takes on so many forms, it seems nearly impossible to say what he really is "in himself"' (Leonard Robbins, 'Zarathustra and the Magician or, Nietzsche contra Nietzsche: Some Difficulties in the Concept of the Overman', *Man and World* 9 [June 1976] p. 180) is simply to beg the question.

reader is afforded a comprehensive and interactive view of those multiple selves - previously seen only in isolation (Z.IV.2-9) - which jointly but not severally constitute the character called Zarathustra. Privy to this intensely personal drama of the soul,[288] the reader does well to recall Nietzsche's observations regarding the hierarchical politics of the soul: 'whichever group of sensations is aroused, begins to speak, [and] issues commands most quickly within a soul, is decisive for the whole order of rank of its values, and ultimately determines its table of goods. The values of a human being betray something of the construction of his soul and where it finds its conditions for life, its real need' (*BGE*.268). The hierarchical anarchy raging in Zarathustra's soul and the real and ineluctable needs thereby expressed will be closely scrutinized in the following three sections.

Last Rites: The Last Supper and The Ass Festival

The higher men's univocal cry of distress that 'greets' Zarathustra upon his return to his cave is expressive of that group of sensations - 'great longing, great disgust, great weariness, and [...] the remnant of God' (Z.IV.11) - commonly associated with despair. Even Zarathustra's animals, innovative and indefatigable sick-nurses in the conscious realm, are impotent in this cavernous underworld of animal instincts and intractable emotions: 'in the midst of this sad company stood Zarathustra's eagle, ruffled and uneasy, for it had been expected to answer many questions to which its pride had no answer; the clever serpent, however, hung about its neck' (ibid.). Despair, then, as the first and therefore the most will(-to-power)ful emotion to manifest itself within Zarathustra's soul, determines both its hierarchy of values and its 'table of goods'.

Accordingly, he who despairs and yet values life over death will place the highest value upon hope, and so it is that hope is the counter-affect which first begins to speak. Hope, of laughter, rest and security, is the first thing that Zarathustra in his welcoming speech offers his despairing higher men. Hope, of redemption from despair, is the expressed yearning of the king on the right: as specific representative of Zarathustra's retrospectively validating nobility of the future and general spokesman for 'all [those] who

---

288. See Introduction (p. 4) where allusion is made to the private publication and allegorical masking of Part IV.

do not want to live unless they may learn to *hope* again - unless they may learn from you, O Zarathustra, the *great* hope' (ibid.), the king on the right snatches greedily at Zarathustra's wanton offer. And once again, hope, of the arrival of a 'beautiful new race' (ibid.) of *Übermenschen*, provokes Zarathustra to disabuse his crippled and crippling higher men of *their* redemptive hopes, and to muse instead over the *coming* of those 'higher, stronger, more victorious, more joyful men', to whom his 'heritage and name belong' (ibid.) and in whom his highest hope resides. Languishing under 'drifting clouds [...] damp melancholy [... and] howling autumn winds' (Z.IV.16), that is, under the 'morning rain-cloud' (Z.IV.2) of Schopenhauerian pessimism,[289] Zarathustra's soul deems the countervailing properties of the 'magnificent' pine-tree - 'tall, silent, hard, solitary, of the best and most flexible of woods, magnificent' (Z.IV.11) - to represent its life-preserving values. With its ability to withstand and provide shelter from howling winds and weeping storms, the pine-tree is to the distressed higher men what *übermenschliche* 'trees of life' (ibid.) are to Zarathustra: a symbol of 'highest hope' (ibid.).

Finally, if life-threatening despair poses the greatest danger, and antidotal hope is thus accorded the highest valorization, then laughter, the most effective restorative known to man, together with the purveyors of laughter, will be transvalued as the greatest good. Indeed, the first thing that Zarathustra promises his melancholy guests is 'someone to make you laugh again' (ibid.), and it is with this promise in mind that Zarathustra places his hermits' pets at his guests' disposal. But given that his animals' restorative powers had but a short time before proven impotent in face of the prouder and cleverer higher men, Zarathustra's offer, while doubtless raising an ironic laugh or two, is little more than a bad joke.

But if in Part IV despair is the first emotion to be aroused, and hope, the one that begins to speak, Schopenhauerian pessimism is the emotion that 'thrust[s itself] forward like one with no time to lose' (Z.IV.12) and that issues commands most quickly within Zarathustra's soul. Scornful of his host's 'idealist mendacity and softness of conscience' (*HH*.II.Pref.3), of his utopian daydreams and patronizing drivel (while Zarathustra dreamed and the rest of his guests looked on in silent consternation, 'the old soothsayer

---

289. It is no coincidence that it is the pessimistic soothsayer who first directs Zarathustra's attention to the howling cries of distress rising from the abysmal depths of his manifold soul.

made signs with his hands and mien' Z.IV.11), the 'starving soothsayer' demands wine. That insatiable pessimist, whom even Zarathustra's animals despair of satisfying (normally such excellent suppliers of spiritual sustenance, especially honey, 'they saw that all they had brought home during the day would not be enough to fill this one philosopher' Z.IV.12), demands wine, for '*that* alone brings sudden recovery and improvised health!' (ibid.).

Food, wine, and declamatory speeches - which, in the figurative language of *Zarathustra*, amount to the same thing - are, of course, the staple ingredients of any 'Last Supper' deserving of that name.[290] It is the poor quality of the wine, however, that the soothsayer objects to and that leads him to suspect a miraculous turning of wine into water: 'And though I hear water splashing here like speeches of wisdom, that is, abundantly and incessantly: I - want *wine*' (ibid.). Like Zarathustra, the soothsayer wants vintage 'wines of wisdom' (Z.III.14), wines with the 'gold-wine scent of ancient happiness' (Z.IV.19.6). But, as we saw in 'The Shadow', one's choice of wine, like one's preferred "brand" of wisdom, is entirely a matter of taste, and the wine provided by the two kings - 'a whole *ass*'s load' (Z.IV.12, emphasis added) of admittedly very old wine, but which, given the kings' predilection for visionary utopianism, will require laying down for at least another millennium or two - is unlikely to be to the soothsayer's, or anybody else's, taste. In the event, it is only Zarathustra - that 'gloomy man' and 'dreamy fellow' (ibid.) - who is intoxicated by what has long been his favourite tipple: the dreamy vision of '*laughing lions*' (Z.IV.11) and laughing, dancing *Übermenschen*. Weary of sitting alone, 'thirsty amidst drunken folk, and nightly lamenting: "Is it not more blessed to receive than

---

290. On the basis of his view that 'Nietzsche's comic correction of the one-sided spirituality of Christian parables reaches its peak in Zarathustra's parody of the Last Supper', Cantor urges a literal reading of this section (see Paul Cantor, 'Friedrich Nietzsche: The Use and Abuse of Metaphor', in David S Miall (ed.), *Metaphor: Problems and Perspectives*, [Brighton: The Harvester Press, 1982], p. 83). But, aside from the sheer unexpectedness (noted by Cantor) of Zarathustra's purported shift from a figurative mode of speech to a literal one, Cantor's literal interpretation is, on his own earlier admission, necessarily speculative: 'What is distinctive [...] about Nietzsche's style is that one is never quite sure whether to take his language literally or metaphorically [...] Nietzsche deliberately blurs the distinction between the literal and figurative meanings of his terms. By allowing his language to hover between the literal and figurative, he keeps his readers off-balance, and prevents them from ever comfortably settling into any dogmatic interpretation of his thought' (p. 81).

to give?" ' (Z.III.9), Zarathustra now sits alone, drunken amidst thirsty higher men who on this most significant of nights lament that it is apparently more blessed for the host to give than to receive. But appearances can be deceptive, and in the way that an animal or plant is host to a parasite, Zarathustra is a kind of sacrificial host: he gives to his disciples his body and his blood, but his body is broken and his blood is thin. Indeed, so liberal is Zarathustra with his sacrificial "wine of wisdom" (his *spirited* valedictory address involves no less than twenty toasts[291] to his higher men - Z.IV.13), and so sober do his parasitic disciples remain, that one cannot help but suspect fool-play, and perhaps recall his earlier remark that 'it is strangest in a wise man if he is also clever and not an ass' (Z.IV.12).

Zarathustra is, of course, clever, wise *and* an ass, but while the heady spirit of idealism keeps the ass in his cups, it is the wisdom of failure that dilutes Zarathustra's speech 'Of the Higher Man' (Z.IV.13). Appealing to the divine in man, the asinine sage - with his brave and beautiful convictions (*BGE*.8) - calls for heroic courage, for antinomian individualism, and for Christ-like suffering (Z.IV.13.4-6 respectively). The truly wise man, on the other hand, addresses the beast in man and reminds him of his burden of natural and, in particular, genetic determinism (Z.IV.13.8 and 13.13 respectively): of the overweening will that must break upon the wheel of fate (Z.IV.13.10) and of the unclean and unsightly business of giving birth to one's bastard child of proud and foolish wisdom (Z.IV.13.11 and 13.12). It remains, therefore, the beguiling task of the cunning, clever sage to offer if not a solution then at least a practicable response to the problem of the divided higher man: buffonic dissimulation (as prefigured in the parable of the ropedancer).

As everyone and no one, wise man and fool, the clever actor-sage reaches for his cap and bells and climbs the back stairway to the 'gods', for it is only from their distant perspective that one can 'play and mock' (Z.IV.13.14); it is only from the vantage point of ironic distance that one can laugh and dance beyond oneself (Z.IV.13.20) and beyond the tragic fate of all higher men being played out on the paltry stage below. From these godly heights, tragedy takes on the appearance of comedy, and just as Zarathustra had seen through the lion-skins worn by the famous philosophers (Z.II.8), so the 'madcap' (Z.IV.11) in the gallery, upon witnessing the histrionic heroics of the diminutive tragic actor below, will see more ass than lion. For

---

291. Zarathustra's speech entitled 'Of the Higher Man' is divided into 20 sections.

although the asinine sage would like to weave his own destiny and play all the heroic parts, especially that of the lion, he must, like Nick Bottom in *A Midsummer Night's Dream*, nevertheless accept the part allotted to him by fate.

Taking their cue from Zarathustra, the higher men respond to their dramaturge's high jinks and 'theatrical rhetoric' (*CW*.8) with playful mockery; and once again, a close look at the group of sensations aroused by Zarathustra's speech will give a good indication as to the pecking order within the clever ass's soul. Most instructive of all the responses, however, is the reaction of the speaker himself to his own windy discourse, significantly delivered 'near the door of his cave' (Z.IV.14.1) - the door of his cave symbolizing the boundary between the unconscious (cave[292] and resident higher men) and conscious (Zarathustra's eagle and serpent) realms. Finding his own hot air unbearably oppressive (an attack of 'after-dinner nausea' perhaps?)[293] and having, in the true spirit of 'do as I say not as I do', hurled his 'laugher's crown' (Z.IV.13.20) to his bemused higher men, Zarathustra escapes into the fresh air with his final words still on his lips: 'I have canonized laughter; you higher men, *learn* - to laugh' (ibid.). But no sooner is he free of his cramping higher men than he requires the reassurance of his sick-nurses that sterile repression is healthier than the stale air of the sick-room (Z.IV.14.1). But if repression is the better part of the convalescent's valour, insurrection is sickness's best form of counter-attack, and chief among the insurgents within Zarathustra's soul is the insidious old sorcerer. As representative of that melancholy spirit (Z.IV.14.2) which afflicts all the higher men in common and seizes Zarathustra's soul every evening, especially at midnight (see Z.Prol.7; Z.I.3; Z.I.8; Z.II.9; Z.II.19; Z.III.1; Z.III.9; Z.III.15.2-3; Z.IV.2; Z.IV.14.2; Z.IV.15; and Z.IV.19), the old sorcerer is the first one to speak and to issue commands within Zarathustra's soul. (Not forgetting, however, that it is the soothsayer who holds the highest order of rank within Zarathustra's soul. As the personification of romantic pessimism - the diagnosed disease of which the other higher men are but symptoms - and the one sent by intellectual conscience to warn Zarathustra of the higher men's imminent resurgence [Z.IV.2], the soothsayer is the soul's ambassador to its tyrannical "master".)

---

292. In 'Schopenhauer as Educator', Nietzsche speaks of 'the inward cave, the labyrinth of the heart' (*UM*.III.3).
293. This is a deliberate misappropriation of *BGE*.282.

As Zarathustra's arch-enemy of old, the sorcerer is familiar with all his opponent's lame attempts at subterfuge. He knows, for instance, that the 'new names' (Z.III.14) - "higher men" or "free spirits" or "the truthful" or "the penitents of the spirit" or "the unfettered" or "the great yearners" (Z.IV.14.2) - bestowed by Zarathustra upon his afflicted soul are but flattering euphemisms for 'the *great disgust*' (ibid.) from which his soul suffers; he knows moreover that he who calls himself "Zarathustra" is but a sad fool masquerading behind 'the beautiful mask of a saint' (ibid.); and above all, he knows - it is what his 'Song of Melancholy' (Z.IV.14.3) *harps* on - that the prophet Zarathustra is an impostor, a fool and a poet who hides his nihilistic desires 'behind a thousand masks' (ibid.). Like the Marseillaise, the sorcerer's 'Song of Melancholy' is a rousing call to arms and one to which only the conscientious man of spirit offers any resistance (Z.IV.15).

What the "conscientious objector" objects to is ugly truths. Consumed by his fear ('man's original and fundamental sensation' ibid.) of 'the beast within', of the violent affects that stalk 'the forests, caves, steep mountains, and labyrinths' (ibid.) of every human soul, the conscientious man of spirit seeks refuge and false security in the poetic truths purveyed by Zarathustra, and in the half-truths retailed by scientific positivism. Zarathustra also is apparently no lover of 'naked' (Z.IV.14.2) truth: hearing the conscientious man of spirit (Z.IV.15) turn one truth on its head (he *named* Zarathustra the only 'tower' of certainty in a 'tottering' world of uncertainty) and another (the prevalence of primal and instinctual fear) back on its feet, Zarathustra expeditiously turns the latter truth back on its head by *naming* courage rather than fear as 'the whole pre-history of man' (ibid.), and creates a plinth for the former upturned truth by emphatically *naming* himself, Zarathustra, as courage personified.

Hearing this, the higher men 'burst into a great peal of laughter', this most fabulous of "truths" being by far the funniest thing they have heard all day. 'Even the sorcerer', who is momentarily upstaged by Zarathustra's black-humoured buffoonery, 'laughed and said prudently: "Well then! He is gone, my evil spirit!" ' (Z.IV.15). His compassionate good humour stems from the knowledge that Zarathustra's drollery is but an antic disposition put on to alleviate the melancholy malaise, and that comedy will once again collapse into tragedy once evening falls - for 'tragedies [...] have to do with precisely the incurable, inevitable, [and] inescapable in the fate and character of man' (*HH*.II 'Opinions and Maxims' 23). He knows, moreover, that

Zarathustra's love-hate relationship with his higher men is symptomatic of a man at odds with himself, of a man who 'has loved himself as he has despised himself' (Z.IV.7) and who 'loves his enemies [...] but for that takes revenge - on his friends!' (Z.IV.15).

The higher men applaud their chief's magnanimity and Zarathustra, moved and humbled by yet another instance of his soul's compassionate understanding (cf. Z.III.14), 'went round and mischievously and lovingly shook hands with his friends, like one who has to make amends and apologize to everyone for something' (Z.IV.15). But no sooner is Zarathustra reconciled with his higher men than he is overcome with the shame of his 'indulgence and suffering', the two weaknesses (in the private if not in the public sphere) which have always been his 'greatest danger' (Z.III.9); and were it not for his shadow's plaintive cry of restraint, he would certainly have escaped once again into the reassuring realm of his proud and deceptive consciousness.

Bereft of all hope and direction, Zarathustra's shadow is desperate to keep at bay 'the bitter business of our howling and cries of distress' (Z.IV.16.1), if only by maintaining the pretence of gaiety. To this end, he snatches up the sorcerer's harp - the Æolian harp of Zarathustra's soul which is played upon most often by the 'damp air' of evening melancholy (ibid.) - and over its strings breathes 'good, clear, oriental air' (ibid.). Ostensibly about a sexually repressed European man who lusts after oriental desert maidens that dance seductively about him, the harp's shadow-song echoes Zarathustra's earlier reflections upon covetous chastity ('These people abstain, it is true: but the bitch sensuality looks enviously out of all they do' Z.I.13), and it is this secret voluptuousness of the ascetic (alluded to earlier by the conscientious man of spirit - Z.IV.15)[294] that gestures towards the song's metaphoric meaning. It is a metaphor for the 'saints of the desert' of solitude and for 'the beast within' that grows there (Z.IV.13) - hence the song's opening and closing refrain: '*Deserts grow: woe to him who conceals deserts*' (Z.IV.16.2). In other words, the song tells the story of the ascetic hermit who lusts after life but lacks the strength to live it; of Zarathustra, who represses his importunate affects, but nevertheless recognizes them as constitutive of life - 'a subterranean life of struggle' (*GM*.I.12).[295]

---

294. '... those who with their praise of chastity secretly invite voluptuousness!'
295. For a radically different reading of the shadow's song see C A Miller, 'Nietzsche's "Daughters of the Desert": A Reconsideration', *Nietzsche-Studien* 2 (1973), 157-195.

Ignoble Lies and Insolent Truths   157

The shadow's ruse is a resounding success: the 'bright, light air' (ibid.) of the orient has dispersed the melancholy rain-clouds and filled Zarathustra's cave with 'noise and laughter' (Z.IV.17.1). Even Zarathustra, who strongly suspects that their vulgar, derisory laughter is at his own expense, seizes upon this rare moment of merriment to declare, albeit to himself (self-deception is, after all, far sweeter than self-mockery), the day a victory: 'he gives way, he flees, *the Spirit of Gravity*, my old arch-enemy! How well shall this day end that began so ill and so heavily' (ibid.). And herein lies the key not only to Zarathustra's character but to his *raison d'être*: cheerfulness at any cost (see *GS*.Pref.4). The spirit of gravity or melancholy *must* be vanquished: just as Nietzsche had invented for himself "free spirits" (to whom he dedicated his 'melancholy-valiant' book *Human, All Too Human*) and the 'brave companion and phantom' called Zarathustra (the eponymous hero of his other melancholy-valiant book) 'so as to remain among good things while surrounded by bad (sickness, solitude, alienation, apathy, inertia)' (*HH*.I.Pref.2);[296] so Zarathustra *invents* the *Übermensch* and its precursory higher men.

But when all such utopian ploys fail him, Zarathustra alleviates his gloom with malicious self-parody and ironic laughter which together reach their acme[297] in 'the awakening'[298] (Z.IV.17) Ass Festival. Zarathustra is, of course, the ass: it is he who bears the burden of his affective higher men and is their slave; his is the patience that stems from a heart that can never honestly deny its feelings; it is he who would rather praise and affirm his fictive world than openly deny life, for his is the 'shrewdness that does not speak' (ibid.); grey - connoting ambiguity, leadenness, and the 'grey friars' of the Franciscan order - is the 'sober livery'[299] (*Leib-Farbe*) in which he wraps his twilight virtue; redemption from despair is his 'hidden wisdom' (ibid.), hence the affirmation rather than the negation, laughter rather than melancholy, foolish illusion rather than tragic insight; his kingdom 'beyond good and evil' (ibid.) is no more than an innocent "conceit"; his indulgence and suffering indulges 'beggars and kings' and suffers these and other 'little

---

296. Cf. 'Set good little perfect things around you, you higher men! Things whose golden ripeness heals the heart. Perfect things teach hope' (Z.IV.13.15).
297. The subsidiary and archaic meaning of 'acme' is of particular relevance here: 'the crisis of a disease' (*SOED*).
298. In the sense of '*un*consciousness raising'.
299. Cf. 'Now came still Evening on, and Twilight gray / Had in her sober Liverie all things clad', Milton, *Paradise Lost*, Book IV, ll. 598-9.

children' to come unto him (ibid.); and finally, he will eat anything so long as it feeds his metaphysical hunger. In the (speculative) words of the conscientious man of spirit, Zarathustra has 'become an ass through abundance and wisdom' (Z.IV.18.1). And in partial acknowledgment of this, Zarathustra asks that all future celebrations in honour of the ass be commemorative of the tragic buffoon: 'should you celebrate it again, this ass festival, do it for love of yourselves, do it also for love of me! And in remembrance of *me*!' (Z.IV.18.3).[300]

In worshipping their asinine master, the higher men parody Zarathustra's belief in 'godly asininities' (Z.IV.18.1), in laughing, dancing *Übermenschen*. The butt of their satire is Zarathustra's piety: when called to account by their indignant host, the higher men defend their parodic piety with choice Zarathustran maxims especially chosen for their delightful ambiguity, for it is 'the enigmatic character of his art, its playing hide-and-seek beneath a hundred symbols, its polychromy of the ideal, that leads and lures' (*CW*.10) the higher men to Zarathustra in the first place. Appositely, it is the ugliest man (symbolizing Zarathustra's bad conscience) who sums up the general attitude of the higher men towards their slavish god: 'O Zarathustra, you obscure man [...] you dangerous saint, you are a rogue' (ibid.). And it is with characteristic roguery that Zarathustra responds to his bad conscience; for if the roguish higher men had, like Hamlet, thought to catch the bad conscience of their "king" with their satire play, that much greater rogue, Zarathustra, thwarts their plans by feigning naïveté and by treating their play as an innocent piece of buffoonery (Z.IV.18.2-3).

Bad conscience is janus-faced - for all ugly things love to disguise themselves (Z.IV.11) - and just as Zarathustra dissembles so as to conceal his painfully 'awakening' *self*-consciousness, so his ugliest man, in a staggering act of loyalty and compassion, implores his fellow higher men, '[f]or Zarathustra's sake', to feign 'transformation and recovery' by joining with him in a joyful (if unconvincing) affirmation of life's eternal recurrence (Z.IV.19.1). This act of consecration represents the apotheosis of the prophet Zarathustra. But at the moment of canonization, the soul of the 'dangerous saint' departs - 'his soul retreated and fled before him and was in remote distances' (Z.IV.19.2) - leaving only the idol. This recalls the incident of Zarathustra's flying shadow, seen by the sailors in Part II to be heading towards the volcano (Z.II.18), and the possibly related myth of

---

300. Cf. Luke 22:19.

Empedocles. Neither myth offers an explanation of its hero's disappearance, only speculation. Did Empedocles throw himself into the crater of Etna in the hope that his sudden disappearance might make the people believe that he was a god,[301] or was it an act of suicidal despair? Did Zarathustra, given his inability to teach by example ('Zarathustra speaks to his pupils differently - than to himself' Z.II.20), also feel that a sign, like the superlative sign of the cross (*BGE*.46), would be more potent and more persuasive than a fallible and all too often failed exemplar, or did he just lose faith altogether in his calling? In both myths, however, demon-despair seems the likelier motive for absence, and while the faithful naturally inclined towards the mystery of absence as divine presence ('I would rather believe that Zarathustra had carried off the Devil' Z.II.18), the rest of the people were closer to the mark when they opined that 'the Devil had carried off Zarathustra' (ibid.). For despite Zarathustra's resolution to 'keep [his shadow] under stricter control - otherwise it will ruin my reputation' (ibid.), the flight of his soul towards the end of Part IV - suspended there 'between two seas'[302] (Z.IV.19.2): the turbulent inner sea of his all too human past (Z.IV.1) and the smooth, all too distant sea of 'halcyon self-sufficiency' (*BGE*.224) and *übermenschliche* perfection - would seem to suggest abdication following upon the death of hope.

Death: The Nightwanderer's Song[303]

In the penultimate chapter of *Zarathustra*, the suicidal despair of its hero is dramatized in the stage(d)-death of the prophet. Like the death-throes of so many tragic heroes and heroines, Zarathustra's is a long, drawn-out, theatrical affair, a confessional soliloquy typically aware of its audience. 'I would rather die, die, than tell you what my midnight heart is now thinking' (Z.IV.19.4), confesses Zarathustra, whilst the dramatic death knell tolling

---

301. Sayffert, p. 212.
302. This phrase is mysteriously absent from Hollingdale's translation.
303. '*Das Nachtwandler-Lied*'. '*Nachtwandler*' also means 'sleepwalker', but the song *sung* by Zarathustra is about sleeplessness and the terrible clarity of one's midnight-thoughts and, as it were, midnight-wanderings. In 'The Night-Wanderer's Song' the stress falls heavily on 'night' and what it stands for: 'pre-natal darkness preceding rebirth or initiation and illumination, but [...] also chaos; death; madness; disintegration' (Cooper, p. 112). For the nocturnal Zarathustra, night signifies all these things.

the midnight hour resonates his secret despair.[304] 'The usual romantic finale is sounded - break, breakdown, return and collapse before an old faith, before *the* old god' (*AS*.7). With each mournful cadence, the 'old, heavy, heavy booming bell' (*Z*.II.15.2) tolls the tragic fate

> Of all the lost adventurers my peers, -
> How such a one was strong, and such was bold,
> And such was fortunate, yet each of old
> Lost, lost! one moment knelled the woe of years.[305]

Like the quixotic knights of old, Zarathustra's bold and impatient heart, in its 'unconditional search for the true' (*HH*.II 'Opinions and Maxims' 13), suffers shipwreck on the sea of life. His 'untamed wisdom' (*Z*.II.8) had hoped to ravish and tame wanton and coquettish life (*Z*.III.15.1), but life does not conform to the conventions of eighteenth- and nineteenth-century fiction: inconstancy will not be wed to constancy, nor realism to idealism. Were it not for his wild wisdom, Zarathustra might have consummated his torrid affair with life; but just as spiritual cares have a tendency to neglect the needs of the body, so visionary idealism has a tendency to neglect the needs of the age.

The prophet is lost to his age because of his visionary absorption:[306] 'The *Übermensch* lies close to my heart, *he* is my first and only concern - and *not* man: not the neighbour, not the poorest, not the most suffering, not the best' (*Z*.IV.13.3). But to sacrifice *Mensch* to the *Übermensch* and a palpable present to an implausible future is nihilism, while destruction without creation and judgment without mercy is vengeful nihilism. With his divining-rod of *ressentiment*, Zarathustra metes out 'punishment and justice' (*Z*.II.7), but he who seeks revenge upon life will never be able to 'will it thus!' (*Z*.II.20). One must be reconciled with life before one can will its eternal recurrence, for while there are 'higher things beyond reconciliation'

---

304. This desire for secrecy - 'a tendency which is then dualistically reversed in terms of a habit of confession' - is, according to Miller, a typical sign of 'romantic duality' (p. 46).
305. Robert Browning, "Childe Roland to the Dark Tower Came ", ll. 195-198.
306. See Kierkegaard's distinction between the visionary prophet who 'goes hand in hand with his age, and from this standpoint envisages that which shall come', and the ironist who 'has advanced beyond the reach of his age and opened a front against it' (p. 278).

Ignoble Lies and Insolent Truths 161

(ibid.), reconciliation remains the means to these higher ends; but in loving the furthest more than the nearest and the ideal better than the best, Zarathustra has betrayed life and so lost her. In overreaching man he has failed to overcome man; unable to overcome his time and the "signs" of his time within himself, Zarathustra has willed himself beyond time. Consequently, now that he must part with life and leave the world and his proselytizing work undone, Zarathustra bewails his loss of time: 'Woe is me! Where has time gone? Did I not sink into deep wells? [...] Now I am dead. It is gone' (Z.IV.19.4).

At the hour of spiritual death, the soothsayer's pessimistic prophecy - 'In vain was all our work, our wine has become poison' (Z.II.19) - weighs heavy upon the prophet's heart. Cranking up the stage-effects, Zarathustra dramatizes the confession of failure that his heart cannot utter: the moon (Z.IV.19.4), symbolizing cyclic time;[307] the spider (ibid.), symbolizing destiny;[308] and the lugubrious 'midnight-bell' (Z.IV.19.3), tolling the death of hope; together proclaim the 'eternal "too late" ' of failed higher men (BGE.269). And as the spider spins its web of destiny around Zarathustra, the wise sage might well ponder the paradox of free will and determinism: To what extent is self-determination an impossible ideal? Who, indeed, can master his own predetermined world and in so doing will it thus eternally (Z.IV.19.4)?   To the song of life's eternal recurrence (Z.III.15.3), Zarathustra had taught his soul to 'dance *upon* [and] dance across' (Z.III.12.2) the graves of his youth (Z.II.11), 'but a leg is not a wing' (Z.IV.19.5) nor a dirge a gavotte. And whereas in 'the Funeral Song' of Part II Zarathustra still cherished the hope that his '*will*' to self-overcoming would destroy the graves of his youthful dreams and drag his soul away from its pious graveyard vigil (Z.II.11), now, at the hour of his death, such sweet wines of "wisdom" taste like bitter dregs to his jaded palate (Z.IV.19.5). Broken by the greater will to power of his irrepressible higher men, Zarathustra's '*will*' finally submits to the victory of the past and the present, and to history's inevitable determination of the future. Having failed to destroy the graves of his youth and thereby effect his own

---

307. 'Whether male or female the moon is universally symbolic of the rhythm of cyclic time; universal becoming' (Cooper, p. 106).
308. 'The Great Mother, in her terrible aspect as weaver of destiny, is sometimes depicted as a huge spider. All moon goddesses are spinners and weavers of Fate' (Ibid., p. 156).

resurrection (Z.II.11), he now yields to his higher men's will to 'redeem the graves [and] awaken the corpses!' (Z.IV.19.5).

But even as Zarathustra yields to the demands of his higher men and, by implication, of authenticity, the 'worm' of bad conscience, grown fat on the ascetic ideal, continues to 'burrow' in his heart (ibid.). Bad conscience is 'the womb of all ideal and imaginative phenomena' (GM.II.18), and if Zarathustra feels compunction and remorse because a practicable moral injunction - 'Do not ask anything improbable of yourselves' (Z.IV.13.13) - has (not surprisingly) triumphed over an impossible moral ideal - 'Man is something that should be overcome' (Z.Prol.3) - this is due to 'a very high degree of vanity' instinct in the voluptuous ascetic: 'man experiences a veritable voluptuousness in violating himself by means of excessive demands and in then deifying this tyrannical imperious something in his soul' (HH.I.137). This vanity is, in turn, to be found in the mother of bad conscience: intellectual conscience. Out of the tenacious black roots of vanity intellectual conscience blossoms: 'That we are *afraid* of our own thoughts, concepts, words, but that we also *honour* ourselves in them and involuntarily attribute to them the power to applaud, scorn, praise and rebuke us, that we thus traffic with them as with free intelligent persons, with independent powers, as equals with equals' (HH.II 'Opinions and Maxims' 26), explains why Zarathustra would rather traffic with 'higher, stronger, more victorious, more joyful men' than with his so-called higher men (Z.IV.11). Because vanity dislikes the *distorted* reflection of a fool's mirror, Zarathustra would rather be anybody but *himself* (Z.IV.19.9).

'Joy is deeper than heart's agony' (Z.IV.19.8) and even the most abysmal Dionysian despair can be transfigured by the beauty of Apollonian illusion. In the dead of the deadliest night of the soul, the 'artist of decadence' (CW.5) wills 'the *lie* of the grand style' (CW.1) with which to usher out his grand 'counterfeit[er] of transcendence and the beyond' (CW.Postscript): Zarathustra exits to the sound of the poet's 'sweet lyre' (Z.IV.19.6), an instrument closely related to the penitent's melancholy harp. Zarathustra would rather the world remember him as a divine prophet: 'rich, solitary, a treasure pit, a gold chamber' (Z.IV.19.7), than as a tragic buffoon: 'a midnight lyre, a croaking bell that no one understands but which *must* speak' because that is the only way it knows of dispelling its midnight thoughts and nightmare visions (Z.IV.19.8).[309] Above all, though, Zarathustra wants to live to see his divine prophecy come to pass, because 'all that is unripe [...] all that suffers wants to live that it may grow ripe and lusty and desirous / desirous for the far, the higher, the brighter. "I want heirs", thus speaks all that suffers, "I want children, I do not want *myself*" ' (Z.IV.19.9). And as the reader will recall, it was the prophet who, just before 'The Last Supper', begged his higher men - as a token of their love and a sort of *quid pro quo* - to humour him with talk of his 'children'.[310] News of the impending arrival of this 'beautiful new race' of *Übermenschen* - his 'highest hope' - is the succulent and strengthening Viaticum requested by the prophet (Z.IV.11) in return for the so-called 'succulent and strengthening discourse' (Z.IV.17.1) which he will lavish, albeit in vain, on his lovingly indulgent disciples.

As is the case with most last confessions, however, hope has the final word. But even in his last and (given the frankness of his confession) finest hour, the prophet has the 'good taste' (see *BGE*.5) to warn his disciples of his final act of perfidy: a confession of faith in the ideal and thus a breach of good faith. Bidding his higher men hence, 'or you will learn: a wise man is also a fool' (Z.IV.19.10), the prophetic fool expediently offers up his final libation to joyful life and its eternal recurrence. With this Pascalian wager, made in the unthinkable event of life's eternal recurrence, this walking shadow and poor player, having strutted and fretted his last hour upon the stage, finally takes his leave.

Resurrection: The Sign

On the morning after this dark night of the soul, Zarathustra 'sprang up from his bed, girded his loins, and emerged from his cave, glowing and strong, like

---

309. Preaching is to Zarathustra what writing is to his author, namely, an involuntary cathartic exercise: 'A: [...] I am annoyed by or ashamed of my writing; writing for me is a necessity - to speak of it even in a parable disgusts me. B: But why, then, do you write? - A: Well, my friend, to be quite frank: I have hitherto found no other way of getting rid of my thoughts. - B: And why do you want to get rid of them? - A: Why do I want to? Do I want to? I must. - B: Enough! Enough!'
310. 'As a man calls for wine before he fights, / I asked one draught of earlier, happier sights, / Ere fitly I could hope to play my part'. Browning, "Childe Roland to the Dark Tower Came", ll. 86-88.

a morning sun emerges from behind dark mountains' (Z.IV.20). With the passing of the midnight hour and the return of a new dawn, the soul is resurrected[311] and hope springs eternal. Rising with the dawn, and with the renewed optimism vouchsafed to him by his proud and prudent consciousness ('My animals are awake, for I am awake' Z.IV.20), Zarathustra is struck once again (see Z.Prol.1) by his affinity with the sun. Pondering thus the divine mystery of natural supernaturalism, he challenges once more the supremacy of the Transcendent in an attempt to naturalize the supernatural: 'Great star [...] what would all your happiness be if you had

---

311. This resurrection of Zarathustra's soul is not to be confused with White's understanding of the same (pp. 63-104). In a chapter entitled 'The Resurrection of Zarathustra's Soul', White contends: (a) that what is affirmed in the eternal recurrence 'is not a circular course of history, not a cosmic repetition, but rather the resurrection of the Nietzschean soul [...] here and now repeatedly, a re-creation of the soul and by the soul, on an earth that has regained the "innocence of becoming" ' (p. 73); (b) that Nietzsche's affirmative teachings are to be found in Zarathustra's doctrine of eternal recurrence; and (c) that the latter doctrine 'emerges most fully [...] within the sections recounting Zarathustra's interactions with his soul' (p. 74). While agreeing with (b), I would counter (a) with the observation that, even if one finds White's redescription of eternal recurrence to be acceptable (which I do not - see NB), Zarathustra cannot re-create his soul by his soul, simply because the time when the earth will have regained the "innocence of becoming" lies in a distant and utopian future; and (c) by noting that the most explicit conversation (interaction) which Zarathustra has with his soul (Z.III.14) is not only unremittingly negative, but gestures towards the "eternal recurrence" of herd values within Zarathustra's unregenerate soul - a form of eternal recurrence quite distinct from Nietzsche's doctrine but clearly dramatized in Part IV of *Zarathustra*.
NB. White's interpretation of the doctrine of eternal recurrence, so clearly at variance with the doctrine as presented in Nietzsche's works (first, by Nietzsche in GS.341 [and later corroborated in *EH 'The Birth of Tragedy'* 3: 'the unconditional and infinitely repeated circular course of all things']; then, by Zarathustra in Z.III.2; and finally, by Zarathustra's animals in Z.III.13), rests on his belief that 'eternal recurrence' may have more than one meaning. Distracted by this 'multivocity' (p. 159, note to p. 71), White is unable to recognize a clear consonance, both literal and conceptual, between the 'moment', the 'spider', and the 'moonlight' in GS.341 and the gateway 'Moment', the 'spider', and the 'moonlight' in Z.III.2, and so remains baffled by the 'vision' and the 'riddle' of Z.III.2. He is further led to reject any correspondence between the two preceding descriptions of eternal recurrence and the (albeit sanitized) version set forth in Z.III.13 on the grounds that Zarathustra's animals, while clearly *his* animals, 'are also animals' (p. 92) - a somewhat naïve statement given Zarathustra's love of symbols.

not *those* for whom you shine' (Z.IV.20).[312] Whatever the sun is taken to represent, whether intuitive knowledge, enlightenment, or the supreme cosmic power,[313] the defiant tone of Zarathustra's address is unmistakable.

Absent from this act of hubris (the starting point of many a tragedy, including *Zarathustra*), when the soul 'shudder[s] with godlike desires' (Z.II.13), are Zarathustra's higher men, and in their absence resides 'the secret of the soul: only when the hero has left the soul does there approach it in dreams - the superhero' (ibid.). For the hero, however great, is still possessed of a 'violent will' (ibid.), and it is precisely this violent will to power that spurs the struggling heroic soul on to inglorious acts of heroism: the soothsayer to absolute renunciation, the two kings to self-imposed exile, the conscientious man of spirit to a dogged pursuit of "knowledge", the sorcerer to a pretence of greatness, the last pope to criticism of his God, the ugliest man to avenge himself on the witness, the voluntary beggar to throw away great riches, and the shadow to follow Zarathustra into forbidden and forbidding lands. Fundamentally reactive, these heroic acts lack the grace and beauty (ibid.) of those spontaneous *übermenschliche* deeds which, we are told, overflow from a soul that is naturally free from all antagonistic compulsion. The heroic human being is at bottom a man of *ressentiment*, a man 'whose strength lies in forgetting himself' (*UM*.III.4); and one recalls how Zarathustra's two attempted acts of heroism in Part III fail as a result of self-recollection. In 'Of the Vision and the Riddle', Zarathustra pits his affirmative spirit against his spirit of gravity in an endurance test involving the thought of eternal recurrence; but while his shrewd spirit of gravity endures by means of subtle misconstruction, his affirmative spirit falters on his 'own thoughts and ulterior motives (*Hintergedanken*)' (Z.III.2.2).[314] Similarly, in 'The Convalescent', Zarathustra rashly summons up this most

---

312. These words echo the following lines from Byron's *Manfred*: 'Thou material God! / And representative of the Unknown - / Who chose thee for his shadow! Thou chief star! [...] Our inborn spirits have a tint of thee' (III.ii.14-22), and further recall the so-called blasphemies of the Christian mystics, eg. *Gott lebt nicht ohne mich* (I.8) from Angelus Silesius' *Cherubinischer Wandersmann*: 'I know that God cannot live without me / If I become nothing he must of necessity give up the ghost' (*Ich weiß daß ohne mich GOtt nicht ein Nun kan leben / Werd' ich zu nichts Er muß von Noth den Geist aufgeben*).
313. Cooper, p. 162
314. *Hintergedanke* is translated as 'ulterior motive' (*The Collins German Dictionary*). This definition is far stronger and far more revealing about Zarathustra's state of mind than Hollingdale's 'reservations'.

abysmal of thoughts only to reel back in horror and disgust at the sight of it (Z.III.13).

Zarathustra is wont to forget himself when intellectual conscience inspires vanity and moral idealism or when his proud and clever animals occupy the affective space recently vacated by his higher men. Accordingly, now that his higher men are asleep and thus appear to have 'left' his soul, Zarathustra can once again look optimistically towards his proselytizing 'work' (*Werk*)[315] and his teaching of the superheroic: of the *Übermensch*, the eternal recurrence of all things, and the apocalyptic noontide. When, however, Zarathustra does think of himself (particularly his higher men) and of the Herculean task that lies ahead of him, 'he measures the distance between himself and his lofty goal and seems to see behind and beneath him only an insignificant heap of dross' (*UM*.III.4). But this resentment towards the past is, as Zarathustra knows, simply the will to power of the spirit of revenge, and the distance which Zarathustra would have us believe exists between himself and his higher men is merely an imagined distance born out of self-denial rather than self-transcendence, out of affinity rather than difference: 'It is not in how one soul approaches another but in how it distances itself from it that I recognize their affinity and identity' (*HH*.II 'Opinions and Maxims' 251).

Before the prophet can turn to his work, he must first await the sign that the rightful recipients of his teaching are approaching, for (unlike Schopenhauer) Zarathustra does not have 'the courage to be himself [...] to stand alone and not first wait on heralds and higher signs' (*UM*.III.5). As it is written, such visionary signs only appear in epiphanic dreams, and so it happens with Zarathustra. The sign that his hour has come, the hour of his

---

315. In *Nietzsche's Case* (pp. 173-88 and note 2 on pp. 273-4), much is made of Nietzsche's use of the word *Werk* as opposed to *Arbeit* in 'The Sign'. It is argued that, by conflating Nietzsche and Zarathustra (a conflation which is deemed to be justified by Nietzsche's 'remarkable' use of the German word *Werk* for 'work'), Zarathustra's '*Werk*' can be taken to refer to Nietzsche's literary work. This is certainly plausible, but to propose further that Zarathustra's '*Werk*' be regarded as *his* literary work, is to violate the fictional unity of Zarathustra's character. *Zarathustra* is pre-eminently a fictional work and any analysis of its fictive hero must primarily be undertaken within these narrative parameters. According to these latter, Zarathustra appears as a prophet whose pedagogic role is, as far as the reader can tell, a peripatetic and oral one; at no point in the story does Zarathustra engage in literary production of any kind. And while it might be argued that Nietzsche often lets the Zarathustran mask slip, he is never so bad a poet as to let it slip altogether.

"divine" descent - the sign, that is, of 'the laughing lion with the flock of doves' (Z.III.12.1).³¹⁶ - comes to Zarathustra in a trance-like state which 'lasted a long time, or a short time: for properly speaking, there is no time on earth for such things' (Z.IV.20). The laughing lion represents the imaginary light-hearted free spirit who has *freed* himself from the sacrificial suffering and heavy-hearted alienation of the penitential "free" spirit in the same way that the 'burden-bearing and reverential spirit' of the camel metamorphoses into the self-determining spirit of the lion (Z.I.1). This spiritual transformation of one who has liberated himself from the 'morality of custom' (*GM*.II.2) and the decadence of modernity, but not without a 'bad conscience for the extraordinary in his task [of self-determination]' (*GS*.186); this transformation into one who is not only proudly aware of 'the extraordinary privilege of responsibility [to himself]' (*GM*.II.2), but who joyfully undertakes to make instinctual such powers of self-determination, is symbolized by the flock of doves. For until Zarathustra can exemplify his teaching, he is destined to remain either unheard or misunderstood.

With the awakening of the higher men and their appearance at the door of Zarathustra's cave, however, the gay laughter of the lion suddenly turns into a furious roaring. In other (non-metaphoric) words, as Zarathustra's decadent character(istic)s begin to filter back into consciousness, the promise of future emancipation, of genuine free will (in Nietzsche's sense of spontaneous self-mastery - see *GM*.II.2), appears less like self-realization than self-delusion.³¹⁷ Far from experiencing the 'immense and proud composure' of self-mastery (*BGE*.284), Zarathustra feels hostility towards his higher men, 'hostility towards those influences, habits, laws, institutions in which he cannot recognize his goal' (*UM*.III.6). As the mystical moment of easy affirmation gives way to negation and *ressentiment*, the spell is broken and the vision vanishes. Zarathustra returns to his soulful solitude

---

316. The dove traditionally symbolizes the soul and/or its transmutation (Cooper, p. 54), and in the light of Zarathustra's belief in the multiplicity of the soul it is fitting that 'the sign' of transmutation which appears to him is not of a single dove but of a flock of doves.

317. On the strength of Bakhtin's (*Rabelais and His World*) observation that the parodic prophecy was a regular part of carnival festivity, Shapiro decrees that: 'Rather than looking for mysteries in Zarathustra's signs we *should* see them as parodically countering the prophecy of nihilism' (p. 122, emphasis added). I would argue, however, that Zarathustra's prophetic 'sign' is a sign of profound inner need which *could* more plausibly be seen as *exemplifying* the nihilistic prophecy; exemplifying, that is, the 'counterfeiting of transcendence and the beyond' (*CW*.Postscript).

and to the realization that as long as he feels pity (*Mit-leid*) for, and so 'suffers *with*', his higher men (*contra EH* '*Why I am so wise*' 8),[318] he will never succeed in liberating himself from himself for the creation of a new self. This recognition of failure and tragic destiny is the hellish despair out of which Zarathustra repeatedly constructs his redemptive heaven (see *GM*.III.10).

'The Sign' ends with the same powerful image with which it began: '[Zarathustra] left his cave, glowing and strong, like a morning sun emerging from behind dark mountains'. This image is a sign to the reader: a sign that 'A hundred times he threw himself back into life with short-breathed hope and put all spectres behind him. But that he almost always did so with immoderation, was a sign (*Anzeichen*) that he believed neither deeply nor firmly in this hope but was only intoxicating himself with it' (*UM*.IV.3). Above all, it is a sign that Zarathustra is one of those 'ambitious artists who like to pose as ascetics and priests, but who are at bottom only tragic buffoons' (*GM*.III.26).

---

318. Fink (p. 118) makes the same point.

Conclusion

Self-Overcoming as an Impossible Ideal

Self-overcoming is the impossible precept at the heart of Nietzsche's romantic ethics of perfectionism. Like Coleridge's ideal poet who 'brings the whole soul of man into activity, with the subordination of its faculties to each other, according to their relative worth and dignity',[319] Nietzsche's ideal free spirit will, through discipline and cultivation (*Zucht* and *Züchtung*), construct an order of rank within his soul and so overcome himself and his fate. Nietzsche is no ideal poet, however, and Part IV of his epic poem *Thus Spoke Zarathustra*, by revealing the rank disorder that obtains within his soul, proclaims the vanity of self-overcoming.

Zarathustra *signally* fails to overcome his decadent past, and the single unequivocal cause of his failure is psychological determinism. The fundamental structure of the human psyche is *not* susceptible to change, and memory, which retains its psychological history as ineluctably as a rock retains its geological history, serves as a constant reminder of this fact. Nietzsche, like Zarathustra, is an ambitious artist and within the tragic terms of his artist's metaphysics, self-overcoming is simply an affectation of style. There *is* no overcoming; Zarathustra knows it, Nietzsche knows it, and anyone with a modicum of intellectual integrity knows it. There is only an *overwhelming*, of one affect by another, driven by an inexorable will to power.

Nietzsche's philosophy stands or falls with the efficacy of self-overcoming. Man can only become an innocent child of becoming *if* he can overcome his past and embrace the eternally recurring present; man can only become a lover of fate *if* he can overcome his fate; man can only become an *Übermensch* *if* he can overcome man, but man can only overcome man *if* he can overcome his proud and deceptive consciousness. Man can only

---

319. Samuel Taylor Coleridge, *Biographia Literaria*, Ch. XIV.

become a dancer on the edge of the abyss *if* he can overcome his abysmal pessimism (soothsayer); man can only become sovereign over himself *if* he can overcome his plebeian values (two kings); man can only become a lover of knowledge *if* he can overcome his will to divine truth (conscientious man of spirit); man can only become an artist of abundance *if* he can overcome his penitential spirit (sorcerer); man can only be faithful to himself if he can overcome his faith in the ascetic ideal (last pope); man can only become a stalwart of intellectual conscience *if* he can overcome his shameful and pitiful bad conscience (ugliest man); man can only become a true giver of gifts *if* he can overcome his hunger for requital (voluntary beggar); and finally, man can only become the epiphanic noonday sun *if* he can overcome the shades of his shadow-self (shadow).

If, however, as this book claims, self-overcoming is an impossible ideal, and becoming what one is but an eternal recurrence of the same, then it is 'high time' that Nietzsche's entire philosophical output underwent serious re-evaluation.

Texts and Translations

I have relied primarily on *Sämtliche Werke, Kritische Studienausgabe in 15 Bänden* (*KSA*), eds. Giorgio Colli and Mazzino Montinari (Berlin: de Gruyter, 1980), but have also consulted the translations listed below. In all references to Nietzsche's works, the numbers refer to sections, not pages.

A   *The Anti-Christ*, trans. R J Hollingdale (Middlesex: Penguin, 1968).
AS   'Attempt at a Self-Criticism', in *The Birth of Tragedy*, trans. Walter Kaufmann (New York: Vintage, 1967).
BGE   *Beyond Good and Evil*, trans. Walter Kaufmann (New York: Vintage, 1966).
BT   *The Birth of Tragedy*, trans. Walter Kaufmann (New York: Vintage, 1967).
CW   *The Case of Wagner*, trans. Walter Kaufmann, (New York: Vintage, 1967).
D   *Daybreak*, trans. R J Hollingdale (Cambridge: Cambridge University Press, 1982).
DD   *Dithyrambs of Dionysus*, trans. R J Hollingdale (London: Anvil Press Poetry, 1984).
EH   *Ecce Homo*, trans. Walter Kaufmann (New York: Vintage, 1969).
GM   *On the Genealogy of Morals*, trans. Walter Kaufmann and R J Hollingdale (New York: Vintage, 1969).
GS   *The Gay Science*, trans. Walter Kaufmann (New York: Vintage, 1974).
HH   *Human, All Too Human*, trans. R J Hollingdale (Cambridge: Cambridge University Press, 1986.
NCW   *Nietzsche Contra Wagner*, in *The Portable Nietzsche*, trans. Walter Kaufmann (New York: Viking Penguin, 1954).
TI   *Twilight of the Idols*, trans. R J Hollingdale (Middlesex: Penguin, 1968).
TL   'On the Truth and Lies in a Nonmoral Sense', in *Philosophy and Truth: Selections from Nietzsche's Notebooks of the early 1870's*, ed. and trans. Daniel Breazeale (Atlantic Highlands: Humanities Press, 1979).
UM   *Untimely Meditations*, trans. R J Hollingdale (Cambridge: Cambridge University Press, 1983).
Z   *Thus Spoke Zarathustra*, trans. R J Hollingdale (Middlesex: Penguin, 1969).

Bibliography

Ackerman, Robert John. *Nietzsche: A Frenzied Look* (Amherst: The University of Massachusetts Press, 1990).
Agosti, Stefano. 'Coup upon Coup: An Introduction to *Spurs*', in Jacques Derrida, *Spurs: Nietzsche's Styles*, trans. Barbara Harlow (London: The University of Chicago Press, 1979).
Aiken, Henry David, 'An Introduction to *Zarathustra*', in Solomon (ed.), *Nietzsche: A Collection of Critical Essays* (New York: University of Notre Dame Press, 1973), pp. 114-30.
Alderman, Harold. *Nietzsche's Gift* (Athens: Ohio University Press, 1977).
Alford, Steven E. *Irony and the Logic of the Romantic Imagination* (New York: Peter Lang, 1984).
Allison, David B. (ed.), *The New Nietzsche: Contemporary Styles of Interpretation* (London: The MIT Press, 1988).
Andersen, Hans Christian. *Fairy Tales*, trans. H L Braekstad (London: William Heinemann, 1937).
Ansell-Pearson, Keith. *An Introduction to Nietzsche as Political Thinker* (Cambridge: Cambridge University Press, 1994).
Barth, Karl. 'Humanity without the Fellow-Man: Nietzsche's Superman and Christian Morality', trans. G.W. Bromiley, in O'Flaherty, Sellner and Helm (eds.), *Studies in Nietzsche and the Judæo-Christian Tradition* (London: The University of North Carolina Press, 1985).
Barzun, Jacques. *Classic, Romantic, and Modern* (London: The University of Chicago Press, 1975).
Bataille, Georges. *On Nietzsche*, trans. B. Boone (New York: Paragon House, 1992).
Beatty, Joseph. 'Zarathustra: The Paradoxical Ways of the *Creator*', *Man and World* 3 (February 1970), 64-75.
Beckett, Samuel. *The Theatrical Notebooks of Samuel Beckett*, Vol. 1, *Waiting for Godot*, eds. McMillan and Knowlson (London: Faber and Faber, 1993).
Behler, Ernst. '*Nietzsches Auffassung der Ironie*', *Nietzsche-Studien* 4 (1975), 1-35.
Behler, Ernst. '*Nietzsche und die Frühromantische Schule*', *Nietzsche-Studien* 7 (1978), 59-87.
Behler, Ernst. 'The Theory of Irony in German Romanticism', in Frederick Garber (ed.), *Romantic Irony* (Budapest: Akadémiai Kiadò, 1988), pp.43-81.
Bennholdt-Thomsen, Anke. *Nietzsches Also sprach Zarathustra als literarisches Phänomen, - Eine Revision*, (Frankfurt am Main: Athenäum, 1974).
Bergmann, Frithjof. 'Nietzsche's Critique of Morality', in Solomon and Higgins (eds.), *Reading Nietzsche* (New York: Oxford University Press, 1990), pp. 29-45.
Berkowitz, Peter. *Nietzsche: The Ethics of an Immoralist* (London: Harvard University Press, 1995).

Biser, Eugen. 'The Critical Imitator of Jesus: A Contribution to the Interpretation of Nietzsche on the Basis of a Comparison', trans. T.F. Sellner, in O'Flaherty, Sellner and Helm (eds.), *Studies in Nietzsche and the Judæo-Christian Tradition*, pp.16-28.

Blake, William. *Poetry and Prose of William Blake*, ed. Geoffrey Keynes (Bloomsbury: The Nonesuch Press, 1927).

Blanchot, Maurice. 'The Limits of Experience: Nihilism', in Allison (ed.), *The New Nietzsche*, pp. 121-27.

Bloom, Harold and Trilling, Lionel (eds.), *Victorian Prose and Poetry* (New York: Oxford University Press, 1973).

Booty, John E. (ed.), *The Book of Common Prayer, 1559* (Charlottesville: The University Press of Virginia, 1976).

Bourgeois, René. 'Modes of Romantic Irony in Nineteenth-Century France', in Garber (ed.), *Romantic Irony*, pp. 97-120.

Brinton, Crane. *Nietzsche*, (Cambridge, Massachusetts: Harvard University Press, 1941).

Büchner, Georg. *The Plays of Georg Büchner*, trans. Victor Price (Oxford: Oxford University Press, 1986).

Burgard, Peter J. (ed.), *Nietzsche and the Feminine* (Charlottesville: The University Press of Virginia, 1994).

Cantor, Paul. 'Friedrich Nietzsche: The Use and Abuse of Metaphor', in Miall (ed.), *Metaphor: Problems and Perspectives* (Brighton: The Harvester Press, 1982), pp. 71-89.

Cauchi, Francesca. 'Nietzsche and Pessimism: the Metaphysic Hypostatised', *History of European Ideas*, 13:3 (1991), 253-67.

Cauchi, Francesca. 'Figures of *funambule*: Nietzsche's Parable of the Ropedancer', *Nietzsche-Studien*, 23 (1994), 42-64.

Cauchi, Francesca. 'Rationalism and Irrationalism: A Nietzschean Perspective', *History of European Ideas*, 20:4-6 (1995), 937-943.

Chesterton, G K *St Francis of Assisi* (London: Hodder and Stoughton, 1924).

Clark, Maudemarie. *Nietzsche on Truth and Philosophy* (Cambridge: Cambridge University Press, 1990).

Coleridge, Samuel Taylor. *The Oxford Authors*, ed. H J Jackson (Oxford: Oxford University Press, 1985).

Conant, James. 'Nietzsche's Perfectionism: A Reading of 'Schopenhauer as Educator' ' (unpublished).

Conway, Daniel W. 'Overcoming the *Übermensch*: Nietzsche's Revaluation of Values', *Journal of the British Society for Phenomenology*, 20 (October 1989), 211-24.

Coomeraswamy, Ananda K. 'Cosmopolitan View of Nietzsche', in *The Dance of Shiva* (London: Peter Owen, 1958).

Cooper, J C. *An Illustrated Encyclopædia of Traditional Symbols* (London: Thames and Hudson, 1990).

Danto, Arthur C. *Nietzsche as Philosopher* (New York: Columbia University Press, 1980).

Danto, Arthur. 'The Eternal Recurrence', in Solomon (ed.), *Nietzsche*, pp. 316-21.

Del Caro, Adrian. 'The Immolation of Zarathustra: A Look at "The Fire Beacon" ', *Colloquia Germanica* 17 (1984), 251-56.

Del Caro, Adrian. *Nietzsche Contra Nietzsche* (London: Louisiana State University Press, 1989).
Deleuze, Gilles. *Nietzsche and Philosophy*, trans. Hugh Tomlinson (London: The Athlone Press, 1986).
De Man, Paul. *Allegories of Reading* (London: Yale University Press, 1979).
Derrida, Jacques. *Spurs: Nietzsche's Styles*, trans. Barbara Harlow (London: The University of Chicago Press, 1979).
Eldard, Israel. 'Nietzsche and the Old Testament', trans. Yisrael Medad, in O'Flaherty, Sellner and Helm (eds.), *Studies in Nietzsche and the Judæo-Christian Tradition*, pp. 47-68.
Fink, Eugen. *Nietzsches Philosophie* (Stuttgart: W Kohlhammer, 1960).
Fink, Eugen. 'Nietzsche's New Experience of the World', trans. Michael A Gillespie, in Gillespie and Strong (eds.), *Nietzsche's New Seas* (Chicago: The University of Chicago Press, 1991), pp. 203-19.
Foot, Philippa. 'Nietzsche: The Revaluation of Values', in Solomon (ed.), *Nietzsche*, pp. 156-68.
Foot, Philippa. 'Nietzsche's Immoralism', *The New York Review*, 38:11 (June 13, 1991).
Foucault, Michel. 'Nietzsche, Genealogy, and History', in P Rabinow (ed.), *The Foucault Reader*, (Middlesex: Penguin, 1984).
Freud, Sigmund. *Civilization and its Discontents*, in *The Pelican Freud Library*, Vol. 12 (Middlesex: Penguin, 1985).
Friedman, Maurice. 'The Atheist Existentialist: Nietzsche and Sartre', in *To Deny Our Nothingness* (London: Victor Gollancz, 1967).
Frye, Northrop. *Fools of Time* (Toronto: University of Toronto Press, 1967).
Furtwängler, Wilhelm. 'The Case of Wagner', in Ronald Taylor (ed. and trans.), *Furtwängler on Music* (London: Scolar Press, 1991).
Gadamer, Hans-Georg. 'The Drama of Zarathustra', trans. Thomas Heilke, in Gillespie and Strong (eds.), *Nietzsche's New Seas*, pp. 220-32.
Garber, Frederick., (ed.), *Romantic Irony* (Budapest: Akadémiai Kiadó, 1988).
Gillespie, Michael Allen and Strong, Tracy B. (eds.), *Nietzsche's New Seas* (Chicago: The University of Chicago Press, 1991).
Gilman, Sander L. *Nietzschean Parody: An Introduction to Reading Nietzsche* (Bonn: Bouvier, 1976).
Ginsberg, Mitchell. 'Nietzschean Psychiatry', in Solomon (ed.), *Nietzsche*, pp. 293-315.
Goedert, Georges. 'The Dionysian Theodicy', trans. Robert M Helm, in O'Flaherty, Sellner and Helm (eds.), *Studies in Nietzsche and the Judæo-Christian Tradition*, pp. 319-40.
Gooding-Williams, Robert. '*Metaphysics and Metalepsis in* Thus Spoke Zarathustra', *International Studies in Philosophy* 16 (1984), 27-36.
Gooding-Williams, Robert. 'Literary Fiction as Philosophy: The Case of Nietzsche's Zarathustra', *The Journal of Philosophy* 83 (November 1986), 667-675.
Haar, Michel. 'Nietzsche and Metaphysical Language', in Allison (ed.), *The New Nietzsche*, pp. 5-36.
Habermas, Jürgen. *The Philosophical Discourse of Modernity*, trans. Frederick Lawrence (Cambridge: Polity Press, 1987).

Halévy, Daniel. *The Life of Friedrich Nietzsche*, trans. J M Hone (London: J Fisher Unwin, 1911).
Handwerk, Gary J. *Irony and Ethics in Narrative* (London: Yale University Press, 1985).
Harries, Karsten. 'Boundary Disputes', *The Journal of Philosophy* 83 (November 1986), 667-75.
Harries, Karsten. 'The Philosopher at Sea', in Gillespie and Strong (eds.), *Nietzsche's New Seas*, pp. 21-44.
Hayman, Ronald. *Nietzsche: A Critical Life* (London: Weidenfeld and Nicolson, 1980).
Heidegger, Martin. *Nietzsche* Vols. I-IV, trans. David Farrell Krell (San Francisco: Harper & Row, 1991).
Heidegger, Martin. *What is Called Thinking?*, trans. J Glenn Gray (New York: Harper & Row, 1968).
Heidegger, Martin. 'Who is Nietzsche's Zarathustra?', in Allison (ed.), *The New Nietzsche*, pp. 64-79.
Heidegger, Martin. 'Nietzsche as Metaphysician', trans. Joan Stambaugh, in Solomon (ed.), *Nietzsche*, pp. 105-13.
Heller, Erich. 'The Importance of Nietzsche', *The Artist's Journey into the Interior and Other Essays* (London: Secker and Warburg, 1965).
Heller, Erich. *The Importance of Nietzsche: Ten Essays* (London: The University of Chicago Press, 1988).
Hesse, Hermann. 'Zarathustra's Return', in Solomon (ed.), *Nietzsche*, pp. 375-85.
Higgins, Kathleen Marie. *Nietzsche's Zarathustra* (Philadelphia: Temple University Press, 1987).
Higgins, Kathleen Marie. 'Reading *Zarathustra*', in Solomon and Higgins (eds.), *Reading Nietzsche*, pp. 132-51.
Hollingdale, R J. *Nietzsche: The Man and His Philosophy* (Baton Rouge: Louisiana State University Press, 1965).
Hollingdale, R J. *Nietzsche* (London: Routledge and Kegan Paul, 1973).
Horace. *The Complete Odes and Epodes*, trans. W G Shepherd (Middlesex: Penguin, 1983).
Howey, Richard Lowell. 'Some Reflections on Irony in Niezsche', *Nietzsche-Studien* 4 (1975), 36-51.
Hume, David. *An Enquiry Concerning the Principles of Morals* (Oxford: Oxford University Press, 1989).
Hunt, Lester H. *Nietzsche and the Origin of Virtue* (London: Routledge, 1993).
Immerwahr, Raymond. 'The Practice of Irony in Early German Romanticism', in Garber (ed.), *Romantic Irony*, pp. 82-96.
Irigaray, Luce. *Marine Lover of Friedrich Nietzsche*, trans. Gillian C Gill (New York: Columbia University Press, 1991).
Jenkins, Keith. 'Two Dogma of Nietzsche's Zarathustra', *Journal of Philosophy of Education* 16 (December 1982), 251-54.
Jung, C G. *Nietzsche's Zarathustra*, Part I, ed. James L Jarrett (London: Routledge, 1989).
Kant, Immanuel. *Groundwork of the Metaphysic of Morals*, trans. H J Paton (London: Harper & Row, 1964).
Karrer, Otto. (ed.), *The Little Flowers, Legends, and Lauds*, trans. N Wydenbruck (London: Sheed & Ward, 1984).

Kaufmann, Walter. *Nietzsche: Philosopher, Psychologist, Antichrist* (New Jersey: Princeton University Press, 1974).
Keats, John. *The Complete Poems* (Middlesex: Penguin, 1983).
Kierkegaard, Søren. *The Concept of Irony with constant reference to Socrates*, trans. Lee M Capel (London: William Collins Sons, 1966).
Klossowski, Pierre. 'Nietzsche's Experience of the Eternal Return', in Allison (ed.), *The New Nietzsche*, pp. 107-20.
Knight, G Wilson. *Christ and Nietzsche: An Essay in Poetic Wisdom* (London: Staples Press, 1948).
Kofman, Sarah. 'Baubô: Theological Perversion and Fetishism', trans. Tracy B Strong, in *Nietzsche's New Seas*, pp. 175-202.
Kofman, Sarah. *Nietzsche and Metaphor*, trans. Duncan Large (London: The Athlone Press, 1993).
Köhler, Joachim. *Zarathustra Geheimnis: Friedrich Nietzsche und seine verschlüßelte Botschaft* (Nördlingen: Greno, 1989).
Krell, David Farrell and Wood, David (eds.), *Exceedingly Nietzsche: Aspects of Contemporary Nietzsche-Interpretation* (London: Routledge, 1988).
Küng, Hans. 'Nietzsche: What Christians and Non-Christians Can Learn', trans. Edward Quinn, in O'Flaherty, Sellner and Helm (eds.), *Studies in Nietzsche and the Judæo-Christian Tradition*, pp. 341-52.
Lampert, Laurence. 'Zarathustra and his Disciples', *Nietzsche-Studien* 8 (1979), 309-33.
Lampert, Laurence. 'Zarathustra's Dancing Song', *Interpretation* 8 (May 1980), 141-155.
Lampert, Laurence. *Nietzsche's Teaching: An Interpretation of* Thus Spoke Zarathustra (London: Yale University Press, 1986).
Lea, F A. *The Tragic Philosopher* (London: Methuen, 1957).
Leiter, Brian. 'Nietzsche and Aestheticism', *Journal of the History of Philosophy* 30, (2 April 1992), 275-90.
Lermontov, Mikhail. 'Author's Preface', *A Hero of Our Time*, trans. Paul Foote (Middlesex: Penguin, 1987).
Lewis, Charles. 'Morality and Deity in Nietzsche's Concept of Biblical Religion', in O'Flaherty, Sellner and Helm (eds.), *Studies in Nietzsche and the Judæo-Christian Tradition*, pp. 69-85.
Lippitt, John. 'Nietzsche, Zarathustra and the Status of Laughter', *British Journal of Aesthetics* 32:1 (January 1992), 39-49.
Luke, F D. 'Nietzsche and the Imagery of Height', in Malcolm Pasley (ed.), *Nietzsche: Imagery and Thought*, pp. 104-22.
Magnus, Bernd. *Nietzsche's Existential Imperative* (Bloomington: Indiana University Press, 1978).
Magnus, Bernd. 'The Use and Abuse of *The Will to Power*', in Solomon and Higgins (eds.), *Reading Nietzsche*, pp. 218-35.
Magnus, Bernd. 'The Deification of the Commonplace: *Twilight of the Idols*', in Solomon and Higgins (eds.), *Reading Nietzsche*, pp. 152-81.
Magnus, Stanley & Mileur, *Nietzsche's Case: Philosophy as/and Literature* (London: Routledge, 1993).
Mann, Thomas. 'Nietzsche's Philosophy in the Light of Contemporary Events', in Solomon (ed.), *Nietzsche*, pp. 358-70.

Midgley, Mary. *Wickedness* (London: Ark Paperbacks, 1986).
Miller, C A. 'Nietzsche's "Daughters of the Desert": A Reconsideration', *Nietzsche-Studien* 2 (1973), 157-195.
Miller, J Hillis. '*Gleichnis* in Nietzsche's *Also sprach Zarathustra*', *International Studies in Philosophy* 17 (Summer 1985), 3-15.
Miller, Karl. *Doubles* (Oxford: Oxford University Press, 1987).
Milton, John. *The Poetical Works of John Milton*, ed. H C Beeching (London: Oxford University Press, 1904).
Muecke, D C. *The Compass of Irony* (London: Methuen, 1966).
Nehamas, Alexander. *Nietzsche: Life as Literature* (Cambridge, Massachusetts: Harvard University Press, 1985).
Nicholson, Reynold A. (trans.), *The Mathnawi of Jalalu'ddin Rumi*, Book II, (Cambridge: University Press, 1982).
O'Flaherty, James C. 'The Intuitive Mode of Reason in *Zarathustra*', in O'Flaherty, Sellner and Helm (eds.), *Studies in Nietzsche and the Judæo-Christian Tradition*, pp. 274-94.
Ogilvy, James. *Many Dimensional Man: Decentralizing Self, Society and the Sacred* (New York: Oxford University Press, 1977).
Olafson, Frederick A. 'Nietzsche, Kant, and Existentialism', in Solomon (ed.), *Nietzsche*, pp. 194-201.
Parkes, Graham. 'The Overflowing Soul: Images of Transformation in Nietzsche's *Zarathustra*', *Man and World* 16 (1983), 335-48.
Parkes, Graham. 'The Wandering Dance: *Chuang Tzu* and *Zarathustra*', *Philosophy East and West* 33 (July 1983), 235-50.
Parkes, Graham. *Nietzsche and Asian Thought* (London: The University of Chicago Press, 1991).
Parsons, Kathryn Pyne. 'Nietzsche and Moral Change', in Solomon (ed.), *Nietzsche*, pp. 169-93.
Pashman, Jon. 'The Pale Criminal', *Man and World* 4 (May 1971), 169-73.
Pasley, Malcolm (ed.), *Nietzsche: Imagery and Thought* (London: Methuen, 1978).
Pasley, Malcolm. 'Nietzsche's Use of Medical Terms', in Pasley (ed.), *Nietzsche: Imagery and Thought*, pp. 123-58.
Peckham, Morse. *Beyond the Tragic Vision* (Cambridge: Cambridge University Press, 1981).
Pippin, Robert B. 'Irony and Affirmation in Nietzsche's *Thus Spoke Zarathustra*', in Gillespie and Strong (eds.), *Nietzsche's New Seas*, pp. 45-71.
Pirandello, Luigi. *Three Plays*, trans. Julian Mitchell (London: Methuen, 1986).
Plato. *The Republic* (Middlesex: Penguin, 1955).
Pollard, David. 'Self-annihilation and Self-overcoming: Blake and Nietzsche', in Krell and Wood (eds.), *Exceedingly Nietzsche*, pp. 63-79.
Pope, Alexander. *Poems in Facsimile* (Aldershot: Scolar Press, 1988).
Quigley, Michael. 'Which Allegory for Religious Truth: Plato's Cave or Nietzsche's Zarathustra?', *The Thomist* 42 (October 1978), 625-48.
Quine, Willard van Orman. 'Two Dogmas of Empiricism', *From a Logical Point of View* (New York: Harper & Row, 1963).

Reed, T J. 'Nietzsche's Animals: Idea, Image and Influence', in Pasley (ed.), *Nietzsche: Imagery and Thought*, pp. 159-219.
Reinhardt, Karl. *'Nietzsche's Lament of Ariadne'*, trans. Gunther Heilbrunn, *Interpretation* 6 (October 1977), 204-24.
Reinhold, H A. (ed.), *The Spear of Gold: Revelations of the Mystics* (London: Burns Oates, 1947).
Robbins, Leonard. 'Zarathustra and the Magician or, Nietzsche contra Nietzsche: Some Difficulties in the Concept of the Overman', *Man and World* 9 (June 1976), 175-95.
Rousseau, Jean Jacques. *The Social Contract*, trans. Willmoore Kendall (Chicago: Regnery, 1954).
Sadler, Ted. *Nietzsche: Truth and Redemption* (London: The Athlone Press, 1995).
Sallis, John C. 'Nietzsche's Homecoming', *Man and World* 2 (February 1969), 108-16.
Schacht, Richard. *Nietzsche* (London: Routledge and Kegan Paul, 1983).
Scheier, Claus-Artur. *Nietzsches Labyrinth: Das ursprüngliche Denken und die Seele* (Freiburg: Alber, 1985).
Scheler, Max.*'Ressentiment'*, in Solomon (ed.), pp. 243-57.
Schlegel, Friedrich. *Kritische Ausgabe*, ed. Ernst Behler (Paderborn: Ferdinand Schöningh, 1967).
Schopenhauer, Arthur. *The World as Will and Representation*, Vol. I, trans. E F J Payne (London: Dover, 1969).
Schopenhauer, Arthur. *The World as Will and Representation*, Vol. II, trans. E F J Payne (London: Dover, 1966).
Schrift, Alan D. 'Comments: Parody and the Eternal Recurrence in Nietzsche's Project of Transvaluation', *International Studies in Philosophy* 16 (1984), 37-40.
Schutte, Ofelia. *Beyond Nihilism: Nietzsche Without Masks* (Chicago: The University of Chicago Press, 1984).
Seyffert, Oskar. (ed.), *A Dictionary of Classical Antiquities*, rev. and ed. Henry Nettleship and J E Sandys (London: William Glaisher, 1894).
Shakespeare, William. *The Complete Works*, ed. Charles Jasper Sisson (London: Odhams Press, 1954).
Shapiro, Gary. *Nietzschean Narratives* (Bloomington: Indiana University Press, 1989).
Shaw, George Bernard. 'Nietzsche in English', in Solomon (ed.), *Nietzsche*, pp. 371-74.
Smith, Ronald Gregor. *J G Hamann: A Study in Christian Existence* (London: Collins, 1960).
Soll, Ivan. 'Reflections on Recurrence: A Re-examination of Nietzsche's Doctrine, *die Ewige Wiederkehr des Gleichen*', in Solomon (ed.), *Nietzsche*, pp. 322-42.
Solomon, Robert C. (ed.), *Nietzsche: A Collection of Critical Essays* (New York: University of Notre Dame Press, 1973).
Solomon, Robert C. 'Nietzsche, Nihilism, and Morality', in Solomon (ed.), *Nietzsche*, pp. 202-25.
Solomon, Robert C. and Higgins, Kathleen M. (eds.), *Reading Nietzsche* (New York: Oxford University Press, 1990).
Sophocles. *The Oedipus Tyrannus of Sophocles*,ed. Sir Richard Jebb (Cambridge: Cambridge University Press, 1955).
Stack, George J. *Nietzsche and Emerson: An Elective Affinity* (Athens: Ohio University Press, 1992).

Staten, Henry. *Nietzsche's Voice* (London: Cornell University Press, 1993).
Stern, J P. 'Nietzsche and the Idea of Metaphor', in Pasley (ed.), *Nietzsche: Imagery and Thought*, pp. 64-82.
Stern, J P. *A Study of Nietzsche* (Cambridge: Cambridge University Press, 1979).
Sterne, Laurence. *The Life and Opinions of Tristram Shandy*, Vol. II (London: Hutchinson & Co).
Tanner, Michael. 'Wagner, Nietzsche, and the Romantic Agony', *Syracuse Scholar* (1982), 75-88.
Tanner, Michael. *Nietzsche* (Oxford: Oxford University Press, 1994).
Thatcher, David. 'Eagle and Serpent in *Zarathustra*', *Nietzsche-Studien* 6 (1977), 240-60.
Thiele, Leslie Paul. *'Friedrich Nietzsche and the Politics of the Soul'* (Oxford: Princeton University Press, 1990).
Trilling, Lionel. *Sincerity and Authenticity* (London: Oxford University Press, 1972).
Tymms, Ralph. *Doubles in Literary Psychology* (Cambridge: Bowes and Bowes, 1949).
Vaihinger, Hans. 'Nietzsche and His Doctrine of Conscious Illusion' in Solomon (ed.), *Nietzsche*, pp. 83-104.
Warnock, Mary. 'Nietzsche's Conception of Truth' in Pasley (ed.), *Nietzsche: Imagery and Thought*, pp. 33-63.
White, Alan. *Within Nietzsche's Labyrinth* (London: Routledge, 1990).
Willeford, William. *The Fool and His Sceptre* (London: Edward Arnold, 1969).
Williams, W D. 'Nietzsche's Masks', in Pasley (ed.), *Nietzsche: Imagery and Thought*, pp. 83-103.
Wordsworth, William. *The Prelude: A Parallel Text*, ed. J C Maxwell (New Haven: Yale University Press, 1981).
Yeats, W B. *The Poems*, ed. Richard J Finnerman (London: Macmillan, 1983).
Young, Julian. *Nietzsche's Philosophy of Art* (Cambridge: Cambridge University Press, 1992).
Zeitlin, Irving M. *Nietzsche: A Re-examination* (Cambridge: Polity Press, 1994).
Zuboff, Arnold. 'Nietzsche and Eternal Recurrence', in Solomon (ed.), *Nietzsche*, pp. 343-57.

Index

References from Notes indicated by 'n' after page reference

acedia 135
Ackerman, R. 3
actor(s) 13-14, 34, 47, 51-2, 61, 76, 94, 109, 116-7, 153
aesthetics 70, 112
Agosti, S. 15
Alderman, H. 7-8
amor fati 22, 57, 97-8, 169
Ansell-Pearson, K. 56
Apollo 4, 20-3, 38, 65, 69, 76 (*see* artifice; illusion)
and Dionysus 20-3, 65, 69, 76-7, 162
Apuleius 5
Arnold, M. 80
artifice 28, 40, 47, 94, 100-1
Apollonian 21, 71, 77, 135
will to 18, 94, 99, 162
artist(s) 33, 61, 70, 75, 92, 102, 109, 116, 122, 132, 140n, 141n, 162, 168-70
asceticism 45, 81, 85n, 101 and *passim*
atheism 77, 115

Bakhtin, M. 5-6, 167n
Baubô 137, 139
beast(s) *passim*
beauty 17n, 101, 121-2, 162, 165
Beckett, S. 25
becoming 41, 62, 144-5, 149, 161n, 169-70
benevolence 10, 64, 127, 132-4, 141
Bible 90
Old Testament 90, 122
Genesis 60, Exodus 95, Isaiah 121-3, Zechariah 122, 126, Psalms 112, 135n
New Testament 90
Matthew 86-7, Luke 158, Romans 89-90, Corinthians I 112, Peter I 114
Blake, W. 23, 39, 40n, 49-50, 55, 55n, 73n, 86n, 89, 92, 121, 123
Bourgeois, R. 31
Brant, S. 23
Browning, R. 13n, 19, 160, 163n
Büchner, G. 25, 51
Buddhism 21, 80-1
Byron, G. 34, 78, 101, 117, 119, 165n

Cagliostro, A. *see* modernity
casuistry 39, 50, 116, 124
Celano, T. 130n, 132, 134n, 135
Ceprano, G. 133
chance 92
chastity 156, 156n
Chesterton, G.K. 131, 134-5
Christ 86-9, 92, 121, 125, 135, 153
Christians, Christianity 10, 14, 18, 38 and *passim*
Church 6n, 50, 89-90
Cicero 89
Coleridge, S.T. 17, 137, 169
conscience 29, 34, 52 and *passim*
bad 9-10, 14, 64, 91, 107 and *passim*
intellectual 28, 30, 49, 51 and *passim*
Minotaur of 31, 56, 105
consciousness 9-10, 38 and *passim*
contempt 25, 41 and *passim*
convention 59, 81, 137n, 160
conviction(s) 45, 86-7, 95-6, 153
Coomeraswamy, A. 82, 145
counterfeiter 49, 98, 109, 114, 116, 125, 162
courage 21, 34, 39 and *passim*

criminal, pale 82, 109, 140
cruelty 16, 33, 39, 62, 69, 100-11 *passim*, 138
culture 18, 76, 106-7
  modern 7, 10, 64, 69 and *passim*
  ancient 7, 10, 50, 64, 112 and *passim*
  higher 16, 93
cunning 9, 26, 37 and *passim*

dance 23, 48, 60, 62, 64, 84, 113, 145, 153, 156, 161, 170
death
  will to 24, 99, 120
decadence 7, 10, 22, 25, 51 and *passim*
deed 64, 69, 82, 109, 128, 130-3, 138, 140, 141n, 165
Deleuze, G. 40, 40n
democracy 90
determinism 102, 153, 169
  and free will 161
devil 13, 18, 27, 30, 47, 57-8, 106, 159
Diderot, D. 31
Dionysus 13, 26-7, 71, 88n, 107, 118, 135, 141n (*see* insight, tragic)
  and Apollo *see* Apollo
  Dionysian man 20, 23, 26, 31
discipline 89, 106, 109, 169
disgust 48 and *passim*
distance
  artistic 18, 32, 69 and *passim*
  ironic *passim*
  pathos of 88, 94, 103
dogmatism 24, 99
Doppelgänger 15, 20, 30, 136n
dreams 22, 28, 30, 48, 79, 95, 98, 110, 149-66 *passim*

egoism
  egoistic/unegoistic 80-1, 89, 138n
Empedocles 58, 83, 159
Erasmus 23
error(s) 5, 23, 31, 38, 41-5 *passim*, 87n, 99n, 120, 137, 142, 142n
eternal recurrence 56-8, 62-4, 71, 135, 149, 158-66 *passim*, 170
evil *see* good and evil
experience 7-8, 33, 69, 74, 80, 86n, 114, 127, 145

faith 10, 17, 64, 77, 89 and *passim*
Faust 119, 141
fear 15, 33, 39, 50, 59, 79, 96-8, 100, 112, 136, 155
Feuerbach, L. 42n
Fichte, J.G. 42n
Fink, E. 3-4
fool, folly *passim*
forgetfulness 34, 48, 52, 61-2, 71, 118n, 144, 165-6
Francis, St. 130-6
freedom 18, 32-4, 40, 59, 89, 120-2, 139, 141, 165, 167
  free spirit(s) 29, 44, 94, 112n, 155, 157, 167, 169
  free will 139n, 167 (*see* man, sovereign)
  free will and determinism 161
Freud, S. 29, 39, 40n
Frye, N. 5

genius 38, 77, 92, 94, 109
goal 16, 21, 54, 65, 144, 166-7
god(s) *passim*
God 32, 45, 50, 87, 92-3, 98, 112-19 *passim*, 165, 165n
  death of 14-15, 22, 25, 47, 50, 77, 112, 144
  remnant of 93, 113, 150
Goedert, G. 107
Goethe, J.W. 21, 83n
Gogol, N. 34
good and evil 24, 37, 41, 50, 56, 82, 93, 119, 157
gratitude 133, 138
gravity
  law of 28, 30, 96
  spirit of 27-32, 53-4, 93, 96, 105-6, 120, 123, 157, 165
greatness 16, 89, 94, 97, 165
  great men 55, 63 and *passim*
  great poets 34, 75
  great philosophy 8
guilt 91, 108-9, 112
Gurewitch, M. 74

Halévy, D. 29, 62
Hamann, J.G. 16, 119

Hamlet 8, 20-1, 134n, 158
happiness 44, 61, 71 and *passim*
health 16, 26, 29, 34, 127, 131, 142,
   152, 154
   will to 20, 34
Hegel, G.W.F. 42n, 45
Heidegger, M. 1-2, 42n
height(s) 4, 18, 84, 94, 108n, 116, 133,
   138, 140, 143, 153
Heller, E. 62, 73
Heraclitus 78, 83n, 144, 149
herd 17, 48, 52, 90, 97
hermit(s) 29, 47, 52, 71, 84, 96, 104n,
   108, 156
hero(es) *passim*
Higgins, K. 5-6
Holbein, H. 23
Hollingdale, R.J. 2
home 86, 143-5
homeric 95
honesty 33, 72, 110, 122, 124
   irritable 73, 82
   unconditional 33, 51
   will to 18, 34, 94, 106-7
honour 69, 75, 138, 162
hope 10, 14, 32, 50 and *passim*
Horace 51, 82
Hume, D. 74, 99n

idealism and realism *passim*
illusion 20, 61, 71 and *passim*
   Apollonian 4, 21-2, 27-30, 71, 83,
      162
   will to 20, 31, 107, 127
imagination 9, 17, 28, 37 and *passim*
immoralism *see* morality
immortality 91, 113
individualism 19, 145, 153
insight 5, 76, 82, 94
   tragic 4, 76-8, 82, 94, 96, 105, 107,
      157
instinct(s) 39 and *passim*
integrity 31-2, 73, 76-7, 89, 112
   intellectual 21, 92, 169
   moral 124-5
   will to 20, 34
intellect 59, 61
irony *passim*

Romantic 31-4
world-historical 90

Jesus *see* Christ
justice, spiritualization of 16

Kant, I. 41-3, 45, 97, 99
   categorical imperative 17n, 43, 55n,
      56
Keats, J. 121n, 144
Kierkegaard, S. 6n, 33-4, 160n
Kleist, H. 34
knowledge *passim*
Köhler, J. 18n, 30

Lampert, L. 2
language 21-3, 60-1, 65, 93, 104, 152
laughter 6, 22, 34, 54, 79, 93, 110,
   120, 134-5, 150-7 *passim*, 167
law 39, 140, 167
   moral 17, 43, 92, 95
Lea, F.A. 3
Leibniz, G.W. 42n
Leopardi, G. 22, 34
Lermontov, M. 74
Lessing, G.E. 47
lie *passim*
   noble 17, 41-5, 142, 149
longing 48, 54, 93, 113, 118, 139-43,
   150
love 10, 64, 69, 80, 90, 108-41 *passim*,
   156, 163
   self- 34, 50, 140, 156, 158
Luke, F.D. 56

madness 24-5, 93, 107
Magnus, B. 19, 57
man
   last 25, 41, 44, 71
   sovereign 89, 91, 139-40
Mann, T. 108
mask(s) *passim*
mediocrity 18, 90
meditation 10, 64, 130-2
memory 27, 34, 48, 70-8 *passim*,
   106-9, 119, 128, 165, 169
Mephistopheles 106, 141

metaphysics 2, 38-46 *passim*, 99n, 126, 143-4, 169
　hangman's 120, 125
　metaphysical comfort 14-15, 32 48 and *passim*
Mileur, J-P. 19
Miller, K. 15, 19, 107
Milton, J. 119, 121, 137, 157
Minotaur *see* conscience
misanthropy 134
modernity 7, 10, 45, 64, 70 and *passim*
　Cagliostro of 102, 105
morality *passim*
　master and slave 88-94 *passim*
　immoralism 89, 108, 114-15, 118, 125, 140
Moses 92, 95
Muecke, D.C. 31
Munch, E. 79
music 38, 59, 104
Musset, A. 34
mysticism 165n, 167

Napoleon 91
Newton, I. *see* gravity
Nietzsche: Works
　Antichrist, The 28, 33, 50, 63, 71, 83, 87, 89-91, 98, 100-1, 112, 114-16, 121, 140
　'Attempt at a Self-Criticism' 55, 100, 160
　Beyond Good and Evil 8, 16-17, 18n, 20, 23, 31, 34, 39n, 43, 45, 47, 49-50, 56, 59, 63, 70n, 76, 79, 82-3, 85-9, 89n, 90-2, 94, 96-7, 100, 103, 105-7, 110, 112n, 113n, 115-16, 120, 122, 125, 128, 132, 136, 142, 150, 153, 154n, 159, 161, 163, 167
　Birth of Tragedy, The 20-1, 23, 27, 30, 64-5, 69, 71, 77-8, 98-100, 120, 125
　Case of Wagner, The 21, 51, 92n, 94, 102-4, 109, 114, 119, 154, 158, 162, 167n
　Daybreak 85n, 87n, 90, 107, 127, 140, 140n

Dionysus Dithyrambs 46, 73, 105n, 108, 149
Ecce Homo 8, 14, 15n, 16, 22, 45, 49, 60, 75-6, 97, 100, 105, 108, 113-15, 128-31, 144, 164n, 168
Genealogy of Morals, On the 8, 13, 16, 21, 39, 69, 71, 77, 80-1, 88, 90-1, 98-102, 107-8, 113, 115-16, 120-1, 123-6, 130n, 136, 139, 139n, 140, 144, 156, 162, 167-8
Gay Science, The 13-16, 17n, 18, 20-1, 26, 28, 32-3, 44, 46, 49n, 50-1, 55, 63-4, 69-70, 70n, 71-8, 79n, 81, 81n, 82, 85, 87-8, 97-9, 103, 106, 112, 114, 116, 118, 121, 125, 127, 134n, 135, 137, 140n, 142, 142n, 144n, 145, 157, 164n, 167
Human, All Too Human 7-8, 18, 26, 29, 34, 38, 48, 63, 69, 71-2, 74, 75n, 76-7, 78n, 79-81, 83, 87, 93n, 101, 103, 105, 108-9, 120, 125, 130, 132-5, 137, 137n, 138, 139, 141, 141n, 144, 151, 155, 157, 160, 162, 166
Nachlaß 19, 22, 42n, 71n, 81, 82, 83n, 95, 99, 141n
Nietzsche contra Wagner 105, 111
Twilight of the Idols 17, 22, 41, 80, 88, 118, 120, 123-4, 128, 144
'Truth and Lies in a Nonmoral Sense, On the' 38, 45, 59, 61, 100
Untimely Meditations 16-17, 51, 55, 58, 70n, 71-2, 74, 83, 99-101, 104-5, 111, 115, 154n, 166-8
nihilism 9, 20, 30 and *passim*
nirvana *see* nothingness
nobility 17-18, 87n, 88-96 *passim*, 124
nothingness 21, 33-4, 80

Oedipus 64
optimism 15, 20, 99-101, 127, 164
overcoming, self- 22, 53, 69, 97, 161, 169-70

passing by 48-9
Paul, St. 89-90, 93 (*see* Bible)

184 Zarathustra contra Zarathustra

perspectivism 8
pessimism *passim*
  courageous 81, 83
  Romantic 64, 76 and *passim*
Peter, St. 114 (*see* Bible)
philanthropy 10, 64, 86, 127-34
piety 42, 75, 90, 112, 118, 137, 158, 161
  pia fraus 112, 119, 122, 143
Pirandello, L. 24, 51
pity 10, 49, 56, 64, 70 and *passim*
Plato 41-6, 89, 98, 123, 128n
Poe, E.A. 34
poet(s) 3-4, 8, 17, 19, 25-34 *passim*, 60, 75, 100n, 105, 109, 118, 143, 155, 162, 169
Pope, A. 38, 45
positivism 42-5, 100n, 127, 155
pride *passim*
  proud composure 76-7, 86, 167
priest(s) 41, 50, 112, 116, 130n, 132, 168
Prometheus 64
prudence 37 and *passim*
Pythagoras 46

Quixote, Don 87n
  quixotic 9, 95, 142, 160

rank, order of 88-9, 150, 154, 169
Raphael, S. 92
realism and idealism *passim*
reason 9, 37 and *passim*
  age of 77, 93, 120
  practical 17, 41, 43
redemption *passim*
reflection *passim*
  poetic *see* Schlegel
  transfiguring mirror 21, 33, 71-2
religion 90, 115
ressentiment passim
revenge, spirit of 34, 69, 108 and *passim*
reverence 20, 81, 89n, 137n, 138
rhetoric 1, 52, 56, 94, 97, 106, 121, 141, 149, 154

Romanticism 9, 15, 19, 21, 30, 64, 76, 81, 95, 102, 111, 136, 141, 160, 169 (*see* irony; pessimism)
Rousseau, J.J.
  general will 91
  noble savage 39, 95

sacrifice 79n, 80-1, 89-91, 101, 118n, 120-4, 160
saint 75, 102, 108, 111, 116-17, 124, 140, 142-3, 155-6, 158
salvation 89, 93, 112, 114, 141
satyr 4
savage, noble *see* Rousseau
Schauerroman 136
scepticism 43, 80, 87, 115-16, 142n
Schelling, F.W.J. 42n
Schlegel, F. 31-4
  poetic reflection 32-3
Schleiermacher, F. 42n
Schopenhauer, A. 20, 22, 42n, 48, 54 and *passim*
science 10, 64, 77, 86, 96, 98-101, 107, 122, 127, 137, 155
sensuality 156
Shakespeare: Works
  Hamlet 8, 20-1, 122, 134n, 158
  2 Henry IV 40
  King Lear 24, 74, 136-7
  Midsummer Night's Dream, A 7, 154
  Richard II 86
shame *passim*
Shandy, Tristram 136
Shapiro, G. 5-7
sickness 29, 46, 54, 61 and *passim*
Silesius, A. 165n
Socrates 101, 123-4
solitude 18, 29, 49n, 55, 59, 71 and *passim*
Sophocles 77, 108
soul *passim*
  German 16
  modern 74, 103
Spinoza, B. 83n
spirit *passim*
  conscientious of 10, 64, 75, 96-127 *passim*, 155-8, 165, 170

penitent of the 4, 10, 105 and *passim*
spirit of gravity *see* gravity
Stewart, S. 19
Strauss, D. 42n
Sufism 53n
suffering *passim*
  will to abolish 118, 125
sympathy 26, 76, 82-3, 125, 128

taste 92n, 112n, 141, 152, 161 (*see* wisdom)
  bad 26, 118
  good 34, 92n, 163
Tennyson, A. 70, 119
theology 42, 89
tragedy 4, 4n, 21, 23, 64-5, 69, 76, 153, 155, 159, 165
Trilling, L. 31
truth 17, 22, 26, 31 and *passim*
  immoral 77-8, 100
  will to 26, 31, 98-9, 121-31 *passim*
Tymms, R. 30

Übermensch *passim*

values *passim*
  herd 14, 24, 88-95 *passim*, 170
  vanity 26, 59, 109, 118, 122, 144-5, 162, 166
  virtue(s) 19, 24, 38, 49, 76 and *passim*
  Christian 14, 49-50, 89, 126, 139, 157

Wagner, R. 48-9, 64, 92n, 102-11 *passim*
war 39-40, 47, 59, 81-2, 85, 88, 94-5
Wieland, C.M. 143n
will *passim*
  will to power 40, 61, 78, 91, 96, 99, 115-16, 125, 136, 161, 165-6, 169
Willeford, W. 18, 23
wisdom *passim*
woman 43, 49
Wordsworth, W. 48, 138
Yeats, W.B. 19, 143

For Product Safety Concerns and Information please contact our EU representative GPSR@taylorandfrancis.com
Taylor & Francis Verlag GmbH, Kaufingerstraße 24, 80331 München, Germany

www.ingramcontent.com/pod-product-compliance
Lightning Source LLC
Chambersburg PA
CBHW052121300426
44116CB00010B/1749